The Family Letters

of

Christina Georgina Rossetti

Christina Georgina Rossetti.

From a tinted-crayon drawing by Dante Rossetti 1877.

The Family Letters

of

Christina Georgina Rossetti

With some Supplementary Letters and Appendices

Edited by

William Michael Rossetti

She stands there patient, nerved with inner might,
Indomitable in her feebleness,
Her face and will athirst against the light.

HASKELL HOUSE PUBLISHERS Ltd.
Publishers of Scarce Scholarly Books
NEW YORK, N. Y. 10012
1968

First Published 1908

HASKELL HOUSE PUBLISHERS Ltd.
Publishers of Scarce Scholarly Books
280 LAFAYETTE STREET
NEW YORK, N. Y. 10012

Library of Congress Catalog Card Number: 68-24915

Haskell House Catalogue Item # 237

Printed in the United States of America

THESE LETTERS

BY

CHRISTINA ROSSETTI

ARE INSCRIBED BY HER BROTHER TO THE

MEMORY OF OUR MOTHER

TO WHOM HER OWN BOOKS WERE

CONSTANTLY DEDICATED

PREFACE

THE object aimed at in this volume is to present a selection from the family-letters of Christina Georgina Rossetti, supplemented by a very few letters of hers addressed to persons out of the family, and by a quite moderate number of those addressed to herself—as for instance by her brother Dante Gabriel. The total number of letters now extant, addressed to herself, is truly small; for throughout her life her ordinary practice was to destroy such missives as soon as read and answered. On the other hand it seems probable that a very considerable number of letters written by herself to a variety of persons are still in being; for she was a highly punctual correspondent, and, from an early period of her life, there were many who regarded her with predilection, and who thought her likely to do something of note, and it may be surmised that several of these have preserved what she wrote. To letters of this miscellaneous kind I have not had access, save in the rarest instances, and therefore the present collection is practically, though not absolutely, limited to family-correspondence.

Some readers will probably think that I have admitted into my volume various letters the interest of which is extremely slender. As to this I can only say that, slender or not, they appear to me admissible, as tending to define and complete the picture of my sister's mind and feelings; also that I have excluded *many* letters—perhaps a good deal more than the number here given—which I acknowledge to be (more or less) below the requisite standard for publication. From the letters here printed I have omitted a large number of passages which the public could obviously not care for: and this although it seems to me that letters read better when uncurtailed, even if some portions of them may have very little to plead for themselves.

Are the letters, taken as a whole, interesting or uninteresting? Do they relate to important or to unimportant matters? Of this I must leave the reader to judge. My own view is that Christina Rossetti, by her work in poetry and authorship, made herself interesting to a great number of persons; and that anything which tends to show forth her genuine self, her personality and tone of mind and feeling, cannot therefore be totally insignificant. Nothing could evince these more perfectly than her family-letters do. I am certain that I here set before readers a beautiful and lovable character; and, as this is the character of a person widely cherished for her writings, and even intensely valued by many lovers of poetry and many religious devotees, I await with some confidence the verdict which may be passed upon my compilation.

The correspondence in my collection, belonging to the earlier period of Christina's life, is rather scanty, owing to the fact that eighteen of her letters, of dates ranging from 1845 to 1854, are now the property of her sympathetic biographer Mr. Mackenzie Bell, and are thus not at my disposal; moreover two or three of her family-letters, of later date, have been published in Mr. Bell's book. Besides all these, the letters by my sister printed in the *Rossetti Papers*, 1862 to 1870 (Sands & Co., 1903), and (with one exception) those addressed to her by Dante Rossetti included in the volume of his *Family-Letters* (Ellis, 1895), are not reproduced in the present collection.

It will be found that literary matters, and also religious convictions, form an element in the correspondence here published. By far its chief constituent however is family affection, of which the warm glow can be felt incessantly renewed throughout. It is mingled with a constant tone of courteous considerateness, and even definite politeness, more than one would consider essential in family-letters; for Christina—as I have had occasion to say elsewhere—was rather punctiliously polite from her early girlhood onwards, and she saw no occasion for stinting this quality to members of her family, while she gave it in full measure to other people. Brightness as well as ever-present depth of feeling is vividly apparent, along with many neat, sprightly, and engaging turns of expression.

I am conscious that every now and then the letters contain some phrase not only of affection but likewise of commendation to myself —what I was or what I did. If I ought to have cut out these passages, I must apologize for leaving them in. My motive for so doing is too obvious to bear exposition. To have earned, or to have received, the praise of such a woman as Christina Rossetti, is a thing which no man would prefer to hide under a bushel. Apart from the personal and predominant motive for leaving these passages on record, it may truly be said that the excision of them would have diminished the completeness of the self-portrait which my sister has presented in these letters ; for, if she loved other members of her family, she assuredly loved me as well.

I have not thought it needful to reproduce in type the signatures to the letters, and the subscribing words. The signature is almost invariable, " Christina G. Rossetti," but in a very few instances there are only initials. Of the subscribing words, the most usual is " Your affectionate sister " ; every now and then something more marked occurs : " Your most grateful loving sister—Your dismal sister—Truly, as well I may be, your affectionate sister—Lovingly your sister —Affectionately your old sister—Your unchangeable affectionate sister "—and the like.

When I produced the complete *Poetical Works* of Christina Rossetti in 1904, I wrote a compendious Memoir of her uneventful and rather secluded life. I have no mind to go over the same ground now in the same sort of way : but, in order to supply a guide to the reader as to the main stages in the career which the letters indicate in a more or less scattered form, I append here a list of dates and occurrences.

1826, April. Gabriele Rossetti, a political exile from the kingdom of Naples, a poet, literary man, and professor of Italian, with his Anglo-Italian wife, Frances Mary Lavinia (Polidori), settled in No. 38 Charlotte Street, Portland Place, London, now called No. 110
b

Hallam Street. A memorial disk for Dante Gabriel Rossetti has recently been set up on this house: it ought to include, but does not, Christina Georgina Rossetti.

1830, December 5. Birth of Christina in the above house, following the births of Maria Francesca, Dante Gabriel, and William Michael. She, like the other children, was baptized in the English Church.

1836, January. The family remove to No. 50 Charlotte Street.

1842, April. Christina writes her first verses, a birthday address to her mother.

1847. A booklet of her *Verses* is privately printed by her grandfather, Gaetano Polidori.

1848, September. Formation of the Præraphaelite Brotherhood, or P.R.B.

1848, Autumn. James Collinson, a painter and member of the P.R.B., originally belonging to the English Church but now a Roman Catholic, proposes marriage to Christina. She, being reluctant to marry a Roman Catholic, declines.

1848, ? November. Collinson re-enters the English Church, renews his proposal to Christina, and is accepted.

1850, January to May. Christina publishes various poems in *The Germ*: her first publications, save for two pieces in *The Athenæum*.

1850, ? May. Collinson reverts to the Roman Catholic Church, and Christina cancels her engagement to him.

1851, January. The family remove to No. 38 Arlington Street (now merged in Arlington Road), Mornington Crescent, and Christina acts as assistant to her mother in a day-school there.

1853, Spring. Mrs. Rossetti goes with Christina to Frome, Somerset, to set up another day-school. Later on Gabriele Rossetti joins them, the rest of the family remaining in London.

1853, April and December. Deaths in London of Mrs. Rossetti's parents, Anna Maria and Gaetano Polidori.

1854, April. I take a house for the whole family except Dante Gabriel—45 Upper Albany Street, now 166 Albany Street.

1854, April 26. Death of Gabriele Rossetti in this house.

1861, February. Christina publishes in *Macmillan's Magazine* a poem, *Uphill*, which secures a good deal of attention.

1861, Summer. Christina's first foreign trip with her mother and me. Paris, Coutances, and other parts of Normandy.

1862. She brings out her first published volume, *Goblin Market and other Poems*.

1862. She now begins to see pretty frequently Charles Bagot Cayley, a scholar, author, and linguist, translator of Dante's *Divina Commedia*, &c., whom she may have first met in 1847. She falls in love with him.

1865, Summer. Christina's second and last foreign trip, again with her mother and me, through France, over Mount St. Gothard, into Italy—Pavia, Verona, &c. : back by the Splügen Pass, Schaffhausen, &c.

1866, June. She brings out her second published volume, *The Prince's Progress and other Poems*.

1866, ? Summer. Cayley proposes marriage to Christina, and she would gladly accept him : but on some religious ground, apparently that he is not a Christian of an orthodox type, she declines the offer.

1867, June. My mother and two sisters, with myself, remove to No. 56 Euston Square, afterwards called No. 5 Endsleigh Gardens.

1870. Christina brings out her first prose-volume, *Commonplace, and other Short Stories*. This was followed, 1874 to 1892, by seven other prose volumes, the last being *The Face of the Deep, a Devotional Commentary on the Apocalypse.* ı Five of them were published by the Society for Promoting Christian Knowledge.

1871, April. After various other illnesses, beginning towards the age of fifteen, Christina is prostrated by a very dangerous malady, exophthalmic bronchocele, or Dr. Graves's disease. Many months of suffering ensue, and several crises of peril; but the illness gets tolerably subdued by the summer of 1873.

1872, June. Dante Gabriel falls into a bad state of health, which continues, in one phase or another, for the remainder of his life. Christina publishes another volume of poems (for children), *Singsong*.

1873, Summer. Maria Rossetti becomes a novice, and afterwards a professed sister, in All Saints' Sisterhood (Anglican), London.

1874, March. I marry Lucy Brown. We continue living in No. 5 Endsleigh Gardens, along with my mother and Christina.

1876, October. They two remove to No. 30 Torrington Square, along with my mother's two sisters, Charlotte and Eliza Polidori.

1876, November 24. Death of Maria.

1881, Summer. Christina publishes another volume, *A Pageant and other Poems.*

1882, April 9. Death of Dante Gabriel at Birchington-on-Sea, near Margate, after Mrs. Rossetti and Christina had been nursing him for several weeks.

1885, December 5. Charles Cayley dies in London.

1886, April 8. Death of our mother, Frances Rossetti.

1890, January. Death of Charlotte Polidori, who, as well as Eliza Polidori, had continued living in the same house with Christina.

1892, May. Christina, being pronounced to be suffering from cancer on the left side of the chest, undergoes a severe operation.

1893, June. Death of Eliza Polidori.

1893, September. Publication of Christina's last volume, *Verses,* being a collection of the various pieces of poetry scattered through her volumes previously issued by the Society for Promoting Christian Knowledge.

1894, April 12. Death at San Remo of Lucy Rossetti, Christina's sister-in-law.

1894, December 29. The cancer having recurred, complicated by dropsy in the left arm, Christina, after being confined to bed for more than four months, dies at No. 30 Torrington Square. Buried in Highgate Cemetery.

Besides the letters by Christina which form the substance of this volume, along with the few samples of letters addressed to her, I add in an appendix:

1. Extracts from my Diaries, 1871 to 1895, relating to Christina. I regret that so large a proportion of the extracts should have to do with illnesses which affected my sister from time to time, and not with her literary or other interests. Many entries about illnesses have,

however, been omitted, as only going over the same cheerless ground again and again.

2. Extracts from a Diary kept by Christina from 1881 to 1886. This, as the wording shows, purports to be the diary of Mrs. Rossetti, our mother; but my sister, acting on her behalf, was, with a few exceptions in the earlier dates, the real writer of the diary, so far as handwriting is concerned, and no doubt the composition or diction is often hers as well.

WM. M. ROSSETTI.

London, *April* 1907.

CONTENTS

xv

CONTENTS

CONTENTS

CONTENTS

CONTENTS

CONTENTS xxi

LETTERS ADDRESSED TO CHRISTINA ROSSETTI

CONTENTS

APPENDIX

LIST OF ILLUSTRATIONS

CHRISTINA GEORGINA ROSSETTI'S BIRTH-HOUSE.

110 Hallam Street, Portland Place; formerly 38 Charlotte Street.

Photograph taken in 1908.

[*To face p.* 1.

THE FAMILY LETTERS

OF

CHRISTINA GEORGINA ROSSETTI

To GABRIELE ROSSETTI, *Hastings* (translation).

[This is the earliest letter by Christina extant in the family. The original is in Italian, and was (as she says) only the second letter which she had ever indited in that language, her age at this date being twelve and a half. She apologizes for blunders, which are tolerably numerous, but not such as to affect the sense. She must have written various letters in English before this time, yet by no means many.—Mr. Leader was Mr. John Temple Leader, a radical M.P. who lived to a great age, dying near Florence in 1903. He had taken of late much interest in Gabriele Rossetti's health, which was then gravely shattered, and which had driven him to Hastings for relief—soon afterwards to Paris. Mr. Rovedino was a musician, a family-friend ; he was a sprightly man, indulging in small jocularities, at which Christina appears to glance. Dr. Adolf Heimann was the Professor of German in the London University College, and was in all those years a very affectionate friend to all of us. Mr. Parodi was our dancing-master : an estimable and in several respects sensible man, who spoke a curious lingo, compounded of Italian, English, and whatsoever else. The postscript (written by Christina in English), saying that Gabriel had gone to Austin Friars, refers to the cashing of a cheque, or some such matter.]

[50 CHARLOTTE STREET, PORTLAND PLACE, LONDON.]

26 *June* 1843.

DEAREST PAPA,

I hope you will excuse all the blunders which I make in this letter, and that you will recollect that this is only (I think) the second letter that I ever wrote in Italian.

Yesterday Mr. Leader came, and asked how long you expected to remain at Hastings. William replied that he believes that, if the place does you good, you had spoken of remaining some two months. He had not been gone a minute when Mr. Rovedino entered, and he asked when you had gone off; and then, sending you his salutation, and saying some other things which are not worthy of insertion in this epistle, he left.

On Saturday Dr. Heimann came ; and he speaks of taking Gabriel and William for a walk, and asks to be remembered to you and mamma.

Maria sends her love ; Aunt Margaret sends the same. Also Mr. Parodi sends you his respects. And I, thanking mamma for her letter, and sending the love of Aunt Margaret and Maria and myself to mamma and Aunt Charlotte, sign myself Your &c.

Gabriel has gone to Austin Friars.

To WILLIAM ROSSETTI, *Pleasley Hill, Notts.*

[At the date of this letter Christina was engaged to marry James Collinson, a painter and member of the Præraphaelite Brotherhood ; and I, along with Collinson, had gone to pay a visit (it proved to be my only one) to Mrs. and Miss Collinson, the mother and sister of my friend, living at Pleasley Hill, near Mansfield and the site of Sherwood Forest. "The celebrated portrait" is a small oil-portrait of Christina then recently painted by Collinson, and now in my possession; so far from being "flattering," it does not do justice to her face, though fair enough as a likeness. The quotation, "drinking deep-throated of the life of life," comes from one of the numerous *bouts-rimés* sonnets which I wrote in those years; and the reference to "snobbishness" indicates that I had been reading to the Collinson ladies from Thackeray's *Book of Snobs*, a prime favourite in our family.—Mrs. Charles Collinson was the wife of James Collinson's elder brother, a Bookseller in business at Mansfield. "A real live castle" was recommended to me because I had begun some blank verse concerning a castle : the piece was eventually published in *The Germ*, but I may probably have had some idea of offering it to *The Athenæum*, of which Mr. T. K. Hervey was Editor. The banter about chiaroscuro &c. refers to some very faint and unpromising attempts I was then making to see whether I could do anything in the way of drawing.]

50 CHARLOTTE STREET, PORTLAND PLACE, LONDON.

23 *November* 1848.

DEAR WILLIAM,

The postman's knock this morning made evident a most humiliating state of my own mind, for, though not sufficiently philosophical to regret the arrival of your letter to-day, I was quite enough of a baby to mourn over my losing that pleasure to-morrow, when I had calculated upon receiving it. From all this you will draw the conclusion that your hint of a second communication must quite have consoled me, and believe in the sincerity of my thanks both for performance and promise.

Permit me to paraphrase the beginning of your note. "After a journey spent in pointing out to the commiseration of my fellow passengers the unsound state of my mind as more particularly developed at various Railway Stations, I am securely housed." It is a real comfort to think that this is the case.

I had fancied Mrs. Collinson the very reverse of *prim ;* but, as you conjecture, kind-hearted. I am glad you like Miss Collinson, but have a notion that she must be dreadfully clever. Is either of these ladies *alarming?* not to you, of course, but would they be so to me ? I wish that they could be convinced that the celebrated portrait is flattering, and that "the thoughtful and pleasing expression" of my face is indeed "as developed in the portrait." You probably not only *profusely banqueted* but surfeited your victims with my *poetry ;* but in this you may not have been the sole culprit. I dare say that your astonished hostesses are drinking "deep-throated" of snobbishness, which, in one sense, may be called "the life of life." All I have to recommend is that, when you have concluded the European work that treats thereof, you do not begin again. Though not very deeply versed in the rules of social etiquette, I should imagine that

your introduction to any amount of acquaintances were quite
parliamentary. Pray in your next give me a detailed account of
Mrs. Charles Collinson and baby.

But for my superiority to all mean passions I might envy you your
delightful country-walks. Do not forget that in the present stage of
your literary malady a *real live* castle is highly to be recommended.
Perhaps when you are backed by tumbling battlements, moss-grown
stones, and such like, Mr. T. K. Hervey will be compelled to
capitulate. I had imagined "the house" too neat to be very
comfortable; and was troubled with "a foreshown agony" of
windows kept open in winter. (N.B. You must not consider me
responsible for the correctness of my own quotations.) Perhaps if
you were not in company with an artist I might follow up my *N.B.*
by a very emphatic hand pointing a long way round the corner; as
it is, you must either do without one, or sketch it in yourself, with
that masterly touch and intimate knowledge, not to say perfect command of *chiaroscuro*, which all your works display. From his name,
I imagine the bull-terrier to be hideous enough for even my taste.
If his manners have not a *soupçon* of the savage tinging their
cordiality, doubtless we might be excellent friends. . . .

Pray, if you think it expedient, present my respects to Mrs.
Collinson and love to Miss C. Why I have left off calling the latter
Mary is not easily explained except on the score of feeling awkward.
Mamma sends her love. Will you remember me most particularly
to Mr. Collinson? In the firm faith that this overgrown epistle must
elicit a reply, I am &c.

Is your address written rightly?

To WILLIAM ROSSETTI, *London.*

[It will be observed that this letter was written from Pleasley
Hill, Christina being on a visit there to Mrs. and Miss Collinson:
James Collinson was not present—I think not even for a day. Mr.
[John] Orchard was a painter of very infirm physique, who died in the
following year: he contributed to *The Germ* a *Dialogue on Art* of
some marked interest, and one or two poems. His "most peculiar
criticism on Gabriel's picture," *The Girlhood of Mary Virgin*, was I
think in a private letter addressed to Gabriel, not as yet personally

known to him. "His two sonnets" on the same theme are in my possession, and excessively bad they are, considered as sonnets or as verse. The first begins

"Musing, not seldom to my eye of mind":

the second,

"Thy guileless modesty of soul full sure."

"Sol," named by Christina, was a dog :—"My dreary poem" would appear, judging from dates, to have been *Three Nuns*.—"The Kings" were a family—father, mother, and three daughters well grounded in the ancient classics—whom I knew through the introduction of Mr. Alfred Chaworth Lyster : the father conducted a school of good repute in the Maida Hill district : a son of Charles Dickens was seen by me as a boarder there. Mr. Lyster, besides being a colleague of mine in the Inland Revenue Office, was nephew of our old family-friend Mr. Thomas Keightley. "As I lay a-thinking" is a pathetic poem by Barham, author of *The Ingoldsby Legends*.— "Hannibal Fitch" receives some explanation (if he requires it) in an ensuing letter.—"Any two of my brethren" would obviously be Dante Gabriel and Collinson.—Mr. Holman Hunt was thinking of visiting Paris, and in the early autumn he did so in company with Dante Rossetti.]

PLEASLEY HILL.

[25 *August* 1849.]

My dear William,

I *did* see Mr. Orchard's most peculiar criticism on Gabriel's picture : but is it possible you would have expected the author of such prose to excel as a poet? If you are in a very charitable humour you will send me a copy of his two sonnets, your account of which excites my curiosity ; also a notice of Gabriel's excursion to Greenwich, should it take place. Though my visit here is extremely tolerable, still the postman is quite an event in my existence ; and Sol is my other sol-ace. Quite equal to *Punch*. The period of my return home appears altogether doubtful ; so you need not make yourself uneasy yet awhile. I have only had one walk since my arrival ; but hope for a second to-day, as I am getting strong and hearty.

Neither Mr. nor Mrs. Charles has yet appeared ; but I cannot count on this continuing. Local converse wearies me somewhat ; yet this advantage it possesses—I cannot join in it ; so may, during

its continuance, abandon myself to my own meditations.   My dreary.
poem is not completed, but a few appropriate stanzas have been
added since my leaving town.   You will easily believe that, whatever
other merit it lacks, it possesses unity of purpose in a high degree.

The talk of *beaus* is as perpetual here as at Mrs. Heimann's :
however, fewer jokes (?) have been passed on me than might have
been anticipated ; and of these Mary is entirely innocent.   Do you
know, I rather like Mary ; she is not at all caressing, but seems real.
Do you ever see the Kings ? news of them, or of the Brotherhood,
or of anything else, thankfully received.   *Apropos* of receiving, would
you be so kind as to let me have at your convenience "As I lay
a-thinkinge" ?   In my desperation I knit lace with a perseverance
completely foreign to my nature.   Yesterday I made a dirt-pudding
in the garden, wherein to plant some slips of currant.   The
unbusinesslike manner in which the process was gone through
affords every prospect of complete failure.   Ah Will! if you were
here we would write *bouts-rimés* sonnets, and be subdued together.
Mary has told me a capital story of three bears, with which I may
perhaps solace you on my return ; you will stand in need of some
comfort.

From Mansfield on to Pleasley I had for travelling companion a
very correct Titmarsh-looking man.   In one of the railway-carriages
was a young man the very image of Hannibal Fitch when he was
superlatively riled.   Do you recollect the portrait of that individual
as he appeared in the condition above alluded to?

Love to Papa, Mamma, Maria, and any two of my brethren you
choose to select, from Your &c.

Has Mr. Hunt vacated London for Paris ?

To WILLIAM ROSSETTI.

[As the letter implies, the sonnet here appended was a *bouts-rimés*
affair written to rhymes supplied by me.   I wrote a sonnet (but it
need not be reproduced) to the rhymes which Christina forwarded.
These rhymes begin with the word "rose," and end with "hence,"
and I do not identify them as pertaining to any of Christina's "old
things."—The words "your first *Thought*" relate to *The Germ*, the
proposed title of which was at this date *Thoughts towards Nature*.

The "rabid chartist" who was expected to contribute to that magazine must have been William North (mentioned at some length in my book of *Reminiscences*): he did not in fact contribute. Then another expected contributor is alluded to, and the epithet "Blissful" ensues: this was a Mr. Bliss, son of an eminent barrister; but he also did not contribute.—*Arthur Gordon Pym* will be recognized as the title of one of Edgar Poe's most impressive tales.—"C. C." is Charles Collinson, whom Christina had ere this seen once in London: he was not much to the taste of any of us.—The suggestion that I might "fail to decipher this" refers to the fact that that closing part of the letter was "crossed." Otherwise the suggestion would have been absurd, for Christina's handwriting was of the clearest and neatest conceivable.]

[PLEASLEY HILL.

31 *August* 1849.]

My DEAR WILLIAM,

Many thanks for "As I lay, &c." To your rhymes I have written a rather intense sonnet, which cannot miss your approbation. The notion of *life* turning to *must* is not hackneyed. On the back are some rhymes for you to fill up; they belong to one of my old things.

"Have you forgotten" Mr. Hannibal Fitch in Thackeray's Punch's review of one year's Exhibition? There was a portrait of him. I long to see your first *Thought*. That such a magazine as yours will be clever is beyond a doubt, but you must excuse my joining one which numbers among its contributors a "rabid chartist," and one "who thinks of nothing but politics" and "the negation of religion." Your plan is far too *Blissful* for my taste.

Arthur Gordon Pym must be beyond measure interesting; I hope to see it on my return. Mary desires me to kindly remember, or something of the sort, "us" to you. To-morrow she and I go to Mansfield: she prophesies my being a *favourite* with C. C. on account of my unalterable self-possession. Fancy the inflated state in which I shall re-enter London, should this flattering preference result from my visit. . . . Though this is anything but an equivalent for your last delightful letter, I must hope that you will charitably consider it in that light, and continue your epistolary favours to your correspondent, believing her to be ungrateful *only* in deed and not in will.

There are four unanswered notes awaiting my attention, and unable
to obtain it this morning. Still I cannot endure the idea that I may
be losing some possible communications through neglect. Besides
these four impending answers I much wish to write to Aunt
Charlotte, not having done so since leaving town; still justice must
take precedence of generosity. Assuring you that if you fail to
decipher this you lose nothing (which implies an acted bull, for
the assurance is no more legible than the rest,) I remain &c.

> So I began my walk of life; no stop
> Was possible; or else my will was frail;
> Or is it that the first stumblings entail
> Weakness no after strength has power to prop?
> The heart puts forth her boughs; and these we lop
> For very wantonness; until the gale
> Is rank with blood; then our life-portions fail
> And we are fain to share another's sop.
> At first my heart was true and my soul true,
> And then the outside world believed me false.
> Therefore my sweets grew bitter, and I thrust
> Life back, till it stood still and turned to must.
> Yet sometimes through the great stagnation calls
> Of spirits reach me : is it so with you?

To WILLIAM ROSSETTI.

[My proposed "pleasant excursion" was with James Collinson to
the Isle of Wight; hence the reference to "bathing" towards the
close of the letter. We went together to Cowes and elsewhere, and,
after Collinson's return to London, I was at Ventnor.—The "puzzle"
which terminates the letter strikes me as a very easy one to solve : it
must run—"Sir Humphrey Davy, Hyde Park Corner, Piccadilly."]

MANSFIELD.

8 *September* 1849.

MY DEAR WILLIAM,

In the first place let me wish you a pleasant excursion next
week, and petition for an occasional continuance of your epistolary
favours. To-day Miss Collinson and self return to Pleasley; so I
anticipate having more time for the carrying on of my extensive
correspondence. Quite contrary to my expectations, I have greatly
enjoyed my Mansfield visit; and but for certain toilet-difficulties
should be very happy to prolong it. Mrs. Charles is delightful;

the most to my taste of any one I have met down here: her sister too, Carrie Maltby, seems a nice girl.

Yesterday evening we spent with the Fosters . . . Miss Rosanna sang sosoishly; and Mr. Foster went to sleep in a coat more usually seen in morning private life than at a *soirée*. Will you give Mamma my warmest thanks for her darling letter, which I trust to answer very shortly; also my very best love; also will you tell her that, if any one is devoted enough to see about sending it, the portfolio should be directed to me at Pleasley Hill, and that I should very much like to have it, as a ring cannot be offered a person who never wears one?

I *had* mentioned to Mary the sweet prettiness of "As I lay a-thinkinge:" but she does not appreciate it; at least not as we do.

The *must* to which my life has turned is the substantive. You cannot imagine the grief which filled me on learning that you could answer *Yes* to anything connected with my sonnet: yours is less bad, but also less uncommon. Have you yet received ocular demonstration of the existence of H. Fitch? I am perfectly convinced that he is not only an empty name. I still entertain a dreamy hope of seeing Mr. Orchard's sonnets through your kind agency: if I wait to make their acquaintance till my return home, the probability is that they will never meet my longing eyes.

When you are in the country on no account neglect bathing: be a little less lazy than on occasion of our last year's stay at Brighton: and do not forget that the succulent Abernethy should precede your matinal dip. You see I am turning quite into an old nurse. Did you play at chess with C. C. when you were down here? We are tolerably equal: he has conquered once oftener than myself, but I won the last game.

Will you give my love to Papa, Maria, and Gabriel? In a P.S. I will put a curious puzzle for your torture; I only succeeded in deciphering the first line. Wishing you better success, I remain &c.

An English gentleman asked a French one for a London address, and received this:

> Sarumfré Dé Vie,
> Hippocana,
> Piquet dé lait.

To WILLIAM ROSSETTI, *Ventnor.*

[The affairs of James Collinson were regarded as "unpromising" chiefly, I think, on the ground that his pictures did not sell: it may be also that his sister was aware that he was not unlikely to return to the Roman Catholic Church, which would have been, and in fact it was, fatal to the engagement between him and Christina. Park Village was the residence of our grandfather Polidori and his family.]

[50 CHARLOTTE STREET, LONDON.

19 *September* 1849.]

MY DEAR WILLIAM,

Last night we saw Mr. Collinson, who gave us your address, and this at length enables me to answer your last note. I have not yet filled up your rhymes, but still hope to do so; only I will not delay writing till the inspiration comes.

Let me congratulate you on the retirement of Messrs. North and Bliss from your literary concern: without them it appears to me to have more prospect of success. Many thanks for Mr. Orchard's sonnets: your comment on them is not too severe; but there is a good feeling about them . . . By the by I have not told you all this time that I came home on Monday, after exactly a month's stay in Notts. From all acquaintances there I have received unvarying kindness and hospitality; on your return you will probably witness (not watch) the progress of a piece of work of which I hope some day to beg Mrs. Charles' acceptance. I have already given Miss Collinson my Nice portfolio, so need not on that account hesitate to make my next present where I like. . . .

My correspondence with Mary Collinson has come to an end by her desire. Do not imagine we have been quarrelling: not at all: but she seems to think her brother's affairs so unpromising as to render our continuing to write to each other not pleasant. Does not this sound extraordinary? We are all much surprised.

Yesterday I called in Park Village; to-day I hope to visit Mrs. Heimann, but rather dread this interview for very natural reasons.

Mamma wishes me to give you her love; and to say that she will not write to-day as I am doing so, but contemplates doing so soon. Time fails; so with Mrs. Collinson's respects (this really was the message) I remain &c.

I shall have much to talk about on your return: my visit was very pleasant for some reasons, but not exclusively so. In haste, good-bye.

To WILLIAM ROSSETTI, *Ventnor.*

["The Potters" were a family that we had known ever since early childhood; Mr. Cipriani Potter being the Principal of the Royal Academy of Music, and my godfather to boot.

The proposal of bestowing the title *The P.R.B. Journal* upon the magazine which was ultimately named *The Germ* did not come to effect. I think the suggestion was soon dropped by my colleagues in London, and I, the appointed Editor, was not in its favour.]

50 CHARLOTTE STREET, LONDON.
[26 *September* 1849.]

DEAR WILLIAM,

Gabriel, being pressed for time, has commissioned me to write as follows.

You need not hasten your return home on account of the magazine, as the prospectus can wait. You already know all the contributions except Mr. Stephens'; which is at present on divers scraps, in a highly chaotic state. Mr. Hunt's etching is in two compartments; the first represents Mr. Woolner's man and woman gathering flowers by the water-side; the second, the man throwing himself on the woman's grave. These are all his messages, to the best of my remembrance . . .

Your *bouts-rimés* is one of the best you have written: my own has fared very much better than its intrinsic value merits. My overwhelming business consists of nothing more important than needle-work and such like.

Maria and self passed yesterday very pleasantly with the Potters. You really should visit them on your return: they are so friendly, so *pressing* to see you; besides Henry is very nice, and might very probably suit your taste as well as mine. He is nothing at all of your abomination a boy, though only sixteen.

I have heard of *The Saint's Tragedy* from Mr. Collinson. Whether he will be at the Heimanns' to-morrow I know not. Mamma sends her love.

P.S. Mrs. Potter ardently desires to borrow the Snobs, and you are to take it her some evening.

P.P.S. From Gabriel.

Several are thinking of calling it the P. R. B. Journal. Think maturely and write result at once to Stephens. You need not hasten back, as he will manage till your return. All communications are to be addressed to him.

To William Rossetti, *Excise Office.*

[Christina here alludes to various small points, applicable to Brighton, with which she and I had been familiar when there together in 1848. There was somebody whom we had called "Riba," which is the name of a marauding personage in the drama of *The Miller and his Men*, familiar to us in childhood through the medium of *Skelt's Theatrical Characters* and otherwise.—If I was at this date thinking of going to France, I gave up the intention, and went instead to Edinburgh and Newcastle-on-Tyne: did not reach France (Paris) until 1853.—"The execution" refers to a small matter which I have mentioned elsewhere—the seizure of Dante Gabriel's goods in a house in Newman Street, where he rented a studio, owing to the levanting of his landlord, a dancing-master: he was not himself in any arrears of rent.—The reference to Collinson and his picture of *St. Elizabeth of Hungary* shows that by this date Christina had ceased to be in personal relations with Collinson. Their engagement had been broken off at some such date as May or June 1850, owing to his having reverted from the Anglican to the Roman Church.]

34 WEST STREET, BRIGHTON.

[8 *August* 1850.]

My dear William,

Seized with my usual longing for news, I as usual resort to you ; somewhat ashamed indeed of the empty letter system, yet not enough to make me give it up.

Yesterday walking up Western Street I recognized the familiar shop of Pratt, Hairdresser; and the neat abode of Humphry where *Mangleing* is done. The other evening I am convinced I saw Riba on the beach, but have not yet discerned " our nose."

Do you still think of going to France in your holiday? Wishing is foolish, but I could almost wish you to be content with some place in England. I suppose I shall be back before your expedition, but if not do not forget to send me your then address : however the utmost limit of our absence will probably be the completion of the month. How does Gabriel's studio business proceed? I was much surprised to hear of the execution.

Have you seen the *St. Elizabeth* lately? and do you yet know what is to be done with the figure of the old woman whose position was not liked? Whilst I am here, if you can manage without too much trouble, I wish you would find out whether Mr. Collinson is as delicate as he used to be : you and Gabriel are my resources, and you are by far the more agreeable.

I direct this to the Excise that Mamma may not know of it. Do not be shocked at the concealment; this letter would not give her much pleasure. Do have patience both with the trouble I occasion you and with myself. I am ashamed of this note, yet want courage to throw it away; so must despatch it in its dreary emptiness with the sincere love of Your &c.

To WILLIAM ROSSETTI.

[Christina was not quite correct in surmising that Collinson's picture of *St. Elizabeth of Hungary* "must be very beautiful " : it was however meritorious up to a certain point.—As to her writing " two or three scraps," I find only two poems of hers which are dated about this time; they are *Annie* in September, and *St. Elizabeth of Hungary* in November.—Mrs. Sortain was a lady married to a dissenting minister of much note as a preacher : she was a member of one of the families in which my mother had been governess—the Macgregor family.]

34 WEST STREET, BRIGHTON.

14 *August* 1850.

MY DEAR WILLIAM,

Many thanks for the news your letter contains, though you do not seem to consider it much.

Gabriel's position appears not particularly pleasant; but, if his whereabouts is to be kept secret, pray do *not* let me have his address. Mr. Brown appears invariably kind.

Thank you for the St. Elizabeth news : it must be very beautiful. Is it intended to be ready for next Exhibition? I quite wish to see it, and examine into all its beauties. I conclude you may not improbably come in : has some one yet been found for St. Elizabeth's future mother-in-law?—I think her name was Sophia. But from what you say it would seem that St. Elizabeth herself is to be painted from the same head as one of her maids of honour : is this the case? I hope not. . . .

I have written two or three scraps, none of which may very likely be finished. We have not set cognizant eyes on a single speaking acquaintance, and altogether our days and nights and days go by, bearing a considerable resemblance between themselves. We called on Mrs. Sortain yesterday, who has very goodnaturedly lent us books, with the offer of more as wished for. I have got the first volume of Layard's *Nineveh*, and Maria a Life of Crabbe and some book on China; I will not tell you how much I have read of my borrow.

Maria unites with me in love to Papa, Mamma, and Brothers.

To WILLIAM ROSSETTI, *Edinburgh.*

["Mr. Cayley" was Mr. Charles Bagot Cayley, who at a much later date than this proposed marriage to Christina. At present he was known to us as a pupil of my father for Italian, and as author of the beginning of a MS. translation of Dante's *Divina Commedia*, afterwards completed and published. I got some specimens of it published in the weekly review entitled *The Critic* (named towards the close of Christina's letter).—What the "unhappy little fragment" may have been I know not : I presume it was some verse written in the tone of despondency or life-weariness not unusual with Christina. —Priscilla Townsend was a member of a large family well known to us, not in affluent circumstances, who all emigrated at this date to Canterbury Settlement, New Zealand : some of them still are, or recently were, in that dominion.—About the "Scotch beggar," I have some faint recollection that such a personage in Edinburgh handed me some verses, professedly of his own composition : the verses themselves have vanished from my memory.—Mr. (Benedetto) Sangiovanni, by profession a modeller of picturesque figures in clay &c., was an old family-friend of ours, held in much regard, who had recently quitted London for Brighton : the "small clay dog" is, I suppose, the same which remained with Christina up to her death, and which is now mine. The "busto romano" is unknown to me. "Mr. Ciocci," whom it is said to have resembled, was an Italian with a very insignificant but prettyish face : one of those disfrocked priests who beset my father in these years, teasing him (with overmuch success) to write anti-catholic tirades and expositions. We did not ourselves know any particular harm of Ciocci : but it is a fact that, not long after this date, he was tried and convicted at Brighton for something much in the nature of housebreaking.—Mr. (Filippo) Pistrucci was, like Sangiovanni, a family-friend who, leaving London, had settled at Brighton : he lived by teaching Italian, and was also a painter.— The review in *The Guardian* of *Art and Poetry* (*The Germ*) was, if I remember right, written by Coventry Patmore, not at the solicitation of the writers concerned therein.]

50 CHARLOTTE STREET, PORTLAND PLACE LONDON.

3 September 1850.

My DEAR WILLIAM,

To commence with the one useful sentence of my letter : will you in your next let us know whether you have yet received Mr. Cayley's MS. translations from Dante, which we posted for you last Saturday ?

In Mamma's letter allusion was made to one I wrote you from Brighton, which arrived on the day of your departure. As a whole it was not perhaps a peculiarly interesting document : but it contained an unhappy little fragment which so totally disgusted Mamma that I very speedily made away with it.

One evening Priscilla Townsend called to take leave of us before quitting England, and left her remembrances for my brothers. Poor girl, she seemed somewhat depressed as the time for departure drew near. I think of writing to her sometimes, which cannot fail to console her for all privations. But nonsense apart I sincerely regret losing her: she was a very nice girl, cordial and goodnatured. . . .

There seems to me nothing improbable in the fact of your Scotch beggar having composed the verses you sent. There is something I like about them. Before leaving Brighton we took tea with Mrs. Sortain, on which occasion we did not get enough to eat. Mr. Sangiovanni presented me with a small clay dog, and Maria with a *busto romano* which reminds us both of Mr. Ciocci: and we met Mr. Pistrucci by appointment at Mr. S.'s; he is looking better than I ever remember to have seen him. A favourable review of the defunct *Germ*, or rather *Art and Poetry*, appeared in last week's *Guardian*: incidental mention is made of Gabriel's last picture: and I am not sure whether unmixed but certainly high praise is awarded to the Præraphaelite School of painting. Mamma, who possesses the newspaper, is much gratified at all this: not the less perhaps as the pre-eminence of *mind* is not attributed to Mr. Millais. A *Critic* came for you this morning.

I have no further communications of any sort present to my mind except that I am &c.

To WILLIAM ROSSETTI.

[Aylott and Jones, a firm in Paternoster Row, had been the publishers of the first two numbers of *The Germ*. I don't exactly remember what I was proposing to do in relation to them: perhaps to see whether they would publish *Maude*. This was a prose-story (for girls rather than adults) written by Christina, with some verse interspersed: it remained unpublished until after her death, 1897.— Mrs. W. B. Scott was not a poetess or authoress in the ordinary sense: but she had recently shown me some verses of her composition, chiefly on religious topics. Her opinions on such topics were at that time shifting and uncertain: hence an expression in Christina's letter. —" The Gilfillan case" and the " abominable row " are not now clear to me. I was then writing some literary reviews in *The Critic*, and the Rev. George Gilfillan, a rather prominent critic of those days, was taking a leading part in that weekly serial : *possibly* I had surmised that I might come into some sort of collision with him—or (not less probably) the row has no relation to Gilfillan or to *The Critic.*—It will be observed that this letter was written from Longleat, the seat of the Marquis—at this time of the Marchioness Dowager—of Bath. Our Aunt Charlotte Polidori was a governess, and afterwards a "companion," in the Marchioness's family, and had been authorized to receive Christina as a temporary visitor.]

LONGLEAT, WARMINSTER, WILTS.

28 *July* 1851.

MY DEAR WILLIAM,

Many thanks for your kind intention of writing on the subject of Aylott and Jones. Perhaps our letters will cross. I think *Maude* may await my return. She is lying perdu in a drawer, several removes from undergoing a revise. Perhaps I shall some day produce something better in the first instance. I am far from blind to the poetry of Mrs. Scott's verses. They are very superior to my preconceived notions of them, and indicate talent and feeling : if such poetry may be trusted for telling a true tale. Perhaps a *real* tale would better express my meaning, as I have no intention of insinuating falsehood. Do you select the middle of August for taste or convenience, for your projected visit to Newcastle? or did your hosts elect propose it? How have you arranged matters in the Gilfillan case? It is very easy to set down matters as "nonsense and a bore" to me : but I defy you to prove that I do not want your letters, *even* such as they are. But how can you have any taste for an abominable row? I do not approve of the specimen of signature you append to your last letter : it is very easy to say it is W. M. Rossetti.

When next you see them, you may remember me not only to Mrs. but also to Mr. Scott. This is avoiding the hurry of the last moment. Is Mr. Scott a good judge in art? Of course, if not, his opinion may still occasionally be right. There is a (to me) singular plant in the garden : one flower of it swarms with ants. Its appearance is something like that of a thistle.   Did you ever taste bread-fruit?   We. had some yesterday : it reminded me of an indifferent pear.   Will you tell Mamma, with my love, that I regularly have arrowroot in my own room of a night: and that at dinner in the schoolroom I mix my wine with that unpleasant and salutary compound hop-tea ?

Thinking it possible you may not wish me to go on to the genuine history of my week's work, I remain &c.

The other day Lady Bath let me ride home from church, and herself walked in the rain.   She shows herself very amiable in certain little everyday matters.

To WILLIAM ROSSETTI, *Newcastle-on-Tyne.*

[The address here given by Christina had become our family-residence since the beginning of 1851.   Our Uncle Henry Polydore, Articled Clerk to a firm of solicitors, lived in Gloucester, and I visited him on my return homeward from Newcastle, where I was the guest of Mr. and Mrs. W. B. Scott.—The only verse-compositions by Christina which I find dated towards this time are *A Fair World though a Fallen*, in August, and *Behold I stand at the door and knock*, in December.—The phrase " I have not made out North yet " becomes a little less hazy on reading the next-ensuing letter. —" Little Fanny Grey " I have forgotten : she may perhaps have been some small girl, in a humble sphere in life, known to Christina in connexion with church-work.]

38 ARLINGTON ST. CAMDEN TOWN.

23 August 1851.

MY DEAR WILLIAM,

Do not feel aggravated at the sight of my mark.   I write to enclose a note from Uncle Henry to Maria, part of which regards you.   Do you not think it would be possible to take Gloucester in your way home?   I think you might give pleasure by the proceeding ; Uncle Henry is by no means well, and Gloucester is a fine old city well worth seeing.   If you go, try to manage the ascent of Robin Hood's Hill in the vicinity ; the view is magnificent.   There is a delightful walk, too, to Hempstead, such a pretty village.   You can go along by the Bristol Channel, and returning you pass Lanthony Abbey, and an ancient well. . . .

I have written nothing whole since you left, but have begun a piece that, I fancy, might prove nice.

I have not made out North yet. Will you remember Mamma, Maria, and self, cordially to Mr. and Mrs. Scott? How do you all get on, and what do you do?—also how was your present liked? I have not attempted the Heimanns yet; perhaps *the* letter may stand in the place of intercourse for some months to come: but honestly I am not in a condition to walk so far. Little Fanny Grey told us one day that a goose had no legs, a cat two, and a canary four: however she assigned the proper complement to a three-legged stool.

Mamma sends a maternal love, Maria a do. adapted to circumstances.

To WILLIAM ROSSETTI, *Newcastle-on-Tyne.*

[I did, as expected, " proceed to the Lakes by Carlisle," staying for a day or two at Pooley-bridge by Ulleswater: and this was the only occasion when I have visited the Lake-country, except that, shortly after Ruskin's death, I was at his house overlooking Coniston.— Some arrangement had been made for the convenience of William North, who was now either changing lodgings in London, or else preparing to go to the United States. He was not " married," but perhaps he ought to have been.—As to the ballad of *The Hermit of Warkworth*, I believe that I was right in ascribing it to Bishop Percy: it is not the same thing as the ballad of *The Hermit*, written by Goldsmith. I had recently made an excursion to Warkworth Hermitage, and had by mischance left my pocket-book there.]

38 ARLINGTON ST. CAMDEN TOWN.

29 August 1851.

MY DEAR WILLIAM,

Many thanks for your nice long letter. Your time seems full indeed, and pleasantly so. Do you think you shall exceed your fortnight at Newcastle? At any rate I hope my note may arrive before your departure. If you proceed to the Lakes by Carlisle (a near Railway point) and return thither preparatory to continuing your tour, you could thence go to Gloucester by a very direct route. . . .

Yesterday Mr. North sent for his box. To-day Mamma has consented to take in letters for him : how long this is for I know not. Is he married? a young lady with a child in a cab left the message. Begging your pardon, was it not Oliver Goldsmith who versified *the* Hermitage, and not Bishop Percy? You may thank your third-class tastes for the delightful duration of your journey, I conjecture. I dare say Lincoln Cathedral is grand : once I was told that Gloucester and Worcester were reckoned the two finest in England. But how delightful Hexham Church must be : and I like the Sexton.

Did all its furniture depart along with your pocket-book? Could you not make enquiries for it, Mamma suggests? If you have not yet got a new one, on no account do so. Maria and I hope to present you with one for your next birthday. You need not answer per post, as we hope to see you before then. . . .

Have you chilly weather? We have, say I.

From DANTE ROSSETTI *to* CHRISTINA ROSSETTI, *Darlaston Hall, Staffordshire.*

[This letter (with some minor omissions of words, and especially of its drawing) has previously been published in *The Family-letters of D. G. Rossetti.*—As to the statement that Christina was "perpetrating portraits," it may be observed that towards this date she had a certain disposition to cultivate any aptitude which she might possess for art-work. She never carried the attempt far, but could catch a likeness pretty well.—"The Sid" was Elizabeth Eleanor Siddal, whom my brother married in 1860.—His things sent from Highgate were probably forwarded from the house rented by Mr. E. L. Bateman, a decorative artist who had emigrated to Australia with Thomas Woolner and others. Mrs. and Miss Howitt (the late Mrs. Howitt-Watts) were then staying in the house, and were on very cordial terms both with my brother and with Miss Siddal.—The magazine with which Mrs. Howitt was connected was named (I think) *Aikin's Year*: Christina published in the magazine the composition *Behold I stand at the door and knock*: not perhaps anything else.

SKETCH BY DANTE GABRIEL ROSSETTI.
See p. 22.

[*To face p.* 21.

Her *Ruined Cross* was a very early affair, included in the privately printed *Verses* of 1847.—Christina was at this time on a visit to Mr. Swynfen Jervis and his family, at Darlaston Hall, Staffordshire : she was, I think, bringing on one or other of the daughters in conversational Italian. Mr. Jervis, a connexion of Lord St. Vincent, had been in parliament : our father had taught Italian in his family, who had kept up some acquaintance with us otherwise. The pen-and-ink sketch of Mr. Jervis and Christina, and the description of it, were not intended as seriously ill-natured to this gentleman, but as banter which a sister would understand. Mr. Jervis was something of a Shakespearean commentator, and something also of a verse-writer.— My brother's proposed trip to Hastings was for the purpose of rejoining Miss Siddal, who stayed there at times for health's sake.]

LONDON.

4 *August* 1852.

MY DEAR CHRISTINA,

Maria has just shown me a letter of yours by which I find that you have been perpetrating portraits of some kind. If you answer this note, will you enclose a specimen, as I should like to see some of your handiwork. You must take care however not to rival the Sid, but keep within respectful limits. Since you went away, I have had sent me, among my things from Highgate, a lock of hair shorn from the beloved head of that dear, and radiant as the tresses of Aurora, a sight of which perhaps may dazzle you on your return. That love has lately made herself a grey dress, also a black silk one, the first bringing out her characteristics as a "meek unconscious dove," while the second enhances her qualifications as a "rara avis in terris," by rendering her "nigro simillima cygno."

I am rejoiced to hear of your improved health, and hope it may prove lasting. I was lately in company with Mrs. and Miss Howitt, with whom you are a considerable topic. I believe Mamma forwarded you an intelligent magazine by Mrs. H. to which you are at liberty to contribute. That lady was much delighted with your printed performances, and wishes greatly to know you. Her daughter likewise yearns in your direction. She has by her, singularly enough, a drawing which she calls *The End of the Pilgrimage*, made by her some years back, which furnishes an exact illustration of your *Ruined Cross.*

On the opposite page is an attempt to record, though faintly, that privileged period of your life during which you have sat at the feet of one for whom the ages have probably been waiting. The cartoon has that vagueness which attends all true poetry. On *his* countenance is a calm serenity, unchangeable, unmistakeable. In yours I think I read awe, mingled however with something of that noble pride which even the companionship of greatness has been known to bestow. Are you here transcribing from his very lips the title-deeds of his immortality, or rather perpetuating by a sister art the aspect of that brow where poetry has set up her throne? I know not. The expression of Shakespear's genial features is also perhaps ambiguous, though doubtless not to him. Westminster Abbey, I see, looms in the distance, though with rather an airy character.

I shall very possibly be going to Hastings in a few days. Meanwhile, till I hear from you or see you again, believe me &c.

I forgot to say that Mamma considers 2/6 sufficient to give the maid, in which I may add I do not coincide. Mamma, however, says *you* must judge.

To FRANCES ROSSETTI, *London.*

[Not long after settling in Frome-Selwood, Somerset, Mrs. Rossetti had to return to London, to attend the deathbed of her mother, Mrs. Polidori, aged eighty-four or thereabouts. Christina remained behind at Frome; to which town she and our mother had very recently gone to arrange for opening a day-school. The Rev. Mr. Bennett was Vicar of Frome. He had been appointed to that living by the Marchioness Dowager of Bath, after exciting in London some commotion by his "high-church" practices : and it was conjectured that, with some countenance from him, Mrs. Rossetti, with Christina as her assistant, might be able to do something better with a day-school at Frome than they had managed with a like school at No. 38 Arlington Street.]

probably been waiting. The cartoon has that vagueness which attends all true poetry. On her countenance is a calm serenity, unchangeable, unmistakeable. That yours I think I read also. mingled however with something of that noble pride which even the companionship of greatness has been known to bestow. Are you here transcribing from his very life, the title-deeds of his immortality, or rather perpetuating by a vision but the aspect of that from whence poetry has set-up her throne? I know not. The expression of Shakespeare's genial features is also perhaps ambiguous, though doubtless not to him. Westminster Abbey, I see, looms in the distance though with rather an airy character.

I shall very possibly be going to Hastings in a few days. Meanwhile till I hear from you or see you again.

Believe me, dear Christina,
your affectionate brother
D. G. Rossetti

FACSIMILE FROM ROSSETTI'S LETTER.
See p. 22.

[To face p. 22.

BRUNSWICK PLACE, FROME.

28 *April* 1853.

MY PRECIOUS MAMMA,

Thank God indeed that dear Grandmamma died without pain, and also that you left Frome when you did; another delay would have made you too late, at any rate unless you had had even more night-travelling. I am very glad she mentioned me, but hardly hope she understood my love. I have managed to put on nothing contrary to mourning to-day, and shall be glad to have the proper things, as you kindly say you will order them.

Now I want you to consider about my going to town, and only to consider your own wishes in the matter. In the first place, trusting in the goodness of my intentions, I shall defer setting off till Monday morning at any rate: this will enable me to complete the current week, and to make our shortcoming exactly a fortnight. On the other hand, if you are only requiring my presence in London to save me trouble, pray do not let this weigh with you: I am managing very well, and doubt not I shall continue doing so. . . .

Do not let Maria or any one at home labour under the delusion that I do not care to see them ; but rather let them attribute my plan to that strength of mind which characterizes me. . . .

And now for something personal. If I come to London, and am in time, I should like to see Grandmamma again. Pray do not be afraid of the effects of such a sight on me ; I really wish it, unless the lapse of so many days renders it inadvisable. But of course I leave the decision wholly to you. I hope Grandpapa will not suffer in his health.

The weather here continues very ungenial in-doors, but has improved out. Mind you take due care of your wise self: and this exhortation I address to all I love, which includes a considerable number of persons ; each of whom I salute, especially Papa.

To WILLIAM ROSSETTI.

[Christina did not give any address to this letter beyond writing "H. H.," and I do not now well remember where she was—possibly

Hampstead Heath.   It is clear that she was engaged in some sort of tuition, not of a fully defined kind, and that she rejoiced (quite characteristically) in finding her health not strong enough for regular engagements of like description ; and this was, I think, the very last attempt that she made at anything of the sort.—" Henrietta " was Miss Henrietta Rintoul, daughter of the Editor of *The Spectator*, for which I was then the art-critic.—About the Russian book by Harrison I don't know anything ; we had some acquaintance with a family named Harrison, in which the mother and one or two of the daughters were flower-painters.—Mr. Munro was the sculptor Alexander Munro.]

H. H.

[13 *November* 1855.]

MY DEAR WILLIAM,

I hope you are glad to know that I am very comfortable in my exile ; but at any rate I know I am rejoiced to feel that my health does really unfit me for miscellaneous governessing *en permanence*.   For instance yesterday I indulged in breakfast in bed, having been very unwell the day previous : now I am very tolerable again, but do not feel particularly to be depended upon.

May I hope for another letter before my return ?   I dare say you know I have written to Henrietta ; to whom my cordial love *should you chance* to see her.   Since writing to her, I have discovered a charming fact in a note to an amusing Russo book : to wit, the Chinese have three words signifying death ; *sze* (?) for the vulgar, *pang* for the emperor, but for princes and such like *hung ! ! !*   I am so pleased.

Do you know *Hochelaga* by dreary Elliott Warburton ?   I am supposed to be reading it.

But to revert to the Russian book.   It is by a man *called* Harrison, and some particularly bad plates illustrating it are signed *F. Harrison*. I wonder if these have anything to do with our Harrisons.   I have a notion they had a Russian resident brother, and the plates then would be due to the fair Fanny.   Their nature encourages in me a ·suspicion that I could do better myself.

I hear Mr. Munro has dined at home since my departure : I

wonder if I ever shall make his acquaintance, having heard of him these hundred years.

Of course there are numbers of pictures about here, some of which are worth looking at. I wish you could see an extremely quaint one of a little girl holding something in her hand whilst a kitten stretches up towards her : I fancy it must possess merit.

I hear my young charge just come in from their walk : so in haste believe me with love to Mamma and Maria . . .

To G. too, of course, if attainable.

To WILLIAM ROSSETTI, *Freshwater*.

[I spent some little while at Freshwater, seeing much of Mrs. and Miss Rintoul, and something of the Tennysons.—I forget what Dr. Heimann's tale may have been.—*The Crayon* was an American Art-review, edited by Mr. W. J. Stillman (afterwards well known as American Consul in Rome and in Crete, *Times* correspondent in Rome, &c.), and I acted as its informant for British matters.]

45 UPPER ALBANY STREET, LONDON, N.W.

18 *August* 1858.

MY DEAR WILLIAM,

Your letters, showing that you are enjoying yourself, cheer us like sunbeams and produce in us a moon-like content. We heard this morning from Maria, who also appears comfortable : she has promised the Scotts to be with them on Friday evening. . . .

Dr. Heimann's tale proves very superior to my expectations; Heimannic, but agreeably so : I think you will like it. He seems inclined to publish it both in German and English, in the former almost immediately. . . .

Gabriel is so well as to have utterly disappeared from these quarters. His water-cure was prescribed by himself, such treatment having formerly relieved him. No letters for you to-day, as yet.

We have revisited the Z. Gardens. Lizards are in strong force, tortoises active, alligators looking up. The weasel-headed armadillo as usual evaded us. A tree-frog came to light, the exact image of a tin toy to follow a magnet in a slop-basin. The blind wombat and neighbouring porcupine broke forth into short-lived hostilities, but apparently without permanent results. The young puma begins to bite. Your glorious sea-anemones :—I well know the strawberry specimen, but do not remember the green and purple. Beware of putting them into *fresh* water, as the result is said to be fatal and nauseating. Did you thank us for that *Crayon* ? Sometimes `a very mean instalment of occupation is acceptable at the sea-side. . . .

Mamma's love : also hers and mine to Henrietta, with the useless assurance how truly I am &c.

To WILLIAM ROSSETTI, *Newcastle.*

[The statement, "I have promised to go to Highgate," relates to an institution at Highgate for the reclamation and protection of women leading a vicious life : Christina stayed there from time to time, but not for lengthy periods together, taking part in the work. —The "proofs" which she had to attend to must have belonged to her volume, *Goblin Market*, &c.—Olaf and Peter were dogs—the latter at Wallington Hall, the seat of Sir Walter Calverley Trevelyan. —The observation that Paris and other French places were now realities to Christina glances at her having been in France (for the first time) with our mother and myself in the summer of this year.— The "horror" connected with horses in France was, I think, some process of vivisection.—As to Dr. Gray and Mr. Du Chaillu, some readers of the present day may remember an embittered controversy which was carried on regarding Du Chaillu's adventures with gorillas. Ultimately his opponents had to admit the essential truth of his statements, though combined with various inaccuracies of date and locality.]

45 UPPER ALBANY STREET, LONDON, N.W.

25 *October* 1861.

MY DEAR WILLIAM,

. . . I have promised to go to Highgate for a short time, on condition that I shall have leisure to attend to proofs : but expect to be home again about the 13th if not before. Gabriel, in a note to Maria, mentioned that he was going to Yorkshire (last) Wednesday, so now very likely he is gone.

The 2 Misses Cayley called the other day. Sophie (in a bonnet and not very good light) handsome and striking, ready and amusing in conversation; Henrietta you know. . . .

My love to my dear Mrs. Scott: Mamma joins me in everything cordial to both your hosts. How is dear Olaf? And at Wallington has Peter found a worthy successor?

On Wednesday evening we went and heard an amusing schoolroom lecture, Reminiscences of foreign travel; Boulogne, Rouen, and Paris, are realities now for me instead of mere names. The lecturer, a Revd. — Jackson, was one of the recent deputation to Napoleon III on the subject of cruelty to poor horses: and describes the Emperor's reception of the deputation as not merely courteous but apparently even cordial. In a week the horror was put an end to.

The Cayleys I find are connections of Dr. Gray, Du Chaillu's opponent.

From DANTE ROSSETTI.

SIMPSON'S DIVAN.

[July 1862.]

DEAR CHRISTINA,

Here are the 2 notices. I forgot that one puffs me too; so, if you want to show them to any one, I would be obliged if you would copy them and not show them in my writing. I hope you are better, and should come up to-night instead of writing if it were not late. I shall come very soon. With love to all.

British Quarterly, July 1862.

Besides *Goblin Market* this volume contains some miscellaneous poems and a variety of devotional pieces. All of these are marked by beauty and tenderness. They are frequently quaint and some-times a little capricious. The designs by Mr. Rossetti are rich and exquisite. No goblins could be better or more laughable than these; nor could we imagine anything more felicitous than the mixed longing and hesitation pourtrayed in the face and action of the damsel. The poem which the designs illustrate is perhaps the wealthiest in expression of any in the volume, as it is also the one which is most purely and completely a work of art; but the devotional pieces are those we have liked best, and we are only sorry to have no space to quote from them.

National Review, July 1862.

The principal poem has rare delicacy and beauty of a modest kind, and several of the sonnets are fine.

To DANTE ROSSETTI.

[This letter is headed by a primitive portrayal of two hands raised in astonishment, and a note of admiration. It relates to a caricature made by Dante Gabriel, founded upon a phrase in *The Times*, in a critique upon the *Goblin Market* volume, "Miss Rossetti can point to work which could not easily be mended." He chose to misconstrue this phrase, and represented Christina, in a state of senseless excitement, destroying household furniture with a hammer, bank-notes in a firegrate, &c. The caricature was preserved by Christina, and is still extant—now in the hands of my daughter Olivia Agresti.—The Henrietta here mentioned was Henrietta Polydore, daughter of our uncle; she was at this date aged sixteen or thereabouts, and was consumptive. She died in the United States towards the age of twenty-eight.—By "Mac" here and elsewhere Christina meant her publisher Alexander Macmillan, with whom she was always on pleasant terms.]

81 HIGH ST., HASTINGS.

[*December* 1864.]

MY DEAR GABRIEL,
    Such is my attitude vis-à-vis of the historic record of my finished work. The stolid equanimity of the elephant under the loss of his trunk is perhaps my favourite point: though Henrietta justly directed my admiration to the rueful eye which the chip directs to the old block (head).

DANTE, CHRISTINA, FRANCES, AND WILLIAM ROSSETTI.

From a Photograph taken by Rev. C. L. Dodgson (Lewis Carroll) in Dante Rossetti's Garden, c. 1864.

[*To face p. 29.*]

A Miss Smith has asked and obtained Mac's leave to melodize one of my things, I know not which. The other day a Rev. Mr. Baynes wrote begging my permission for him to reprint *House to Home*, in a collection he is preparing to promote a charitable object: after consulting Mac I consented. Jean Ingelow is in his list of contributors; and Dean Alford, not that I rate him very high poetically.

Uncle Henry and Henrietta join in love.

To WILLIAM ROSSETTI.

[This letter is very roughly written in pencil. My recollection concerning it is not exact. Christina was somewhere away from home, but I think not far off nor for long. It is clear that she had by this time, on grounds of religious faith, declined the offer of marriage made by Charles Bagot Cayley: also that I had written making some proposal which she thought liberal—I presume the proposal (which I certainly did make at some time or other) that, if they two were to marry, with means of subsistence inevitably very slender, or indeed next to none, they would be welcome to live as free inmates of my house.]

11 *September* 1866.

DEAR WILLIAM,

I am writing as I walk along the road with a party.

I can't tell you what I feel at your most more than brotherly letter. Of course I am not *merely* the happier for what has occurred, but I gain much in knowing how much I am loved beyond my deserts. As to money, I might be selfish enough to wish that were the only bar, but you see from my point of view it is not. Now I am at least unselfish enough altogether to deprecate seeing C. B. C. continually (with nothing but mere feeling to offer) to his hamper and discomfort: but, if he likes to see me, God knows I like to see him, and any kindness you will show him will only be additional kindness loaded on me.

I prefer writing before we meet, though you're not very formidable.

From CHARLES CAYLEY.

[At the head of this letter Cayley wrote an Italian sonnet by Dino Frescobaldi, date 1311. He afterwards translated it in the *The Pall Mall Gazette* thus :—

> "Advice for him that visits England. Wear
>   No gaudy colours and no lofty mien.
>   In show be simple, and in practice keen.
> Ill may the Briton, if he trips you, fare!
> Spend with bold heart, and shun the miser's air.
>   Keep out of troubles, and give way to spleen.
>   Pay punctually, but with politeness screen
> Your dunning, and protest your pouch is bare.
> By what you ask for be prepared to stand.
>   Purchase betimes, and fortune speed you well.
>   Never with men who trade in wit commune.
> Be duteous to the great ones of the land,
>   And on good terms with your own people dwell,
>   And make your doors fast in the evening soon."]

[? BLACKHEATH.

2 *September* 1868.]

DEAR MISS CHRISTINA ROSSETTI,

        Many thanks to you and William for the extracts you so kindly copied. You might perhaps like, *in its way*, the sonnet I mentioned to him; I will have the pleasure of showing you how I translate it in the P. M. G. or in a proof. . . . On other points your brother convinced me. I must send you some remarkable intimations about our friends the Uommibatti; let us hope that by being eaten they will multiply and earn a livelihood. This is from a *Times* article on the Victoria acclimatization society.

"The Society acts on the principle of reciprocity, and is ready to lend as well as borrow. For instance, it sends us black swans for white, and has, besides, done its best to provide us with the *wombat*, though we fear to little purpose. This animal was recommended some years ago as calculated to supply a particular want—that, namely, of an animal available for ordinary food, and conveniently intermediate in size between a pig and a rabbit. Of its flesh we only heard that it was neither unwholesome nor disagreeable, but what has become of the venture we cannot say. It seems that the creature has been exported to Paris and Calcutta, as well as to London, so that the experiment ought to have had a fair chance."

To Dante Rossetti.

[This letter is imperfect—the first sheet of it has been lost. It would appear that Dante Rossetti had conveyed to his sister a suggestion, made by Mr. Stillman, that she should write some more poems, partaking (in greater or less degree) of "politics or philanthropy." Such would not have been Rossetti's own recommendation: as he was more than commonly opposed to the use of such matter as a subject for poetry. Perhaps I need scarcely translate Christina's Italian words, "*tanto meglio per me,*" "so much the better for me."

[LONDON.
? *April* 1870.]

. . . It is impossible to go on singing out-loud to one's one-stringed lyre. It is not in me, and therefore it will never come out of me, to turn to politics or philanthropy with Mrs. Browning: such many-sidedness I leave to a greater than I, and, having said my say, may well sit silent. "Give me the withered leaves I chose" may include the dog-eared leaves of one's first, last, and only book. If ever the fire rekindles availably, *tanto meglio per me :* at the worst, I suppose a few posthumous groans may be found amongst my remains. Here is a great discovery, "Women are not Men," and you must not expect me to possess a tithe of your capacities, though I humbly—or proudly—lay claim to family-likeness. All this is for you, not for Mr. Stillman, for whom however are all our cordial regards. . . .

A human being wanting to set one of my things to music has at last not fixed on "When I am dead," but on *Grown and Flown.*

From FRANCES ROSSETTI *to* CHRISTINA ROSSETTI, *Folkestone.*

["Nolly" was Oliver (son of Ford) Madox Brown.—Dante Rossetti's "country-lodgings," mentioned at the end of this letter, were the Manor-house at Kelmscott, Oxfordshire, which he rented jointly with William Morris.]

56 EUSTON SQUARE.

19 *August* 1870.

MY DEAR CHRISTINA,

. . . Yesterday I passed a most pleasant day with Gabriel and William at Chelsea : your Aunts and Uncle were invited also. Gabriel is notably, I hope *desirably*, thinner : he seemed well and in spirits. We dined most delightfully in the tent, the pretty deer coming to the entrance, and eating out of our hands : he did not molest two ducks, a rabbit, and a cat, which sported in his wake. He adorns the garden which has quite run wild, and which he browses at his will ; he is master of almost *all he surveys.* We ate mulberries from the venerable tree, and excellent they were. Green figs on a recumbent branch we only looked at. Grouse came to table, also to our house here, a gift from my son Gabriel ; who tells me you are "a more spontaneous poet" than himself . . .

Gabriel has a mole, the gift of Nolly. I cannot think he will have it long, though he provides it with a glass box of good dimension, filled with earth. Nothing short of full liberty in the garden can, I suppose, keep him alive ; and even of that fact there would be no ocular proof, as doubtless he would sink into the ground. His first salute to Gabriel was a bite, more regarded by me than by himself . . . Gabriel continues assiduous in his painting, and will not go yet to his country-lodgings. . . .

To DANTE ROSSETTI.

[Various poems written by Dr. Thomas Gordon Hake are the subject-matter of this note.]

56 EUSTON SQUARE.
[1871—? *End of February.*]

MY DEAR GABRIEL,

Referring to your letter of weeks ago, I wish I could say more about *Madeline;* but I altogether lost myself in its mazes, and perished in its quag. The *Parables* however are quite another matter. *Old Souls*, not to discuss every point in it, has a rugged nobility and beauty which I hope may strike fire out of some flints, and a pathos which may melt some. *The Lily of the Valley* too has continual beauty; the *Deadly Nightshade*, startling awfulness. Perhaps, but I am not sure, the one I care for least is *Immortality*. But in all, unless we except *Old Souls*, I have a habit of missing the thread, if indeed the thread always is there to miss. Even in *Madeline* I recognize beauty—but how about meaning? The *Epitaphs* I have not studied, but the *Resurgam* I read and liked. Perhaps, if I had not been pulled down by my abscess I might be more pointed; as it is, please pardon generalities.

Our Mother's love.

To DANTE ROSSETTI.

[The dreadful illness from which Christina suffered for two or three years—termed exophthalmic bronchocele or Dr. Graves's disease—began in or about April 1871. Here we find the first evidence of it: the handwriting is very much affected. It is like what Christina's handwriting, starting from the standard of March 1871, might have been expected to come to when she should be seventy-five years old or upwards. This collapse of handwriting lasted for some months, but was totally overcome in the long run.]

56 EUSTON SQUARE, N.W.
28 [*April* 1871].

MY DEAR GABRIEL,

Thankyou for forwarding me Dr. Marston's courteous and complimentary letter, which I like. Perhaps you may look at it some day. Sir W. Jenner saw me last Saturday and pronounced me seriously ill: to avoid stairs I am confined to the drawing-room floor.

3

Our Mother sends a love of the magnitude to which we are accustomed.

Please attribute intolerable hideousness in part to weakness.

To WILLIAM ROSSETTI, *Ravenna.*

[This letter was written by Christina chiefly for the purpose of sending on to me any letters which had arrived to my London address after I had left town.—Mr. Arthur Hughes was (but I need scarcely specify it) the illustrator of *Singsong*, and all sorts of people have agreed with Christina in regarding his designs as "charming."— I forget what "the beautiful Greek album" was : probably something coming to me from Mr. W. J. Stillman, who had recently been United States Consul in Crete.—The *Songs of the Sierras* was the first volume of poetry published by Joaquin Miller.—Maria's "frontispiece" appertained to her book, published about this time, *A Shadow of Dante.*]

56 EUSTON SQUARE, LONDON, N.W.

28 *July* 1871.

MY DEAR WILLIAM,

. . . We were setting off to-day, as Sir W. J[enner], having seen me, recommends sea again; but a cold I caught has delayed us at least till to-morrow.

By the by, one other letter has come for you, but it is only from Dalziel with a second proof of *Sing Song*. Mr. Hughes continues charming. I have written now to ask that proofs may be addressed to me, and of course they must follow me out of town. . . .

I could not tell you outside (having forgotten to mention inside) how warmly Miss Heaton and Mr. Cayley thanked you for the beautiful Greek album. He wishes you also a pleasant tour. He called last Wednesday and stayed to dinner, and borrowed my *Songs of the Sierras*. He had just been down to Cambridge for his little niece's birthday.

Maria's love. She received 4 proofs of her frontispiece to choose from, and Gabriel to whom she sent them made the selection. We have not heard from him again. . . .

To WILLIAM ROSSETTI, *London.*

5 GLOUCESTER PLACE, FOLKESTONE.

1 *September* 1871.

MY DEAR WILLIAM,

Thankyou very much for the notes on my last proof, notes which I might not have ventured to make even had I had the wit for their composition. What a charming design is the ring of elfs producing the fairy ring—also the apple-tree casting its apples—also the three dancing girls with the angel kissing one—also I like the crow soaked grey stared at by his peers.

In one way I have certainly gained ground, my appetite has improved; and I walk a little better perhaps. The abscess is a thing of the past. Still I am weak, and less ornamental than society may justly demand. . . .

I hope you now admit that England has its share of heat and sunshine: you might be indignant could you hear even me complaining of the heat as I do now. . . .

Habitual ugliness has overtaken my letters—pardon.

To WILLIAM ROSSETTI, *Roehampton.*

[This letter relates to the very alarming illness of Dante Rossetti, then staying at the house of Dr. Hake at Roehampton. He was at first supposed to be struck down by serous apoplexy, and likely to die, with the "one fearful alternative" of loss of reason.—Mr. [Henry Treffry] Dunn was his art-assistant.—Christina was herself at this time confined to bed with her malady, and not capable of moving; whereas our Mother and Maria, along with myself, were for two or three days housed by Dr. Hake.]

[56 EUSTON SQUARE.

10 *June* 1872.]

MY OWN DEAR WILLIAM,

Thankyou warmly for your note received before 4 last night: it helped me—with its comparatively hopeful news—to get soundly to sleep at last. I have now seen Mr. Brown fresh from Mr. Marshall, but before this reaches you he will have told you what he told me. I know not (having heard of one fearful alternative) what to hope: but with my whole heart I commit our extremity to Almighty God.

My love, please, to dearest Mamma and Maria. I am getting on capitally, and Aunt Eliza nurses me most kindly: her love to all, and mine too if it could reach Gabriel. Lucy called this morning full of grief and sympathy. I have seen Mr. Dunn's telegram to Mr. Brown.

No letter has come to be sent on.

To WILLIAM ROSSETTI, *London.*

[Trowan, a farmhouse near Crieff in Perthshire, was the place where Dante Gabriel was now recruiting his health, in company with Dr. and Mr. George Hake.—The phrase " paint all a lover's smart " &c. refers to a funny poem by Thomas Hood, called *Love Lane*, which afforded many a laugh to Christina and the rest of us from of old. Hood shows how a lover in a rural retreat paid court to his fair one, interrupted by various too-attentive insects, &c.—

> " And painted all a lover's smart,
> Except a wasp gone up his arm."]

GLOTTENHAM.

31 *August* 1872.

MY DEAR WILLIAM,

I have never yet thanked you direct for the loan of those funny German caricatures you sent me a while ago. The stork's nest in a hoop, and the frog ill for three weeks, are good—so indeed are many more.

Mamma, with love and warm expression of joy at the excellent news from Trowan, returns herein the Hake correspondence. Such friends as Dr. Hake and his son are rarer and more precious than gold. I wrote to Gabriel, not quite certain how my letter might answer; but now I am thoroughly re-assured, and rejoice that I did so.

One day here is so very like another that there is not much news for a letter even to my brother of brothers. Two robins haunt the garden—one afternoon emmets (?) appeared in swarms. Here one might from time to time " paint all a lover's smart, except " (happily not a wasp, but say) " a midge gone up his arm. . . ."

We expect to return home on the 11th; and soon after I may keep house with you, as in old days, in much harmony.

To WILLIAM ROSSETTI.

[Mr. Stauros Dilberoglue was a Greek merchant in the City of London, a man of fine character and more than average ability. He had recently lost his wife, and asked Christina to accept one of her belongings, an Indian shawl.—For the wedding of Dr. Francis Hueffer and Cathy Brown, Sir Lawrence Alma-Tadema painted portraits of the couple framed jointly: I have now forgotten what the quotation was, but it was something from which an evil omen might have been drawn.—Christina's "fearful brownness" was one of the symptoms of her illness, and was indeed highly observable.— Madame Bodichon was that excellent lady known earlier as Miss Barbara Leigh-Smith: she had an estate in Sussex not far from Glottenham.—Dante Gabriel was at this date still in Scotland, and there was some likelihood that he would not only not return thence direct to Tudor House, Chelsea, but would even see about wholly quitting that house and living elsewhere in or near London. As a fact, he settled for many months at Kelmscott Manorhouse, Oxfordshire, and then returned to Tudor House.]

GLOTTENHAM.

[5 *September* 1872.]

MY DEAR WILLIAM,

Thankyou for your dear letter received this morning. I am quite delighted with the Indian shawl, Mr. Dilberoglue's generous present; and suppose it may be the handsomest gift I ever in my life received.

I am so glad Maria enjoyed Cathy's wedding-feast, and that your shawl shone amongst the presents. Also I am pleased that the bridal portrait includes my negligée, but not pleased at the inappropriate dismalness of the quotation by Alma Tadema. I hope Dr. Hüffer is not superstitious.

Please do not think me obstinate for returning home with Mamma on the 11th, despite your and Maria's kindness. I feel languid and sometimes low here, besides another inconvenient symptom, and think that I may have to consult Dr. Wilson Fox not long after my return. *Pro* you will find me fatter ; *contra* of a fearful brownness.

Mme. Bodichon's kindness adds considerably to our pleasure here, and certainly she is a charming woman.

Dear old Gabriel—I incline to hope very earnestly that he will not return to Chelsea. I am so sorry for your inconvenience in sleeping at Tudor House.

To DANTE ROSSETTI, *Kelmscott.*

[Though Christina did not comprehend the inscription, there is nothing difficult in it, if only one remembers a certain phrase in Dante's *Paradiso.* The medal, bronze, is a good work of art, done by Signor Cerbara.]

17 ROBERTSON TERRACE, HASTINGS.

28 *April* 1873.

MY DEAR GABRIEL,

. . . Dearest Mamma is very well again, and wonderfully well in her feet, which now bear her about in comfort. *I* am very well too, all things considered.

Winter has been with us again, but to-day gives hopes of spring or summer to come. A Bath chair is to come for me at 12.30, to take me out for the first time since our coming down. We think of returning home on the 20th May, a little before William talks of going abroad.

Very likely, with or before this you will receive from Maria in London the bronze medal of our Father sent from Italy. The likeness is not all we might desire, but still the medal is very interesting to us. The inscription I confess I do not yet comprehend.

Mrs. Madox Brown and Lucy called on us before we left London, the latter looking pale but not complaining of illness. What a delightful person she is ! . . .

Our cordial remembrances, please, to Mr. Hake.

To WILLIAM ROSSETTI, *Venice.*

56 EUSTON SQUARE, LONDON, N.W.

17 *June* 1873.

MY DEAR WILLIAM,

. . . Thankyou for such kind thought of me and my health. I cannot tell you how much better I am ; downstairs again, and with some latitude as to going out. Maria came home from Eastbourne yesterday, looking well, and feeling also better ; though we still have cause for anxiety about her. Her love to you ; and, a size bigger, our Mother's.

Mamma and I are thinking of Kelmscott: Gabriel has been written to, and we are now awaiting his answer. . . .

To-day I got an application for leave to insert *Uphill* in a Tauchnitz vol. of poetry : *Yes*, of course. The letter is apparently from Amelia B. Edwards—at least, I hope it is the autograph. . . .

My looks have met with some amount of approval.

To LUCY BROWN [ROSSETTI].

[This letter was written (as its terms indicate) as soon as Christina had received notice of the engagement between Lucy Brown and myself.]

THE MANOR HOUSE, KELMSCOTT, LECHLADE.

10 *July* 1873.

MY DEAR, DEAR LUCY,

I should like to be a dozen years younger, and worthier every way of becoming your sister ; but, such as I am, be sure of my loving welcome to you as my dear sister and friend. I hope William will be all you desire ; and, as I know what he has been to me, a most loving and generous brother, I am not afraid of his being less than a devoted husband to you. May love, peace, and happiness, be yours and his together in this world, and together much more in the next ; and, when earth is an anteroom to heaven (may it be so, of God's mercy to us all), earth itself is full of beauty and goodness.

To WILLIAM ROSSETTI, *London.*

THE MANOR HOUSE, KELMSCOTT, LECHLADE.

10 *July* 1873.

MY VERY DEAR WILLIAM,

You have brought a fresh spring of happiness and interest into our family, and the kindness with which your letter alludes to me in one general sentence is warm in my heart. Who shall wish you well except the sister whom you have cared for all her life? If dear Lucy and you are as happy as I would (if I could) make you, earth will be the foretaste and stepping-stone to heaven. Her sweetness, amiability, and talent, make her a grace and honour to us —but I need not state this to you. . . .

How much will have to be settled when Mamma returns home! I had a little friendly chat with Mrs. Brown this morning, and find her and hers as full of welcome as we are. I have ventured to write affectionately to Lucy.

To DANTE ROSSETTI, *Kelmscott.*

[Dizi, called more properly Dizzy in some published letters of Dante Rossetti, was a black-and-tan terrier, of ample canine sagacity.]

56 EUSTON SQUARE, LONDON, N.W.

[*July* 1873.]

MY DEAR GABRIEL,

The delightful life at Kelmscott ought not soon to slip from my memory, nor ought I soon to forget whose kindness provided me with so many pleasures. Our mother, with a most maternal love, joins me in recording the pleasures of our visit to you. Our journey home was completely prosperous. Once in the railway carriage, Dizi behaved very well: at Oxford, instead of the servant Mr. Hake had promised to send, two gentlemen (the two Mr. Mackays I conclude) took us all in charge and relieved us of all trouble. Of course you have heard since; but they gave us an excellent account of Mr. Hake, who had his doctor's permission to go out the following day. When you see that most amiable of men pray remember us both most cordially to him; he was a marked element in our enjoyment . . .

To-day all the Browns are engaged to dine here. Yesterday I called in Fitzroy Sq., and already Lucy has paid her respects to Mamma in this house. She is as sweet and engaging as ever in her new position, and there seems promise of happiness to come . . .

To OLIVER MADOX BROWN.

[Oliver Brown, aged eighteen, was now about to publish his first novel entitled *Gabriel Denver*; at a later date it was re-issued (cutting out some alterations which had been introduced to conciliate the publishers) under the name of *The Black Swan*.]

56 EUSTON SQUARE.

[C. *July* 1873.]

MY DEAR NOLLY,

Thankyou very warmly for permitting us to read *Gabriel Denver* in proof. My Mother joins me in admiration of the talent of which it is full; which realizes and conveys so vividly, and wields both power and beauty. I like touches about animals, and sympathy with their poor little cares and fortunes. What I do not like (if you will suffer my boldness) are the characters of your principal personages. Surely they are detestable; unless Laura's weakness saves her from so strong a brand. Still, I am happy the two gained the shore. . . .

To WILLIAM ROSSETTI, *Somerset House.*

[I quite forget what Christina's "ebullition of temper" may have been: can safely say it was a trifle. Her "sleeping in the library" (the back parlour) was remedied by her sleeping, with our mother, in the back drawing-room. Thus, following the date of my marriage, 31 March 1874, things continued until Michaelmas 1876, when they two removed to another house, 30 Torrington Square.]

56 EUSTON SQUARE, N.W.

[5 *November* 1873.]

MY DEAR WILLIAM,

I am truly sorry for my ebullition of temper this morning (and for a hundred other faults), and not the less so if it makes what follows seem merely a second and more serious instance.

My sleeping in the library cannot but have made evident to you how improper a person I am to occupy any room next a dining-room. My cough (which surprised Lucy, as I found afterwards, the other day at dinner), . . . makes it unseemly for me to be continually and unavoidably within earshot of Lucy and her guests. *You* I do not mention, so completely have you accommodated yourself to the trying circumstances of my health : but, when a "love paramount" reigns amongst us, even you may find such toleration an impossibility. I must tell you that not merely am I labouring under a serious relapse into heart-complaint and consequent throat-enlargement (for which I am again under Sir William Jenner's care), but even that what appeared the source of my first illness has formed again, and may for aught I can warrant once more have serious issues.

The drift of all this is that (through no preference for me over you as you may well believe, but because of my frail state which lays me open to emergencies requiring help from which may you long be exempt) our Mother, if I am reduced to forego all your brotherly bounty provides for me, will of her own unhesitating choice remove with me. We believe that from all sources we shall have enough between us, and you know that our standard of comfort does not include all the show demanded by modern luxury. I have very little doubt that an arrangement may be entered into which shall lodge us under one roof with my Aunts ; thus securing to us no despicable amount of cheerful companionship, and of ready aid in sickness.

Dear William, I should not wonder if you had been feeling this obvious difficulty very uncomfortably, yet out of filial and brotherly goodness had not chosen to start it : if so, I cannot rejoice enough that my perceptions have woke up to some purpose.

I do not know whether any possible modification (compatible

with all our interests, and not least with Lucy's) may occur to you as to arrangements ; to me, I confess, there scarcely seems any way out of the difficulty short of a separation. Perhaps in a day or so you will let Mamma or me know what you judge best.

Of course Mamma is in grief and anxiety ; her tender heart receives all stabs from every side.—If you wonder at my writing instead of speaking, please remember my nerves and other weak points.

To DANTE ROSSETTI, *Kelmscott.*

[" My book " is *Annus Domini,* which contains a prefatory poem. —By " a story of mine," Christina meant the *Speaking Likenesses.* Mr. Arthur Hughes was secured as illustrator of the volume. Mr. James Smetham, a painter well known to and valued by Dante Rossetti, is esteemed now in virtue of some of his writings as well.]

SOUTHSEA HOUSE, MARINE PARADE, EASTBOURNE.

4 May 1874.

MY DEAR GABRIEL,

It is worth while molesting you with words, because I can tell you that our dearest Mother really has rallied at this nice place. She goes out for her little walks, her little sits, her church, and I hope is on the mend for this long while to come. Her dear love to you ; and Maria's love as genuinely, though I fear we shall soon lose Maria from our hearth in favour of her new " Home."

Our sitting-room here reminds me of beloved Kelmscott, though I fear you would draw the line at its wall-paper. Its crossbeam in the ceiling you should not demur to.

Thankyou for all the kind thought you have taken in finding what to say of my book. I despaired of your saying aught for its verse. Elsewhere I have had a few pleasant mentions of it, but nothing especially cut out for report to you. I hear Mrs. Scott with Miss Boyd have called in Euston Square since we left, and that the former likes my little book, I having sent it her.

Do you see (what I am told through two or three reporters, for I have not myself *seen* it) that *The Athenæum* has announced a story of mine to come out with Macmillan? Funnily enough, I did not know matters were concluded between Mac and me, but now I hope they are. I tried to get the illustrations for Hughes, and secondarily for Smetham, but know not whether with any result. The story is merely a Christmas trifle, would-be in the. *Alice* style with an eye to the market. . . .

Our remembrances, please, most cordially to Mr. Hake. ˎ I am very much better for this pleasant change.

To WILLIAM ROSSETTI, *Naples.*

[Dr. Littledale may be remembered as a high-church clergyman who wrote various books. He was an Irishman, and, though highly serious in his public capacity, full of agreeable pleasantry in private.]

SOUTHSEA HOUSE, MARINE PARADE, EASTBOURNE.

15 *May* 1874.

MY DEAR WILLIAM,

Most welcomely your nice little card of news has reached our Mother this morning, and has assured us of Lucy and your safe return home. To think that you two now have one home and one heart—may they be full of peace, love, and happiness.

Mamma, Aunt C., and Aunt E., join me in two loves; which two are the largest couple you will know. . . .

We fully expect (D.V.) to dine with you on Saturday 23, and re-pitch our tents at home. My Aunts mean to return to Bloomsbury Sq. the same day. . . .

I have heard again from Mr. Macmillan, and find he is treating with Mr. Arthur Hughes about illustrating my Christmas story; so of course *this* is accepted, to my great contentment. He asked me about illustrators, and I proposed—or rather I expressed my own preference for—A. H.: wherefore I am pleased.

We are particularly well lodged here as to situation, in nice rooms and with nice people. Poor Mamma has caught cold I know not how, but still I hope this will not neutralize the good already achieved: I myself thrive, and show mitigated.looks to boot. I hope *Annus Domini* has met with a fraternal welcome at your hands and

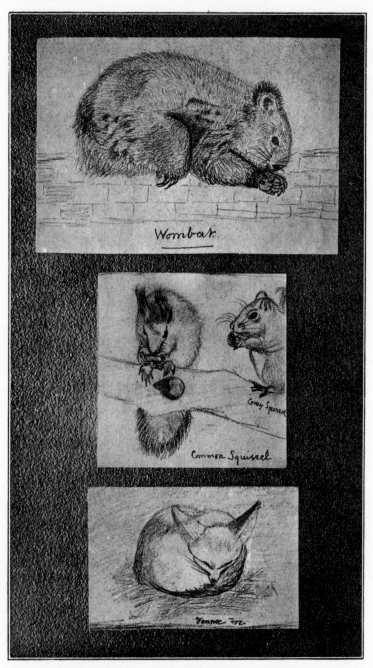

FROM PENCIL DRAWINGS BY CHRISTINA ROSSETTI.

Animals in the Zoölogical Gardens, London, c. 1862.

[*To face p.* 45.

heart. Various more or less pleasant mentions have been made of it, particularly one which has gratified me in a note of acceptance from Dr. Littledale.

I need not "hope" you have enjoyed *this* trip.

To DANTE ROSSETTI, *Kelmscott.*

[If I remember right, this proposed visit of our mother and Christina to Kelmscott did not take effect. My wife and I were there for a few days, and my brother began a well-known head of my wife in coloured chalks; finished soon afterwards when he had re-settled in London.]

56 EUSTON SQUARE, LONDON, N.W.

22 June [1874].

MY DEAR GABRIEL,

Your letters always cheer our Mother, as a country rose cheers a Londoner, or the first Spring day overtakes all the world. With a very warm love she acknowledges the pleasure of your invitation (in which I thankfully claim my share), and, weighing all circumstances on your side and on our own, thinks that Tuesday 30th (*not* this week, but next week) will suit us all for the commencement of our visit. . . .

Mamma understands from William this morning that he and Lucy go to you next Saturday, but of course they write for themselves to you. . . .

To DANTE ROSSETTI, *Kelmscott.*

["My fruitless apple-tree" was a decorative design by Christina, who at rare intervals adventured upon some such performance — *Her Winning Ways* was a novel by Dr. Hake published in a magazine.]

56 EUSTON SQUARE.

[C. 23 *June* 1874.]

MY DEAR GABRIEL,

This is a word to tell you the upshot of my fruitless "Apple-tree." Mr. Morris has written me a truly obliging letter, finding something to praise, but setting-up a standard of such complicated artistic perfection as (I fear) no alterations of mine can ever by possibility attain. " In due season I found no apples there " . . .

Warm thanks to Mr. Hake for *Her Winning Ways*, which Mamma and I are reading and enjoying together. I should not have expected such overflowing punnishness from grave and dignified Dr. Hake. The mystery is an interesting one, and leads one on, but we have not yet gone very far.

To DANTE ROSSETTI, *Chelsea.*

["Your beautiful present" was an old Italian painting, not of large dimensions, which had been sent to Dante Rossetti by some unknown hand, and which he transferred to Maria. It was of some religious subject, and he (I know not on what authority) regarded it as the work of Pietro Laurati.—The reference to chloral as taken by my wife indicates that, during an early stage of our married life, she now and then took a dose to procure sleep. With her it acted perfectly well : but, on learning that the reverse was the case with my brother, she abandoned it, and never resumed its use.—" Poor Nolly " [Oliver Madox Brown] had recently returned, with myself and others, from a brief stay in Margate, where he suffered much from pains, at that time chiefly in a foot. It was the beginning of the disease, pyæmia, which brought his life to a close on 5 November 1874. My brother was now re-settled in Cheyne Walk. The address given by Christina, 12 Bloomsbury Square, was the residence of our Aunt Eliza Polidori, and (when in London) Charlotte. Our mother and Christina, though dwelling with me in Euston Square, were pretty frequently staying with my aunts.]

12 BLOOMSBURY SQUARE, W.C.

28 [*September* 1874].

MY DEAR GABRIEL,

. . . I am quite pleased at the prospect of Maria's so soon receiving your beautiful present, and doubt not she will in the first instance transport it to Margaret St., though thence I dare say it will soon be despatched to Eastbourne—at least, at some time. I hope *we* shall see it first. We saw her on Saturday, when she appeared tolerably well though by no means free from weak points. Mamma continues admirable, and is her own dear gently-active self again. This afternoon William paid her a visit, and reports Lucy and her family home again from Margate : when she can sleep without chloral *well*, I trust she may have recovered to all intents and purposes. Poor Nolly has been doubtfully pronounced on by Mr. Marshall, but his symptoms do not distinctly declare themselves ; only he must take great care. I hope your change of servants will prove a success ; I should regard with an eye of callous philosophy obesity and Hogarthianism, especially if not shared by the housemaid. I have just heard from Mrs. Morris, who asked particulars about Eastbourne Hospital for the sake of a poor young Icelandic woman she is interested in, and who has been quite blind though now somewhat bettered, and happily I was able to impart some details as well as to suggest the way of obtaining fuller information. I hope the poor thing may benefit if sent there by her kind friends. My Aunts join in love to you. . . .

I have now seen all Mr. Hughes's illustrations to my little story, and hope they are pretty enough to please you in due course.

To DANTE ROSSETTI.

12 BLOOMSBURY SQUARE, W.C.

[1 *October* 1874.]

MY DEAR GABRIEL,

There was a visible brightening up amongst us on receiving your good-natured proposal of a second day together : and our family conclave fixes on either to-morrow *Friday*, or next *Monday*. If you do not write at all, we will understand you to accept Monday, and arrive in caravan that afternoon. . . . I hail the prospect of seeing again the *Proserpine*, and for the first time the *Veronica :* where in England and its studios is your peer ?

To DANTE ROSSETTI.

56 EUSTON SQUARE, N.W.

[5 *November* 1874.]

MY DEAR GABRIEL,

Here is my book at last ; and I hope Mr. Hughes will meet with your approval, even if you skip my text.

Do you know that poor Nolly is so extremely ill that I even think it possible that he may not live till this reaches you? He did survive last night, and this morning Sir W. Jenner and Mr. Marshall are making one more effort to save his life, but I know not whether with real hope of success. . . .

My title page has a " thereof" which dismays me; but I missed seeing the proof both of that and of the list of illustrations, of which latter I never thought.

To DANTE ROSSETTI.

[The poems of Canon (Richard Watson) Dixon are the subject of this letter.]

56 EUSTON SQUARE, N.W.

[C. 20 *June* 1875.]

MY DEAR GABRIEL,

Many thanks indeed for bringing Mamma and me acquainted with a poet. She is greatly impressed with the sublime beauty of some part, and I with the frequent excellence; also we echo some of your "!" Do you think the rock, if any, Mr. Dixon tends to split on is dryness? You see which way my verdict inclines, but I honour yours. . . .

I am returning Mr. Dixon's 2 volumes to you, with this.

To WILLIAM ROSSETTI.

[" The three Austins" were relatives of my mother—cousins of some sort. I question whether I myself ever saw any of them.—Dora Greenwell was of course the poetess, tolerably well known to Christina: by me, slightly known and considerably liked.]

ALL SAINTS MISSION HOME, 2 ROYAL PARK, CLIFTON, BRISTOL.

11 [*August* 1875.]

MY DEAR WILLIAM,

It seems a human observance to write and announce our safe arrival and well-being, and so I go on to do; but, as you know, news does not abound on such like occasions. . . . We are most comfortably lodged and entertained here, our one austere point being an absence of carpets : all else abounds and is excellent. Clifton would I think be too Cheltenhamy for you ; yet a nice place it appears, refreshingly tree-full, blossoming right and left, and suggesting a highly advantageous St. John's Wood. The Down, however, far excels any feature known to me of that quarter, and affords a really good drive. The stone quarried hereabouts is varied with fine shades of red, and walls gain greatly by this circumstance. On some houses the great white magnolia blooms, and on one to-day I spied the rare sight of a myrtle in blossom. Our 3 remaining weeks seem to promise much satisfaction, for we still propose returning to London on the 31st.

We have called on or been called on by all the three Austins, but the only one actually seen is old Mrs. Austin. I also have paid private and personal visits to Dora Greenwell, who appears a good deal invalided, but failed not to evince interest on hearing of your marriage. . . . Bristol, by the by, looks a picturesque town; and I find there is a local zoo.

To WILLIAM ROSSETTI.

[Mrs. Greenwell, when I saw her towards 1862, was an old lady of very fine presence and motherly engaging manner.—My wife and I were at present staying for a short while in Fitzroy Square, with Madox Brown and his wife. Probably Miss Mathilde Blind, the poetess, was also there, and we may have offered to take her with us on our returning to Euston Square.]

ALL SAINTS MISSION HOME, 2 ROYAL PARK, CLIFTON, BRISTOL.

[17 *August* 1875.]

MY DEAR WILLIAM,

. . . I called on Dora again yesterday and gave her your cordial remembrances, which she returns in kind. She still recollects your kind attentiveness to her mother, who, old as she was, began reading your Dante ; and now *she* has her mother's photograph of you. Poor thing, her health is apparently very much shattered, though one Dr. appears not hopeless of doing her good.

I recollect *Venus Astarte*, a noble drawing, and one which I

4

hope Gabriel may delight in painting. £2000 too is, I suppose, a good price even for his work.

Very friendly of you to house Miss Blind. I hope you are comfortable in Fitzroy Sq., and am sure you are all the more so by sympathy with Lucy's period of comfort.

To DANTE ROSSETTI.

2 ROYAL PARK, CLIFTON.

[*August* 1875.]

MY DEAR GABRIEL,

I was not thinking of writing to you from this pretty but civilized (and therefore not suitable to you) place,—when, last Saturday, we spent the day some six miles out of Clifton, at Berwick Lodge, a house standing in its own grounds, which include an actual wood, and the house itself and garden and lawn reminding me of dear Kelmscott. Unlike K[elmscott] however, the garden is slopy, and the country round-about hilly : the lawn commands a splendid descent of fields, ending in a good glimpse of the Bristol Channel, this again backed at one part by distant Welsh mountains. The house itself is very inferior to K[elmscott] in outside beauty, but inside (I should say) fully its equal in scale and comfort. A Mr. Lewis is at present the landlord ; he keeps the farm belonging thereto in his own hands, and lets Berwick Lodge with its grounds and furniture (which includes many nice old things, I think, and quaint objects of art) at 4½ guineas per week. . . . I could not see this charming well-wooded place in a fine hilly country without thinking of you : and, if my telling you about it serves no other purpose, it will at least illustrate my impotent good-will. . . . The great drawback I hear of is that in the hunting-season huntsmen overrun the very lawn by the house. I do not know how near the Avon may or may not be. All I know is that it runs through Bristol, Clifton and Bristol forming in fact one town.

Our day at Berwick Lodge took place because "our Superior" is staying there with her family, and invited us all three over for a visit. It came off pleasantly, in spite of such a wet·drive home in an open vehicle as might have depressed a being less buoyant than myself.

I think you know Dora Greenwell. I have been seeing her down here; and am quite struck with her large-mindedness, really liking her. She is far more dilapidated than myself, poor thing.

Do you take any active interest *counter* that horror of horrors, Vivisection? In case you or any of your chums do, and would sign, I enclose a paper to which I am trying to get names,—and which I am sure you will at any rate oblige me by sending me back signed or unsigned. You had better, please, direct it to Euston Square, where (D.V.) we shall be to-morrow.

Mamma and Maria join in love to you. This excursion has suited our healths and our tastes all round.

To DANTE ROSSETTI.

12 BLOOMSBURY SQUARE.

[*September* 1875.]

MY DEAR GABRIEL,

I am the more obliged by your personal kindness to myself which has led you to sign though without thorough agreement. I used to believe with you that chloroform was so largely used as to do away with the horror of vivisection; but a friend has so urged the subject upon me, and has sent me so many printed documents alleging and apparently establishing the contrary, that I have felt impelled to do what little I could to gain help against what (as I now fear) is cruelty of revolting magnitude. Mamma is cut to the heart by details she has read, and has given her dear name also to the cause. I have been much struck by M. Nélaton's verdict on the same question; and, in case his name may have weight with you, I venture to enclose one fly-leaf which has struck me, and which of course I will not trouble you to return.

My date shows that we are at Bloomsbury Square with my Aunts. . . .

We came home from Clifton last Tuesday, and on Wednesday came on here. William and Lucy prosper, though the latter with various drawbacks at this particular moment : perhaps before we get home again you and I may own a small nephew or niece ! . . .

To DANTE ROSSETTI.

12 BLOOMSBURY SQUARE.

21 [*September* 1875].

MY DEAR GABRIEL,

We have a niece! Born about 8 o'clock . . . on yesterday evening, the 20th. Both mother and child safe, and William our informant this morning. . . .

We think Maria will soon now be "professed"—and till then she is likely perhaps to enjoy less leisure than usual: but she still has her Saturday afternoon with our Mother.

Mamma's very best love to you.

I have at last harvested £5 from *Sing-Song*!! Both Aunts send love.

To DANTE ROSSETTI, *Bognor.*

[Rossetti was now staying at Aldwick Lodge, Bognor, whence Christina had recently returned.—By "the Lays" she meant Macaulay's *Lays of Ancient Rome*, a book which had been a great favourite with us in early days.—"Old Mrs. Harrison," the flower-painter, has been previously mentioned in this correspondence.—The term "my unwieldiness" relates to the unwieldiness (as pointed out by Dante Rossetti) of the title of a poem by Christina, *The Iniquity of the Fathers upon the Children*: he had proposed as a substitute simply *Upon the Children*.—Mr. J. H. Ingram is now well known in literature as the biographer of Edgar Poe and of Marlowe, &c.]

56 EUSTON SQUARE, LONDON, N.W.

[1875—C. 30 *November.*]

MY DEAR GABRIEL,

Your letter full of interest has been one of our Mother's pleasures this morning, and she is sending it on to Maria, so it will do double duty of entertainment. She would like to have seen your fine fan of sea-flag; and certainly, if the oyster-shell is as legible as your transcript, its monogram stamps it as all her own. Though we are no longer at Aldwick I assure you we dwell in a semi-arctic

region of our own, and truly sorry I am if your atmosphere is much
colder than ours: I think not merely the sparrows and robin, but
even the thrush, blackbird, and wagtails, may have to capitulate if you
spread their board for them : perhaps the actual tom-tit may present
himself on his least of legs. . . .

All cordial regards from us both, please, to Mrs. Morris. I am
sorry our last parcel proved so barren. For the *Vicar of Wakefield*
(about the size of 3 thumbs, and therefore no burdensome mistake)
I was answerable, as also for the *Lays* which I thought might
possibly have become a book not universally known to a younger
generation than our own. Now I have done up ready for the rail 6
vols. (one entire set, that is) of the Walpole Letters : and if these
please you there are 6 more, and also an additional 3 containing
the Miss Berrys' Journal and Correspondence which have to do with
the same period and circle, at your service . . .

I do not know whether by rummaging for additions you will
discover enough to make you accept a copy of my new edition, but
f so I have one ready for you . . .

Yesterday I received a letter in deepest mourning, telling me of
the death of old Mrs. Harrison, some of whose daughters we must
have known on and off for something like 30 years. Emily, one of
the 2 youngest, wrote to me : her Mother (87 as the *Daily News*
shows) worked almost to the very last, and died most peacefully in
an armchair. The kind old lady whilst I was so ill sent me at
different times 2 of her own drawings—wild roses and violets ; and
I am pleased to find that I am now to receive some little
remembrance.

I fear you are right about my "unwieldiness": yet I am not sure
that the half-title you propose would have been sufficiently intelligible.
William seemed to think not, when he had read your letter this
morning. I might however very likely have chosen something briefer
than one and more lucid than the other. . . .

I have had one favorable review of my new edition in the *Glasgow
News :* I know of no other, at least as yet. Do you recollect our
being unable to identify a certain " Don Felix de Salamanca " who
published my fac-simile in a N.° of the *Pictorial World ?* He turns
out to be a certain Mr. Ingram from whom I have heard once or

twice, and who would now like to send a notice of my fresh edition to the same periodical : I have referred the matter to Mr. Macmillan for decision.

Our kindest remembrances belong to Mr. Hake, whether he be at Brighton or at home. I cannot help thinking B. may be an ill-chosen abode for his neuralgic Father, my first (and very severe) acknowledged fit of neuralgia having overtaken me there when I was 17.

To DANTE ROSSETTI, *Bognor.*

[Christina here replies as to the little poem, *No thank you, John.* She says that John never "existed or exists"; and this she must have alleged in some sense not inconsistent with truth, for I question whether in her whole life she ever "told a lie." Yet John was not absolutely mythical; for, in one of her volumes which I possess, Christina made a pencil-jotting, " The original John was obnoxious, because he never gave scope for 'No thank you!'" This John was, I am sure, the marine painter John Brett, who (at a date long antecedent, say 1852) had appeared to be somewhat smitten with Christina. I presume the point of reconciliation between her two rather conflicting statements is that there never existed any John to whom "No thank you" had been, or could have been, said. John there was, but not a John who was negatived.]

12 BLOOMSBURY SQUARE.

14 [*December* 1875].

MY DEAR GABRIEL,

Your most kind invitation has met with a great sucess *here* though not (alas!) with good Maria. My Aunts join in love and thanks with Mamma and me, and in the hope of seeing you at Christmas. . . .

Now about Mr. Hake, to whom our warm compliments—there is not the slightest pretence for his taking charge of us. *Three* of us will cherish and guard the Mamma adequately, wrap her up like a coachman, and hand her a muff at the right moment. Of course to see his kind face anywhere and at any moment is agreeable, but not to win sight of it by false pretences.

Now for a little bit about my new ed[ition]. It gratifies me much to receive your sympathetic praise, and find you care to accept the copy I store for you. The whole subject of youthful poems grows anxious in middle age, or may at some moments appear so; one is so different, and yet so vividly the same. I am truly sorry if I have judged amiss in including *The Lowest Room ;* which however, I remind you, had already seen light in *Mac's Mag.* To my thinking it is by no means one of the most morbid or most personal of the group; but I am no good judge in my own cause. As to " John," as no such person existed or exists, I hope my indiscretion may be accounted the less; and *Flora* (if that is the "next" you allude to) surely cannot give deep umbrage. The latter I hardly think as open to comment as *My Secret :* but this last is such a favourite with me that please don't retort " nor do I." Further remarks, if any, when we meet. Till when and *en permanence,* Your &c. . . .

To DANTE ROSSETTI, *Bognor.*

12 BLOOMSBURY SQUARE.

[1875—? 22 *December.*]

MY DEAR GABRIEL,

. . . Your letter says " Ford Junction," but of course this is a mere mis-write for "Barnham" ditto. If we are not met, "strong-minded loveliest woman," four strong, can coach herself.

After impervious density I begin to see light (I think) on your objection to *The Lowest Room ;* and I already regret having inserted it, you having scale-dipping weight with me. Bulk was a seductive element. However, as to date, it *was* written before my first volume appeared : so certainly before Miss J[ean] I[ngelow] misled me any-whither. I still don't dislike it myself, but can lay no claim to impartiality.

I met Mr. Cayley at the Museum on Monday, and, hearing we were about to visit you, he asked to be remembered. He is going to pass Christmas with his family at Hastings.

Maria has let us see your charming letter, herself highly appreciating it.

The hideousness of this letter I charge on my paper costing 6*d* for 5 quires.

To DANTE ROSSETTI, *Bognor.*

12 BLOOMSBURY SQUARE, LONDON.
[1876—? *January.*]

MY DEAR GABRIEL,

. . . Our good old friend Mr. Cayley has just lost his mother, aged 80. She died on the 30th. I do not know whether you will offer him a word of sympathy at such a moment, but in case you will (I think he is sensitive to friendly kindness) I add his address :—

4 South Crescent,
Bedford Square, W.C.

Mamma's love to you, and both Aunts'; and a batch of friendlinesses to Mr. Hake. We carry on rubbers here as at Aldwick, and with similarly varying success ; but here we draw for deal and for partners.

From MARIA ROSSETTI.

[This letter has little intrinsic importance : but, as it is the only one I find from Maria, whose life was now near its end (she died in the ensuing November), I have thought it worth inserting.]

ALL SAINTS, CLIFTON.
14 *July* [1876].

MY DEAR CHRISTINA,

Very many thanks for yours and all enclosures. I am to go to Eastbourne on the 29th—delightful fact—and hope we shall all travel together : arrangements of course hereafter. I have written to S[ister] Anne. This morning I was very low, but am really much better this afternoon, and in a nice room opposite my own to change the air; presently I am actually going down to Vespers. Two of my class, happening to come in, were quite affectionate. They seem getting on fairly with their examination. . . . Really matters are good about *Singsong.* . . . I am now reading *Mlle. Mori,* a very interesting story indeed : no author's name. . . .

Love to the crowned Queen of Dears.

To DANTE ROSSETTI, *Chelsea.*

[This letter indicates, in brief terms, the impending break-up of the common home of our mother and Christina with myself and my wife and child. I have had something to say of the matter in my book named *Some Reminiscences,* and need not enlarge upon it here Several letters in the present collection certify that the relations between my wife and Christina, though not unvaryingly harmonious, had, and continued to have, a solid basis of affectionate good-will.]

56 EUSTON SQUARE, N.W.

18 [*July* 1876].

MY DEAR GABRIEL,

I write because at last our holiday plans seem settled, and we do so want to see you again before leaving town. On the 29th (Saturday week, that is) Mamma and I hope to go with Maria to Eastbourne, and to remain all together for 4 weeks. . . . I hope you like Mme. D'Arblay in moderation : we both do. The *Arabian Nights* is far above my praise.

Our Euston Sq. home-party is broken up !! I suppose we shall actually move asunder between this and (say) Christmas : but no wonder that I do not exactly know William's plans, when I do not exactly know even Mamma's on which my own are wholly dependent. On the whole I suppose it may be best to regroup ourselves, and of course we part friends. William is cut up, I think, at losing our dearest Mother ; but I am evidently unpleasing to Lucy, and, could we exchange personalities, I have no doubt I should then feel with her feelings.

To WILLIAM ROSSETTI.

ALL SAINTS HOSPITAL, EASTBOURNE.

[2 *August* 1876.]

MY DEAR WILLIAM,

You will like to know that our Mother got down very comfortably last Saturday . . . Maria is certainly very far from well ; but I hope this change from Clifton to Eastbourne is in her favour, as cannot but be Mamma's dear company : she has moreover had some advice since coming down.

In the way of news we see no one and do nothing, though for daily intercourse our circle is fairly agreeable and over our daily employments we potter contentedly. I am exercising my old craft of painting despicable sprigs on note-paper corners, for sale at 1*d.* per sheet,—for the good of the house!

Our 3 loves to you 3: fancy you tripled! I hope Lucy will accept our loves with more conscious welcome than will Olivia; but I will not wish her to accept them with a sweeter smile or a prettier little way. . . .

To Lucy Rossetti.

[It will be seen that, in respect of any past differences, Christina here takes blame to herself, and imputes none to her correspondent. There might be something to remark about this, but the less said the better.]

ALL SAINTS HOSPITAL, EASTBOURNE.

[*September* 1876.]

My dear Lucy,

This promises to be my last as well as my first letter, for it merely announces to you that my Mother and I trust to be at home again in the course of next Saturday afternoon. . . .

Mamma's love to yourself, and dear Willie, and her kiss to her dear little grand-daughter: please put me in also. We remembered Olive on the 20th, and I dare say she will look larger than ever on our return.

Perhaps you have heard that what promises to be a comfortable residence has been fixed upon for our home-party in Torrington Sq., No. 30. I hope, when two roofs shelter us and when faults which I regret are no longer your daily trial, that we may regain some of that liking which we had as friends, and which I should wish to be only the more tender and warm now that we are sisters. Don't, please, despair of my doing better.

Our trial here has been and still continues to be poor Maria's very grave indisposition. I know not what to think of it, but hope that first-rate medical advice in London may be blessed to her. She goes home with the All Saints Mother one day before ourselves, on Friday morning. Her love to you and William and baby. She will not at present resume work at Clifton, but I know not whether she may do so ultimately.

No news of Gabriel.

To DANTE ROSSETTI.

[I am not sure whether the photographs here spoken of formed a regular series; perhaps they were rather a number of photographs from a variety of early Italian paintings sent to Dante Rossetti from time to time by his friend Mr. C. Fairfax Murray.—My brother had recently been staying at Broadlands, Hampshire, the seat of Mr. and Mrs. Cowper-Temple, soon afterwards Lord and Lady Mount-Temple. Here he met Mrs. Sumner (a lady married to a son of a late Archbishop of Canterbury), of whom he spoke as resembling the old Roman type of beauty, as embodied in the elder Agrippina.]

56 EUSTON SQUARE, N.W.

[*September* 1876.]

MY DEAR GABRIEL,

I am writing for dear Maria, and with her special love to you, as she finds herself far too low at present for letter-writing. Her grateful thanks to you for the loan of the beautiful photographs, which she hopes to look through and delight in at a future day; as yet she is too weak and exhausted from what she has so lately gone through to venture on so sustained an effort of attention as would be required to do them justice. She also sends kind regards to Mr. Dunn, and her thanks for his obliging kindness towards her. She is, as you may suppose, very sensible of the good will of old friends; and I am glad to say many of these do not forget her in her devout retirement. Mamma and I saw her this afternoon, and at the first moment were very painfully impressed by her exhausted condition; but she rallied somewhat as we sat with her, and was most heartily glad to see us. She agrees with you as to the Jewish cast of the modern Roman type, but feels that an "Agrippina" is quite another matter; and her admiration kindles towards your Mrs. Temple and Mrs. Sumner (so does mine).

We are all expecting to remove very soon now to Torrington Square; my Aunts next week; we (I suppose, perhaps) the week after. Lucy and baby are looked for in the course of to-morrow. . . .

To DANTE ROSSETTI.

56 EUSTON SQUARE, N.W.

[*September* 1876.]

MY DEAR GABRIEL,

We are so glad to have understood that you are better, and to hope the improvement continues,—Mamma and Maria and I, with warm loves.

I write to tell you how charmed Maria is with the photographs you have lent her, delighted by their beauty and at home in their devotion. She has not yet looked through all, her weakened state making her unequal to prolonged effort; but she examines a few at a time; and, having already reached the Pentecost one, shares your admiration of it. Yet indeed it is only one of several which she admires; the sweet Adoration of the Shepherds charmed her, and I noticed her special admiration of the Martyrdom of St. Stephen. I am not sure whether even she will be able to arrange in order the whole series, but we shall see.

Her health, poor dear, continues to make us very anxious, fluctuating frequently but not distinctly rallying. Yet she has regained a measure of strength; but then other symptoms feed our uneasiness and check our hopes. She is so very good and patient that we need only regret her state for our own sakes, not for hers. Mamma and I are going continually to and fro to sit with her.

We expect to move into Torrington Square, No. 30, on Monday, or at latest Tuesday. Aunt Charlotte is in town again.

To DANTE ROSSETTI.

30 TORRINGTON SQUARE.

[*September* 1876.]

MY DEAR GABRIEL,

I really like to let you know a little earlier about dear Maria. We were able to stay with her perhaps a quarter of an hour yesterday, she talking feebly, deeply interested in your letter which she had read before our arrival. . . . The All Saints Mother, talking to Aunt Charlotte, intimated (as I understand) quite clearly her hopelessness of recovery, but describes the dear thing's own mental readiness as such that it would need an act of resignation on her part to resign herself to life; her one grief is on our Mother's account. Surely through the darkness God compasses her around. . . . How loveable of Mrs. Cowper-Temple to propose receiving and nursing our poor darling.

To WILLIAM ROSSETTI, *Bellevue House, Newlyn.*

30 TORRINGTON SQUARE, W.C., LONDON.

[9 *October* 1876.]

MY DEAR WILLIAM,

There is no great change from day to day in our dear Maria, but all I believe tends in the direction we dread. If I do not write again very soon, please conclude that it is because her condition does not vary very appreciably. But her strength has diminished, and her discomfort, I am sorry to believe, has increased. Gabriel paid her a very loving visit last Friday, sitting with her between one and two hours I think, quite composed, tender, and conversible. We left together, he bringing me home in his fly; when he came in, saw Mamma and liked our dining-room. He was by no means looking his best; but was able to report freedom from limb-pains, and continued improvement in sleep combined with greatly diminished chloral.

Mamma joins me in love to Lucy, yourself, and Olivia. . . .

This house is far on towards being comfortable now, and will I think be very much so when thoroughly settled. I dare say Uncle Henry will soon be here on a visit, as both my Aunts have invited him.

To WILLIAM ROSSETTI, *Newlyn.*

[It will be understood that "Sister Eliza" was one of the inmates of All Saints Home: no reference is here made to Eliza Polidori. This Sister Eliza, whom I saw a few times, appeared to me a most excellent woman, a genuine Christian of the cheerful-minded (not naturally ascetic) class. She was not a person of high education, but must have made a mark in her vocation, for in 1907 I saw a little newspaper-paragraph devoted to her, announcing her death.— On receiving this letter at Newlyn, I with my wife and baby resolved to return to London.]

30 TORRINGTON SQUARE, LONDON, W.C.

12 *October* 1876.

MY DEAR WILLIAM,

. . . Poor dear Maria must be tapped once more, so rapidly does the fluid collect; and any day for 3 days to come may be the one for the operation. She is heavenly-minded, brave and calm; indeed the grief is ours, and the dread ours, much rather than hers. The greatest care has to be observed so as not to over-fatigue her now, and her frequent fits of exhaustion make it difficult to be careful enough: even Mamma has once or twice had to curtail her visit. Of course we were with her this afternoon, and we trust to go to-morrow as usual: should the operation intervene and make any difference as to our going, Sister Eliza will write. She (Sister Eliza) is so sympathetic and loving as actually to soothe our dear Mother in her great grief. You must already be prepared without my telling you for *anything* I may have to write: though please God to avert it,—nor do I know but that my apprehensions may be magnifying the immediate risk. . . .

Our move has proved less horrible than I prefigured, and I believe Mamma echoes the sentiment. Now we are far on towards shaking down into our fresh groove, and it promises to prove a suitable and comfortable one. . . .

To WILLIAM ROSSETTI, *Newlyn*.

30 TORRINGTON SQUARE, LONDON, W.C.

[14 *October* 1876.]

MY DEAR WILLIAM,

I make haste to assure you that dear Maria went happily through the second operation this morning, and has experienced great consequent relief. To-day she must be kept extremely quiet :

to-morrow our Mother and I hope to see her in the afternoon. Our first report about her actually came to us from our invariably kind friend Mr. Brown, who had made enquiries with his wife at the Home to-day, and who wrote immediately to comfort Mamma. We are warmed up with affectionate gratitude to him.

We had an enjoyable visit from Gabriel last night, who has now seen more of this house and likes it. He was tenderly concerned for poor Maria, and I have just written to him the good news. Of course however we must expect recurrent exhaustion and anxiety later on, but the present affords ample scope for thankfulness. He himself appeared very fairly well, and still enjoys improved rest at nights.

The other day amongst old music Mamma found a set of airs, accompaniments to our father's improvisations,—and she has transferred them to Euston Sq. thinking you may value them. All always with her dear love to you. Our loves also to Lucy and funny little Baby.

I wonder whether you in Cornwall have less rain than we have in London : *we* have had a good deal, yet this afternoon shows brightness. So let me wish you brightness within, radiating into a correspondent outward brightness, come shine, come storm.

To WILLIAM ROSSETTI, *London.*

[" Mr. Cayley's Homer " is a translation of *The Iliad* in quantitative hexameters : whether an arduous and scholarly enterprise I need not say—nor yet whether a rather exhausting one for a mere English reader to tackle.]

30 TORRINGTON SQUARE, W.C.

[*27 October* 1876.]

MY DEAR WILLIAM,

I am glad to be able to tell you that the little improvement in our dear Maria has continued to-day, at least till we saw her this afternoon. . . . She sends you and yours her love ; and informs you that, if you would like any day to see her about 11 o'clock (the afternoons are reserved for our Mother), your way would be to write to

The Revd. Mother
All Saints Home
82 Margaret St.
W.

. . . That Maria enjoys seeing you is quite certain, and the only uncertainty is whether at a given moment she could indulge herself so far. . . .

The Gladstone has accepted the dedication of Mr. Cayley's Homer: I hope this will help to launch the grand work, which yet needs no such help.

To DANTE ROSSETTI.

30 TORRINGTON SQUARE, W.C.
[24 *November* 1876.]

MY DEAR GABRIEL,
You see my black edge. This afternoon (at between half past 1 and a quarter to 2, about) our dear Maria died peacefully. Part of the morning she suffered a good deal of distress, and her mind seemed to wander: but before quite the end she was quiet, with no more sign of suffering than must go with such a transition. I think even in her confusion of thought that I once perceived her mind to be fixed on you and William.

Our dearest Mother is bearing her sorrow with that peace which the world neither gives nor takes away.

To DANTE ROSSETTI.

30 TORRINGTON SQUARE, W.C.
21 *December* [1876].

MY DEAR GABRIEL,
Mamma is like yourself strongly against externs, and I feel sure Lucy will not fail to restrict herself to family. 6 o'clock is admirable for all, and I trust we shall thus all meet in Euston Sq. I will write now and accept definitively her outstanding invitation, for

we lagged in hopes of ascertaining your plans before clenching ours.

Dearest Mamma's love to you. In one way Christmas, drawing us all together, seems yet to draw us nearest of all to dear Maria keeping her unexampled Christmas.

To DANTE ROSSETTI.

[I am unable to say which of Christina's poems is here referred to.]

30 TORRINGTON SQUARE, W.C.

1 *January* [1877].

MY DEAR GABRIEL,

Our dearest Mother votes for 11.30, and I echo.

You shall see one or two pieces more; but the one I sent you is a favourite of my own, and I doubt if you will unearth one to eclipse it: moreover, if I remember the mood in which I wrote it, it is something of a genuine "lyric cry," and such I will back against all skilled labour. I will either hand you my infinitesimal budget of pieces to-morrow, or I will send it you afterwards: but please respect my *thin skin* and do not start the subject in public. . . .

Dear Mamma's love to you.

From CHARLES CAYLEY.

[This extract comes out of a half-letter without a beginning. I preserve it here because it shows the origin of Christina's little poem, *My Mouse*—i. e. a Sea-mouse. I do not remember the phrase "demons in shrouds" as occurring in any writing by my sister; nor do I know what its application may have been—probably to the appearance of some animal of a low grade in zoölogy. A cuttle-fish in its first preparatory form might perhaps suggest the notion of a demon in shroud.]

2 *January* 1877.

. . . There is another thing I am more diffident about presenting: it is called in Sussex a *seamouse*, but by naturalists more politely Aphrodita aculeata, or needly Venus; and might be received by you as a compatriot of your "demons in shrouds"; it has bright many-coloured scales. On the other hand, I did not see my way to dry it; so I put it in spirits of wine—not without fears for my carpet-bag's contents; this may seem a drawback. With best wishes for the new year.

To DANTE ROSSETTI.

[This letter relates chiefly to the details of my sister's poem, *Mirrors of Life and Death*, published in *The Athenæum* of 17 March 1877. The "La Vallière date" was apparently required in connexion with another poem, *Sister Louise de la Miséricorde*.]

30 TORRINGTON SQUARE, W.C.

[? 12 *March* 1877.]

MY DEAR GABRIEL,

Please remark that I have adopted your *omission of "sun of*," and your *re-arrangement:* and wink at my *mouse* and *mole* from whom I cannot wean myself. I have, however, woven in a few fresh "mirrors," and some of these tone down (I hope) any abruptness of the *m.* and *m.* Now my little piece satisfies myself, and I shall be very glad if it goes under your auspices to the *Athenæum*, though I would have spared you further trouble by acting for myself now that I am old enough and tough enough. The alternative of a declinal I must brave; at the worst it will not be my first experience in the same line. As to my *mole and his fur*, perhaps you have not noticed the fact of his skin having no right-and-wrong way of the grain (as, for instance, a cat's has): it grows like the *biasless* nap of velvet, and as a naturalistic fact this is explained as adapting him to his career of grubbing to and fro. I hope this specialty is well enough known for my couplet to convey its drift; at any rate I will run the risk and enlarge the public mind.—My "la Vallière" date was more tiresome to you than I meant it to be; to myself the omission matters nothing at all, as the verses are of no present use and I can look up my point any day at the Museum:—pardon!

We shall be very glad to see you when you indulge us, our Mother even more than I. Her dear love to you, *mediante.*

A photograph of the family baby being sent to Florence, Teodorico pronounces her a Polidori and like Mamma: I do not see it myself.

I overlooked "Benignantly hot."—Do you know, I like it,—and do not want to be exclusively "dreamily sweet,"—nor fancy that all the rest is so.

To WILLIAM ROSSETTI.

[Dante Rossetti was at this time wretchedly ill, having lately required some surgical attendance from Mr. John Marshall: it was not an illness directly dependent upon abuse of chloral, though this latter may have tended to aggravate and prolong it.—"Mr. Watts" is (I need scarcely say) Rossetti's constant and devoted friend in these years—Walter Theodore Watts, whom we now know as Theodore Watts-Dunton, author of the romance of *Aylwin*, &c.]

30 TORRINGTON SQUARE, W.C.

[6 *August* 1877.]

MY DEAR WILLIAM,

We think you may like to have news of Gabriel directly on your arrival at home (after, I hope, a safe and comfortable journey), so I write to let you find a letter.

We saw him yesterday. I cannot say he is evidently better, though Mr. Marshall who saw him on Friday still considers all perfectly remediable, if poor G. can be induced to do what depends upon himself. As an absolutely essential step he orders him out of town so soon as it is possible to find a house for him,—he must be forced off if he cannot at the critical moment muster the resolution needed, and Mr. Watts says he was similarly forced off to Broadlands last year. Mamma and I have the comfort of finding that he likes to have us with him out of town; so once more all *our* plans are altered, and we are now ready at any moment to precede, accompany, or follow him as the case may be. Mr. Watts is undertaking the arduous work of house-hunting, and is laying himself out in active friendship. Mr. Dunn is also very kind.

These are the main facts. Poor Gabriel is so dreadfully depressed as apparently to give himself no chance of rallying: but one must hope and pray. . . .

To WILLIAM ROSSETTI.

[The "adequate observance of rule" related to chloral, with its accompanying whisky. "Albert" was the man-servant—more, perhaps, in the nature of a male nurse—whom my brother at present employed.]

30 TORRINGTON SQUARE, W.C.
[15 *August* 1877.]

MY DEAR WILLIAM,

You may like to know about our visit to Chelsea yesterday, before paying yours to-day. Poor Gabriel was greatly depressed, but in some points better: he walked and sat a little in the garden, and played a game of chess with me. Warmly and gratefully did he speak of Mr. Brown, who had sat up reading to him, and very affectionately he made mention of the comfort of seeing you. The special incident however to tell you is that whilst we were there Mr. Marshall called and stayed a long time with him. We of course left him alone with his patient: but after a while he joined us in the drawing-room and held an anxious conversation with Mamma, plainly telling us that, though one month of adequate observance of rule would make all the difference in Gabriel's favour, he could not survive many months on the present system. Well: he had spoken I suppose very plainly also to Gabriel, who had owned to him a very serious breach of rule; and Gabriel has now consented to be put in charge of a regular nurse, who will enforce that moderation which his very life now requires. Mr. Marshall knew of a most eligible nurse just set free from another case; and ¦he has furnished G. with a written table of diet &c., admitting of no misunderstanding. The nurse would be in charge all day, Albert at night : of course she (as well, I do hope, as he) will be of the out-of-town party ; and for aught I know she is now already on the spot. . . .

We left Mr. Watts with him, and dinner on the table. I think Mr. Dunn also seems solidly kind, as I hear of his playing chess with poor G., and I perceived he was going to be of the dinner-party. If Mr. Brown is once more inclined to show himself the good active friend he has ever been, his company will be a helpful solace both Mamma and I feel.

Her love to you.

To WILLIAM ROSSETTI.

[As this letter shows, our mother and Christina joined Dante Gabriel in his retreat near Herne Bay—a comfortable farm-residence. They replaced Madox Brown, who had in the first instance escorted the invalid out of town.—" Mr. Shields " is the distinguished painter Frederic J. Shields, an old friend of my brother, and held in high esteem by all of us.—" The F. M. B. gold-watch incident " was this. Mrs. Madox Brown, pacing along the parade or beach at Gorleston, noticed a watch lying derelict on the ground. She picked it up, and found the inscribed initials to be F. M. B., which were her husband's initials. The right owner was soon afterwards found.]

AT MR. SANDS'S, HUNTER'S FORESTALL, NEAR HERNE BAY.

30 *August* 1877.

MY DEAR WILLIAM,

Your letter incites me to take turns in the bulletins, but without wanting you to " respond " except to our Mother, who needs every cheerful influence within reach, not least your loving letters. Yet she keeps very bright and well, all considered, and is the down-pillow of the group.

Poor dear Gabriel had a somewhat less uneasy night last night ; but it seems only shades of difference which are in question, nothing near the contrast between good and bad. His depression is very painful, though sometimes a shadow of the old fun breaks out and lights all up for the moment. Yet some positive advance seems to have been made if we look back a few weeks. The rooms are no longer kept in semi-darkness, he does not now sit in that attitude of dreadful dejection with drooping head, he perspires less, and, if I am not mistaken, the pains in his limbs have lessened. He looks stout, his complexion is florid ; only his eyes have a peculiar appearance which cannot, I fear, be favourable. Sometimes he is unable to listen to reading, but very often he listens for a good while with interest. Generally a little whist helps on the evening fairly. He has not even yet attempted to take Mamma's portrait, and his hand is often visibly tremulous. Just now he has a degree of eruption out, but I hope it is no more than the effect of heat from some cause or other. The weather from dull has changed to sunny. Gabriel is now going to try a French remedy for insomnolence ; Mr. Shields learnt it from Mr. Andrieu and derived relief from it; it is happily one which Mrs. Mitchell feels no difficulty in sanctioning,—butter-milk, to be drunk in the night. It will not supersede the steadily diminishing (but still enormous) dose of chloral, but may be taken in addition. I am not sanguine, but a blessing may be vouchsafed on any means whatsoever. It is to be tried for the first time to-night.

Mr. Shields is here, most unselfish and friendly. I have no idea how much longer he will be able to stay ; but I fear the sacrifice he makes is not trifling, as he does not attempt to carry on any sort of work, indeed he brought none with him. He did bring a copy he made from Fra Bartolomeo's portrait of Savonarola, and Gabriel and I both recognize in it a strong likeness to Maria; this Mamma also observes, but I suspect less forcibly. We take daily drives.

Mamma's love to you. Curious truly is the " F. M. B." gold-watch incident. . . . Please let Mr. Brown know what I tell you about Gabriel, or I ought to write to that staunchest of friends ; but thus one letter may serve. Pray remember us most cordially to him ; and assure him I am selfishly ready to wish him back here a dozen times a day, to hand him over the housekeeping and be encouraged by his influence over Gabriel.

To WILLIAM ROSSETTI.

[This extract comes from a letter not in complete condition. Christina's " short piece," *An October Garden*, appeared in *The Athenæum*.]

HUNTER'S FORESTALL, HERNE BAY.

11 *October* 1877.

MY DEAR WILLIAM,
         . . . We are very anxious indeed about poor Gabriel. All Mrs. Mitchell tells us amounts to the fact that chloral has now been reduced to doses wholly or quasi inoperative, while not a vestige of natural sleeping-power has been regained. Last night he did indeed sleep somewhat more again : but how? His nurse was driven to concede the point, and return to *one* larger allowance of chloral. Another great fear which besets us is that Gabriel will shortly take

matters into his own hands, and order chloral direct for himself from the chemist, emancipating himself from Mr. Marshall's most salutary rule, and of course in consequence from Mrs. Mitchell's supervision. He has, I am told, spoken in this way; though not to Mamma or me. All I thus repeat to you is in strict confidence, but *you* ought to be informed of what is and of what threatens. He has spoken of not continuing here beyond about the end of this month, but has not so said it that I feel any certainty as to our breaking up at any given moment; if he ceases to conform to rule, I know not what to look forward to, whether we stay or whether we leave. God help us. In general health he is wonderfully recovered, but this sleeplessness saps hope and spirits. . . .

Before long perhaps you may see a short piece of mine in the *Athenæum*, as I happened to write one down here, and obliging Mr. Watts has just sent it in on approval. I desire acceptance, as you may surmise,—and cash !

To Frederic J. Shields.

[This note may perhaps belong to some such date as December 1877, when Mr. Shields was working upon some designs of the Prophets for the Duke of Westminster's Chapel at Eaton Hall, Cheshire. The extract which my sister sent to him is not forthcoming.]

30 TORRINGTON SQUARE, W.C.

[*December* 1877 ?]

Dear Mr. Shields,

Our conversation of last evening gave me some subsequent thought and a wish to feel surer of my ground within such sacred precincts. So I turned to 2 commentaries we have at hand, and, though my search failed in great measure, I did light upon one passage in Scott's well-known work which I venture to extract and lay before you,—not as pretending to clash with your view, but simply as explaining why it seems to me that the promised " desert of roses " blossomed not at the voice of St. John Baptist. I think so, of course, on other and wider grounds, and according to Mr. Scott the " soldiers " form no exception to the rule.

It is balm to my Mother and to me to hear a man of genius who is also a Christian, who speaks of the personages and facts of the Bible *as* of personages and facts, and who brings love and devotion to his work for the glory of God. Pray do not think me overbold in expressing myself, but you well know how many men of genius think and speak otherwise. Please remember my Mother and me very cordially to Mrs. Shields, and with our real regards to yourself, &c. . . .

From THE REV. DR. LITTLEDALE.

9 RED LION SQUARE, LONDON.

7 *February* 1878.

'Tis but too true, dear Miss Christina,
　　What publishers to you reply,
A time like this has always been a
　　Time when the frighted Muses fly ;
Inter arma silent leges
　　('Twas Marcus Cicero who said it),
And all but newspapers are tedious
　　When Dizzy wants his vote of credit.
The public likes a *Prince's Progress*,
　　But only in the *Morning Post*,
And makes a *Goblin Market* ogress
　　Of Russia's or of Turkey's host.
The tale of this or that atrocity,
　　Hummed the stretching wires along,
With all the telegraph's velocity,
　　Pitches the key of *its Sing-song*.
'Twon't last for ever, never fret 'ee
　　But wait till war's alarums fail :
Such is the rede, dear Miss Rossetti,
　　Of your true friend

R. LITTLEDALE.

To WILLIAM ROSSETTI.

[Our old friend Frederic G. Stephens, of the P.R.B., was at this time very dangerously ill : Mr. John Marshall, at a grave crisis, saved his life. Mr. Holman Hunt was also ill, and Ruskin in a painful mental condition.—My "Poets" is the volume *Lives of Famous Poets :* my Shelley was the re-edition of the poems, as first edited by me in 1870.—Mr. W. A. Turner, of Manchester, was one of the later purchasers of my brother's pictures : he bought, among others, the *Vision of Fiammetta.*]

30 TORRINGTON SQUARÈ, W.C.

15 *March* 1878.

MY DEAR WILLIAM,

The poor dear Stephenses,—what dreadful suffering and anxiety. Gabriel was here last night, and, hearing from us about his old friend, was full of concern and sympathy. I shall send him on your letter of this morning that he may know all we know. I shall also write to Mrs. Stephens to tell her Mamma and I are feeling with her,— not, of course, to trouble her for any reply. To me blood-poison is amongst the most appalling of diseases. Even poor Holman Hunt's state frightens me less, critical and painful as it is. By the by, Gabriel also spoke with friendly concern about Ruskin. And he looked at your "Poets" with interest, and mentioned having received your Shelley (though that is but a graceless form of acknowledgment). I fear he was not in genuine good spirits, but at any rate he had a vestige of fun in him, witness the following couplet on *me :*—

> "There's a female bard grim as a fakeer,
> Who daily grows shakier and shakier"—

the point was to find a rhyme for "shakier." Scotus and Mrs. Scott had been to see him, and I think he was expecting that Mr. Turner of Manchester to-day. He is getting on again with his *Fiammetta* picture.

Our mother's love to you, and hers and mine to *yours.*

To DANTE ROSSETTI.

[Mr. James Smetham the painter was at this time at some loss for finding purchasers for his pictures, and Dante Rossetti was pushing their sale to the best of his opportunities. Christina had only a very slight acquaintance with Mr. Smetham, but she esteemed him on religious as well as artistic grounds. Miss Heaton (who has been mentioned before) was a lady resident at Leeds.]

30 TORRINGTON SQUARE, W.C.

[? *April* 1878.]

MY DEAR GABRIEL,

I should be charmed to help Mr. Smetham, towards whom I am drawn by esteem and sympathy, but I have so dropped out of society (never having acquired deep foothold therein) that I fear I am also pretty well out of court as regards useful influence. Miss Heaton is the one name that suggests itself to both of us. . . . What I think would be the best chance of attracting her would be to promise that, if she inclines their way, she should, when she comes to London (supposing any to remain on hand so long), visit your studio with me and *there* inspect them; but perhaps friendship will not carry you so far. . . .

Are they in oil or in water-colour?

To LUCY ROSSETTI.

[I *think* this undated letter may belong to June 1878. The occasion for its being written appears to be that my daughter Olivia, aged at that time less than three years, had been reported by her nurse as making herself rather more than sufficiently " at home " at the residence of my sister and mother.—The phrase " crocodile love " is perhaps used in allusion to the fact that Olivia, who happened to see at a friend's house Mr. Boyle, then Editor of *The Daily Chronicle*, had spoken to him of that paper as " the Daily Crocodile."]

30 TORRINGTON SQUARE, W.C.

[? *June* 1878.]

MY DEAR LUCY,

I am heartily glad you have written, because it gives me a chance of doing away with an impression I never meant to create. I quite admire our clever little Olive, and am really glad she should be imbued with *Sing-Songs;* and the more at her ease she is among us, some of her nearest relations, the better; and, if some day she comes to love me as well as to be familiar with me, that will be better still,—only I do not count on such a happy consummation, as I know myself to be deficient in the nice motherly ways which win and ought to win a child's heart. You do not know how much pleasure, moreover, you will retrench from Mamma's quiet days if you check Olive's coming here or her perfect freedom when she is here. *That* is a truly motherly heart, full of warm nooks for children and children's children: and she could not bear *her* gratification in seeing and hearing your little ones to be doubted or misunderstood. This with her love to you and to them. And mine too, please, to all three: not a crocodile love!

"Kiss and be friends" is a very sound old exhortation: get Olive to be my proxy, and I shall not fear to miss the result. Need I?

To DANTE ROSSETTI.

["L. G." was Luigi Gamberale, of Campobasso, who produced some Italian translations from poems by Dante Gabriel and Christina. —Maria's "masterpiece" was the volume named *A Shadow of Dante*. —The Tauchnitz book was a reprint of Dante Rossetti's *Poems* of 1870.]

30 TORRINGTON SQUARE, W.C.

[*August* 1878.]

MY DEAR GABRIEL,

The Gazetteer informs us that Campobasso is the capital of the Neapolitan province of Molise, is situated about 55 miles from Naples, and stands on the ascent of a high mountain,—I therefore doubt not that Campobasso, Naples, will be an adequate address. If you write to L. G., please add my gratified thanks. I agree with you in not being admiration-struck by his translation, and also in being much pleased at his note on dear Maria, and in wishing that her masterpiece could be brought within reach of Italian readers. Were I a rich woman, I really think I should be tempted to give Teodorico the commission, and have it translated and published on my own responsibility: but such luxuries are not for me.

We all send you our loves, dear Mamma *vagheggiando* her prospective Tauchnitz. Still we have not fixed where to go, but Walton-on-Naze seems not impossible; we have written to some lodgings there.

To WILLIAM ROSSETTI.

[The reference to a "head and hand," followed by Maria's quaint idea about the mummy-room, has to do with a mummified relic presented to me by Mr. Peter Lascaridi, who had recently returned from a visit to Egypt. I did not quite know how best to dispose of this abnormal [gift, and had offered it to Christina. Ultimately it was accepted with pleasure by our medical adviser and friend Mr. William Gill.]

21 *August* 1878.

MY DEAR WILLIAM,

Had I an oratory, I might willingly accept the loan of "head and hand" as a *memento mori;* but, as it is, I could not feel easy at keeping bits of fellow-human-creature as curiosities; my preference would be to give them reverent burial. Long ago Maria suggested how awful it would be to be in the Museum Mummy-Room on the day of the resurrection. Don't you think some of the most competent shops for supplying your glass case would be found in Great Russell St.? I seem to remember none more promising.

From CHARLES CAYLEY.

[The "proofs of Petrarch" were proofs of Cayley's translations from Petrarch. He was at this time writing a completion of a book on the subject of religious and political persecutions, by a Spanish republican named Garrido.—The female members of Cayley's family lived ordinarily at St. Leonard's, Hastings.]

4 SOUTH CRESCENT.

4 *September* 1878.

DEAR CHRISTINA ROSSETTI,

If you are still to be some time out of town, I want to ask you, in charity, to send me a few lines about your Naze-al retreat, and how it suits you, and if anything has occurred among our friends. Here I am not only isolated as in the height of the *nomadic* season, but have been kept ten days at home by a bad foot, and am just beginning to creep out; my doctor has been my fellow lodger, and my landlady, I must own, an excellent nurse in all points. What it came of, at least the crisis, was a walk last Thursday week in Windsor park; which should have been of 7 miles, but I made it more, being insufficiently directed. I was glad to see the old castle, though it is like a set of ugly things that a wave tosses up *magnificently*. I left the state-rooms for another occasion, though I have never seen them, and went to the Long Walk—a three-mile line of elms—do you know it?—that will have completed two centuries in 1880, and there are few signs of destruction and decay; it was a grand idea to plant them. After a mile or so the park widens out, then herds of deer appear, then fernbeds, undulating ground, and all varieties of trees. What I had least expected was the very broad and bright patches of heather near Virginia Water, for there was no admixture of furze whatever. And here, as in the colour of the margin of a rainbow, I will relieve you from this dreary letter, except that I will add I have had some proofs of Petrarch (80 pages) and written my chapters on Naples for "Persecutions"—a quarter, I hope, of what I had to do. My sisters have been in Coventry, Shropshire, and Wales, visiting. I await soon a letter from St. Leonard's.

To DANTE ROSSETTI.

30 TORRINGTON SQUARE, W.C.
17 [*September* 1878].

MY DEAR GABRIEL,

. . . I was charmed at the good success of my *Sing-Songs* with you. But it would indeed need a better Italian than I to translate the whole series: think of me writhing helpless before "Heartsease in my garden-bed" or "In the meadow——"! ! The *Pig*, I avow, causes me inward triumph. "Rotolandosi spumando vanno" gave, I thought, something of the accumulative on-come of the waves, mounting on each other's backs: otherwise *I* am not aware of any reason against "spumanti" as you suggest; or one might obliterate the sound yet more by making it "spumosi". . .

To DANTE ROSSETTI.

30 TORRINGTON SQUARE, W.C.

[*January* 1879.]

MY DEAR GABRIEL,

Teodorico has sent over a few *Sing-Songs* and wants them shown to you: so here they are. Of course his affectionate remembrances to you accompanied them. Some are what I have done, and some not: some (truth to tell) I like better of mine, but his No. 5 beats me hollow. 7, 9, 10, 11, 12, 13, 15, he only has tackled: *12* is charming. Of course I only venture to prefer my own in case their Italian could pass muster,—and very likely it could not, which would make all the difference. . . .

From DANTE ROSSETTI.

[The pen-and-ink design which was enclosed in this letter was an illustration of Christina's lines " Passing away, saith the World, Passing away." There is a date in the corner, 1865, and some initials, which I regard as J. Y. : yet I believe that the name of the designer was known to be Rivington, a clergyman. The praise which my brother bestowed upon the design, though it is not the work of an accomplished artist, was fully merited.—The P.S. must relate to Mrs. Henrietta Polydore (our uncle's wife), who was usually settled in the United States of America, but was once or twice over in England.]

[16 CHEYNE WALK.

22 *May* 1879.]

MY DEAR CHRISTINA,

I am enclosing a production which I think I once mentioned to you and you did not seem to remember ; but I fancy you did see it when sent to me by some one long ago as the work of a young amateur or artist whose name I know not. It is certainly poetic and assuredly quite quaint enough. Now you have it, keep it if you care. I turned it up yesterday, and bethought me to send it ere it got buried again in heaps.

I hope our Mother thrives in this bettering weather. I hope to be seeing you soon, but am beset with building-nuisances here.

Is Aunt C. with you now? If so, love to both Aunts and first of all to our Mother.

How about Mrs. H. P. ?

To DANTE ROSSETTI.

["Our man" presents to me no identity : he would appear to have been the author of some verses, desirous of obtaining Christina's address.—*The Prince's Quest* is of course a poem by William Watson.]

30 TORRINGTON SQUARE, W.C.

[*Summer* 1879 ?]

MY DEAR GABRIEL,

Our man (whom I characterize less briefly than do you) wants my address : so I send him simply my visiting-card, and he may do anything or nothing as he prefers. I augur drearily from his poem, and not brightly from his letter.

I have read *The Prince's Quest*, and indeed the whole volume. Marked beauties it has, and yet I don't foresee a great future for its author,—not confidently. May he falsify my verdict ! . . .

To WILLIAM ROSSETTI, *Broadstairs.*

[The book here spoken of is the one entitled *Seek and Find.*]

2 GLADSTONE VILLAS, SEAFORD.

21 *July* 1879.

MY DEAR WILLIAM,

You will like to know that our dear Mother is settled here very comfortably and prosperously, in air that seems to suit her and in very clean wholesome lodgings. Seaford is very quiet, but so are we. It is a rather desolate-looking small place; though it may, I surmise, look somewhat less desolate when more people arrive, a phenomenon talked of for a little further on in the season,—say August 1. We like it better than being at Walton last year, partly because we like these lodgings so much better than those. . . .

At last I can indulge you with a gleam of light on some of those mysterious literary avocations at which you have occasionally caught

me,—for I have just sold a little book (its copyright) for £40 to the
S.P.C.K., which is the same Society as published Maria's *Letters
to my Bible Class* in old days. Mine is a small work on the
"Benedicite," and I promise myself the pleasure of ere long adding
a copy to your family-shelf, if you will accept one. . . .

I hope your bottled monsters are not less long-lived or more
smelly than in the days of our common experiences. I do not
discern any symptoms of "monsters" here, but my investigations
are carried on from a campstool pitched some way from the water's
edge,—so are by no means exhaustive. Shingle I see: and I think
I have heard of sand, under some condition of the tide which I have
not seen. . . .

To DANTE ROSSETTI.

["Mr. Caine's lecture" was a lecture by Mr. Hall Caine, then in
Liverpool and engaged only subordinately in literature, regarding
Rossetti's poems. His sending a copy of the lecture to my brother
was the beginning of their acquaintance.—"The second me"
must be one of the heads of Christina which Dante Gabriel had
drawn—perhaps the downward-looking one done in 1877. The
"first me" would be the well-known and often reproduced head
dated in 1866.]

2 GLADSTONE VILLAS, SEAFORD.

[1879—? 25 *July*.]

MY DEAR GABRIEL,

Sad to say, my little book *Seek and Find* is exclusive
prose: yet I flatter myself some of it is that prose which I fancy our
Italian half inclines us to indite. It is, of course, but a simple work
adapted to people who know less (!) than I do: but I took a keen
interest in writing it, and I hope some may feel an interest in reading
it. One solitary footnote occurs in its course, and the unnamed
personage of that footnote is our dear good Maria. All the proofs
and even the revises have now passed through my hands, so before
so very long I hope a clean copy will come to light.

Thankyou for letting me too read Mr. Caine's Lecture,—a remarkable work by an author who really thinks, feels; and therefore
has somewhat to express. If you come to know him I should like

to know what he is like: conflicting images of him evolve themselves from my inner consciousness, and he cannot be like both!

This place is suiting us capitally. There is at least one country-ish walk, simple and pretty, within our range, besides the inexhaust-ible beach.

Thankyou much for caring to think of having the second "me" photographed. Should a spare *carte* from either negative ever accumulate in your hands, I shall thankfully accept it, and probably transfer it to an American Miss Alger who asked me in vain for one lately.

On a second reading of the Lecture Mamma is so charmed that she means to buy the N⁰.

To DANTE ROSSETTI.

[The phrase, "Mr. Brown has come forward" &c., refers to the fact that Brown, after Dante Rossetti returned to London from Hunter's Forestall late in 1877, held aloof from him for a while, owing to some tiff (entirely on Brown's side) concerning Rossetti's servants. The tiff had now at last subsided, and Brown had re-appeared.—"The extreme tenuity of £270" relates to the sum payable for his paintings in the Manchester Townhall.—Mrs. Laura Valentine compiled a volume entitled *Gems of National Poetry*, in which she was pleased to insert a very early verse-performance of mine called *In the Hill-shadow*.—The sum of £10 was offered and paid by Mr. Fairfax Murray for the MS. of Christina's *Seek and Find*. The other MS. here mentioned, *Singsòng*, with some vignettes from the authoress's hand, remained perdu for years. At last, towards 1900, it came back to me, and rests in my custody. The vignettes are interesting to people who care about Christina and her work, but of course are highly primitive from an art point of view.—"The predellas" belonged to the second and somewhat diminished version of Rossetti's oil-picture, *Dante's Dream*: Mr. William Graham was the purchaser.]

30 TORRINGTON SQUARE, W.C.

[1879—? 18 *August*.]

MY DEAR GABRIEL,

Your charming letter to our Mother followed us up from Seaford this morning, and she *delights* in it (her own word) and sends you her love. We are so glad that Mr. Brown has come

6

forward and met your latent affection, while we agree with you
(keeping the matter to ourselves) in the extreme tenuity of £270.
I hope that the name and fame accruing may serve as ballast to the
light purse.

"Laura Valentine" I identify no further than as working at one
vol. of Warnes's "Chandos" series. From William she culls *In
the Hill-shadow* and 2 sonnets, but which 2 I know not. From
me, *Twilight Calm* and *Sound Sleep*. William foresaw somewhat ruefully figuring in company with really good work of yours
and mine : but half this combination he will be spared—and he
seems to excel me in freedom from vanity ! . . .

And now for your letter to me. I am amazed, amused, and as you
may believe not a little pleased, at the £10 bid for my M.S., and
am lying in wait for the formal communication from William. Alas !
no more such refuse do I retain in stock—for till Mr. Watts enlightened me I laboured under the delusion that printer's copy was
a perquisite of one's publisher ; and now, too late, I deplore the
original *Sing-Song—embellished* with my own vignettes ! ! ! It is
delightful to hear of Mr. Murray's success in life, and to recollect
that you were his early friend and helper.

I hope the predellas are turning out as beautiful as they promised
to become.

Looking forward to our seeing you ere long, &c. . . .

To William Rossetti.

[This note was written soon after our brother had done something
unreasonable with chloral-dosing or what not, and had reduced himself to a very shattered condition. It lasted some few days, but did
not seriously affect him in the long run.]

30 TORRINGTON SQUARE, W.C.

21 [*October* 1879].

My dear William,

We spent a long morning with Gabriel yesterday, and
found him less depressed than I was prepared for. But what a
state his mouth is in, and his voice was wretched. However, he
was very fairly chatty as to books and people, and showed us some
of his beautiful drawings. I wish you could have heard the tender

and grateful warmth with which he mentioned your kindness in illness,—"like a woman," and the sweetness of your disposition.

We are going again to-day, but not for quite so long a period, as the whole affair yesterday proved almost too fatiguing for our Mother. Her dear love to you, and ours if you please to Lucy, whose and whose Father's helpful kindness we thankfully acknowledge.

To DANTE ROSSETTI.

[In consequence of some talks between Dante Rossetti and Mr. Watts-Dunton (who was solicitor as well as author), it was considered that the publishing arrangements between Christina and Messrs. Macmillan were not quite so clearly or accurately defined as they should have been. Hence this letter, and some ensuing colloquies which proved satisfactory to both parties.]

30 TORRINGTON SQUARE, W.C.

17 *December* 1879.

My DEAR GABRIEL,

I certainly have two very brotherly brothers who command my affectionate gratitude by their unfailing care for my small concerns.

Mr. Watts moreover makes me his debtor by such friendly good will. If he and you and William all agree as to the necessity of the step, and if he will kindly take it without my involving myself in heavy law-expenses, I will accept your opinion that it is advisable, and be glad that he should speak to Mr. Macmillan. But only and absolutely in the most amicable manner; as being quite certain that no wrong has either been done or dreamt of, as knowing that I am satisfied with actual arrangements, and as bearing in mind that I stick to my position of cordial personal friendship with my friendly publisher. All which premised, I should of course be glad to have business-matters put—if they are not so already—on a business-footing. Nothing however, not proof positive that I had been pillaged ! would make me have recourse to law : this is a statement at once preliminary and final. Moreover I am hugging hopes of getting together before long enough verse for a *small* fresh volume: so least of all at this moment am I in the mood to alienate the staunch Mac. . . .

Seek and Find has been favourably mentioned in the *Saturday Review.*

To Dante Rossetti.

[Christina presented to our mother for her eightieth birthday, 27 April 1880, a copy of David Main's *Treasury of English
Sonnets*, and Dante Gabriel inserted into it the illustrated MS. of his
own sonnet on *The Sonnet*. From the following letter it is apparent
that he had consulted Christina on the question whether the close of
that sonnet, which refers to death, might be likely to produce any
painful impression on our mother. I do not know what was the
couplet proposed (but not finally adopted) as a substitute.]

30 TORRINGTON SQUARE, W.C.

2 April [1880].

My dear Gabriel,
            . . . I still think the FIRST sonnet-conclusion quite
admissible,—and (with you, so far as I realize the two) poetically
superior, despite an "imperial" something in the second which has
a stately and splendid sound. I hope I am not making any mistake
in my judgment: but our dearest mother has much to brighten and
endear to her the approaching immortality, even beyond those yet
higher and more blessed aspects of it which we all have in common.
Still, I most keenly appreciate the tenderness which makes you
debate such a point at such a sacrifice.

To Olivia Rossetti (Agresti).

[In April 1880 Olivia was aged about four years and a half. She
had asked to have a copy of the sonnet which Christina had written
for her own mother's eightieth birthday: this is the reply, covering
instead a copy of the verses named *Golden Glories*.]

30 TORRINGTON SQUARE, W.C.

27 April [1880].

My dear Olive,
            I find dearest Grandmamma sets so high a value on her
private and personal sonnet that I am not to make a copy of it even
for you! But I hope you will like quite as well the little piece I
enclose, which has never been printed either: so for the present you

FRANCES M. L. ROSSETTI.

From an Oil Portrait by Dante Rossetti, c. 1865.

[*To face p.* 84.

have it all to yourself. And, if at some future day a "golden glory" of art or of poetry should alight on your "head of golden tips," then (if you are at all like old auntie) you will find that almost if not quite its brightest point is that it kindles a light of pleasure in your own Mother's eyes.

To whom please give my love, and to Arthur and Helen, and last but not least to dear Papa.

To Dante Rossetti.

[The ballad here referred to is *The White Ship*. The incident of the boy in mourning-garb who announces to Henry I the death of his son and daughter was (I think) found by Dante Gabriel in Augustin Thierry's history.—The "sycomore" was used for the picture *The Daydream*, now in the Victoria and Albert Museum.]

30 TORRINGTON SQUARE, W.C.

[? May 1880.]

My dear Gabriel,

Mamma, with love, takes your loving advice and does not herself write, but is quite glad I should write and express for her her (*our*) liking and admiration of your fine ballad. Twice she read and once she listened to it, and many times yet she may read it. She looked in Hume for the plain prose of the history, and found most of your facts, but especially *not* that of the mourning boy,—so picturesque and telling. Perhaps when you come you will tell her whence you gleaned so advantageous a point. I am so glad you have written this fine piece, one really worth writing; and I hope it will delight others in print ere long, as us already in MS.

We are pleased your sycomore is so available, and are not without hopes of beholding the beautiful result some day.

To Dante Rossetti.

[Rossetti's sonnet on William Blake is here referred to.—Madame —— was an Anglo-Greek lady of whom he had narrated a painful experience; and James Smetham was in a grievous condition of mind from which he never recovered.]

III PEVENSEY ROAD, EASTBOURNE.

16 *July* 1880.

MY DEAR GABRIEL,

I think it is worth while to date this letter as illustrating that even in 1880 our dearest Mother was well able to leave home on a little holiday excursion, to stroll and sit out for about 3 hours daily, and to be amused on the Parade. The costumes that pass before us in a brisk panorama! One very simply dressed lady whom I saw once showed a face that I fancy might have charmed even you by its natural rare beauty; but I have scarcely noticed one other at all exceptional, if even one. The horrors of this place would certainly overwhelm you,—its idlers, brass bands, nigger minstrels of British breed, and other attractions; but I, more frivolous, am in a degree amused.

Mamma's love to you. She delights in the letter which you have affectionately filled with so many interesting facts, and which you have enriched with a sonnet so pathetic. She, like myself, had no idea that Blake's workroom remained recognizable, much less intact. " Poor Mme.——" she says (figuratively), and "poor good Smetham." We are both very glad of the re-appearance of Burne Jones, and hope that kindly face and genius may contribute something worth adding to your social circle; and it was pleasant to meet him for a moment at the R.A., and to be carried back to days 20 *years old* by this time! What is Philip Jones to be? and is little Margaret growing up pretty? She quite took me by surprise once in her babyhood that I saw her. . . .

Yesterday Mamma procured *the Temple Bar* and the mention of you gratifies her,—so you may feel certain what style of mention it is! Not one phrase does it contain but of admiration; the passage is short, but not unmeaning. . . .

We had not heard of Mr. Tom Taylor's death : may his "charities" follow him.

To DANTE ROSSETTI.

[The Dixon here mentioned was Thomas Dixon of Sunderland, lately deceased, the cork-cutter to whom Ruskin had addressed his letters entitled *Time and Tide*. He was an estimable man, singularly zealous in promoting the cause of literature and art in his own circle. Joseph Skipsey, the coal-miner poet, was a friend of Dixon.—The "*non fit* pun" has been retailed by me elsewhere, and I need not here recur to it.—I think that Mrs. Meynell, when she wrote the article in *The Pen*, was not personally acquainted with any Rossetti, and that she did not afterwards become so.—The reference to Chatterton is consequent upon a sonnet written by Dante Rossetti.]

111 PEVENSEY ROAD, EASTBOURNE.

20 *July* 1880.

My dear Gabriel,

Thanks for your letter in proportion to its welcomeness— what a word!

Poor Dixon: I feel truly concerned, though I earnestly hope he is the gainer. To him, so far as I know, may fairly attach the character (a noble one) of a good citizen. I dare say many will miss him, and I hope not a few will remember him. May I deserve remembrance when my day comes, and then remembered or forgotten it will be well with me. I don't know that I saw him more than once, but one way and another I seem to know a tolerable deal about him. I recollect you have mentioned Joseph Skipsey to us ere now, and surely you showed us his photograph once at your house,—manly-looking, as a "collier" well may be.

Mamma hopes to write you "di proprio pugno," so I only speak for myself. How I wish we knew who did write the *Pen* article. Don't think me such a goose as to feel keenly mortified at being put below you, the head of our house, in so many ways. I much like the mention of our dear Father, and I like also as far as it goes the tribute to Maria: William too fares fairly. In your "non fit" pun I revel. Who can it be who knows so much about our family, and yet in one or two points is positively at fault,—as when he leaves us *no* English element, and seems to make you the eldest of the group? If ever you find out I hope you will enlighten us.

You are in the right as to my, through ignorance, not being able to say anything about Chatterton's literary position; but the dreadful poverty which goaded him to so dreadful a deed I do know something of; and hard must be the heart which feels not for him, however far from feeling with him. You bring the poor boy and his gifts and his career vividly before one : *I*, if I could write thus upon him, should say something more and something less, but I would not abate a tinge of pathos from the sweetly pathetic end.

We could drive to Pevensey Castle, but are much too far off to reach it otherwise : so I do not think we shall reach it at all.   Years ago our good Aunt Margaret treated me to the expedition.

To DANTE ROSSETTI.

[The name " Vanna " is here applied to the picture known as *The Daydream.   Vanna Primavera* was the original title.—I do not think that Christina ever met the Baroness Burdett-Coutts : yet it might be *possible* that at some such early date as 1855 she got a glimpse of her at Highgate.—*La Pia* was an oil-picture begun by Dante Rossetti towards 1867, but only finished towards 1880 : the allusion to "ricordarsi" will be obvious to a reader of Dante's *Purgatorio.*—Mr. and Mrs. Shields's tour, which he at least found intensely dismal, had been made with Aberdeen as its bourne.—Mr. George Hake had ceased to be Rossetti's secretary in January 1877, and they parted in some mutual displeasure ; but my brother had now received him with cordiality.]

III PEVENSEY ROAD, EASTBOURNE.

9 *August* [1880].

MY DEAR GABRIEL,

. . . I hope we shall see the final "Vanna" some day : but indeed she was so beautiful at our last meeting that she fully sufficed me.   Your charming letter has just come to hand, and cheers that " dear one " who sends you love.

Startling, portentous, quasi incredible is the climax of Lady Burdett Coutts's noble life.   Can such ends come of such beginnings ?   If so, may I never have gift, grace, or glamour, to woo me a husband not half my age ! ! !   I had heard of the intended marriage, though I knew not whether truly reported : but of the disparity of years I had not an inkling.   All amazements pale before this : otherwise I also might gasp a moment at the vision of beautiful Mrs. Morris with her family boating on river Thames (?) for a week ; not only (I trust) with a cabin, but (I surmise) needing one.

No, I am sorry to say, I do not recall *La Pia*, of whom it is so obviously seemly to "ricordarsi." But I hope we shall see her also in due course. . . .

Poor Shields, I hope his tour was less dismal than your narrative suggests : *why* it should be so extra-dismal I do not exactly see; but one certainly may walk the world as one's own wet blanket, and perhaps such is our friend's well-known tourist costume. I will hope that at any rate his wife is still young enough to find in life and in his company something not altogether odious, flat, and to be deplored.

No wonder the *White Ship* won Penkill laurels. Scottish laurels, those : I with English feeling tend towards remarking

> "I trust you have within your brain
> 500 good as he."

I wish you would write more such, and on such subjects : surely they are well worth celebrating, and they leave no sting behind. . . .

Very glad I am that you saw George Hake : I think his looks capital now, in their modified and pronounced style. . . .

To DANTE ROSSETTI.

30 TORRINGTON SQUARE, W.C.

14 *August* [1880].

MY DEAR GABRIEL,

We got back quite comfortably on Thursday, and here we are. . . .

No, I was not thinking of arousing envy and spite when I spoke of the innocuous nature of historic ballads (something, of course, being pre-supposed as to theme and treatment),—but rather of one's own responsibility in use of an influential talent. As to "envy and spite," I think they may well (!) be roused by the *White Ship.* . . .

To DANTE ROSSETTI.

[A certain person, quite unknown to Christina, had written to her for permission to set to music some poem or poems of hers, and she assented. This was mentioned to Rossetti; and he, acting upon information which he had received from a credible source, told Christina that there was a scandal (were it well founded or not) in connection with that applicant, and it would be undesirable for her to have anything to do with him. She therefore wrote withdrawing her assent. The present letter shows an ensuing stage of the affair.]

30 TORRINGTON SQUARE, W.C.

[6 *September* 1880.]

MY DEAR GABRIEL,

—— has written in answer. He does not say a word about the setting; but asserts himself "an innocent man" (premising that he "will not affect to misunderstand" my letter), and appears what in one case I consider justly hurt, and in the other resentful. I am very much pained: and think I shall write once more—FINALLY—not of course to reconsider the question of the music, but to make myself less uncomfortable in case (however blindly) I have been unjust. No explanations or details or assertions will be needed: and under no possible circumstance can harm ensue. Do not laugh: I am weighed upon by the responsibility of all one does or does not do; besides, I think our dearest Mother inclines in the same direction practically that I do as to this affair. Her dear love to you.

To DANTE ROSSETTI.

30 TORRINGTON SQUARE, W.C.

[*September* 1880.]

MY DEAR GABRIEL,

Thanks for kind encouraging words where certainly some reassurance is opportune.

Unless we are almost immediately to have the pleasure of seeing you, will you kindly return the ORIGINAL letter by post,—my copy there is no hurry about. But the other I want back because I have made up my mind what to do. —— wrote again enclosing strong evidence on his side. Two documents there were: one I think any candid person would admit carried great weight, the other goes far with me. But I do not feel a right to let them out of my hands, or

even to show them, except to our Mother, who is at least as favourably impressed by them as I am. The practical point to which all
this tends is that I am going to send —— back all his letters and
papers, so that he may feel sure they neither in my lifetime nor
afterwards pass into other keeping; and I delay sending any till I
can despatch all together. Poor fellow, whatever his case may be,
he is infinitely to be pitied. . . .

To DANTE ROSSETTI.

[The book here named is the one entitled *Called to be Saints*.
Mr. (Fairfax) Murray has previously been mentioned as the purchaser of a MS. by Christina.—Mrs. Anna Eliza Bray was a cousin
of our mother on the maternal side, authoress of several books,
including an autobiography. She married in the first instance a son
of the painter Thomas Stothard, and in the second instance a
clergyman.]

30 TORRINGTON SQUARE, W.C.
[29 *December* 1880.]

MY DEAR GABRIEL,

. . . Did William tell you that I am likely before long to
have another volume out with the Christian Knowledge Society?
That very work on the Saints' Days which possibly you may recollect
I composed several years ago, and for which I long failed to secure a
publisher. It is in the press, and I conjecture (but this is a mere
guess) that it may perhaps see the light towards Easter. I do not
know what money it will bring in; but I have hopes not less than
the last, and that was £40. Of course there will be a printer's copy
in time, and Mr. Murray asked me to let him know if one should
accrue: so I must let him know some day.

Presumably our cousin Mrs. Bray turned 90 on Christmas Day!!

To DANTE ROSSETTI.

[I suppose that this letter belongs to 1881. It was in that year
that Christina brought out her volume, *A Pageant and Other
Poems.*]

30 TORRINGTON SQUARE, W.C.

1 *January* [? 1881].

MY DEAR GABRIEL,

Mamma is extremely pleased with your affectionate full letter received yesterday evening, despite the pain sympathy in your difficulties and anxieties arouses in her. Be sure I contribute my mite of sympathy. . . . A thousand thanks for Mr. Watts's sister's admiration, and for your care for my fame. I don't think harm will accrue from my S.P.C.K. books, even to my standing: if it did, I should still be glad to throw my grain of dust into the religious scale. I am seriously hoping, however, to get up a vol. of poems before so very very long. There are a few poems in my Saints' Day book. Mamma's very dear love to you.

From DANTE ROSSETTI.

[The sonnet sent herewith was *Michelangelo's Kiss*.]

13 *January* 1881.

MY DEAR CHRISTINA,

You know my habit of patching up matters by letter-writing. I felt I did not show how much pleased I was to see you to-day. Don't answer on the point, but feel sure I *was* pleased nevertheless.

If Aunt Charlotte should feel inclined, as you indicated, to come here to see the picture, try and let me know when, and I shall be most pleased to show it. Try also for both your sakes to choose a less deadly day.

Love to our dearest Mother and to both Aunts.

As dear Mamma loves sonnets, I put a new one opposite. I think the beautiful anecdote will please her, as told by M.A.'s loving pupil Condivi.

You may observe in the sonnet a pun on Buonarruoti—of course it ought to be ruot*e*, but I suppose it might be perceptible.

To WILLIAM ROSSETTI.

[This relates to the volume *A Pageant and other Poems*. The reference to "twins" was consequent upon a domestic event in my own household.]

30 TORRINGTON SQUARE, W.C.

[28 *April* 1881.]

MY DEAR WILLIAM,

"Io anche—"! At last I took the plunge and sent in some poems to Macmillan, who before he saw accepted them,—for I wrote first on the subject, and he closed with them forthwith. I am somewhat in a quake, a fresh volume being a formidable upset of nerves,—but at any rate, it cannot turn out TWINS !

I am sure you take interest enough in my doings to deem this news worth your hearing. . . .

To DANTE ROSSETTI.

[The "noble sonnet" was the one on the assassination of Czar Alexander II.]

30 TORRINGTON SQUARE, W.C.

[2 *May* 1881.]

MY DEAR GABRIEL,

Thankyou for sight of a noble sonnet towards which our Mother and I do warm as you may think. Would that every one felt with you, even though the bulk of feelers must ever lack such power of expression,—and, most of all, would that our nearest and dearest felt with you. Our Mother sends love, and therewith expresses her admiration and her sympathy. . . .

I am quite pleased about Macmillan, because he said *yes* without asking to see the M.S. or making a single enquiry as to either bulk or subject. I hope the apparent lag of your proofs is merely because the publishing moment (October?) must now be awaited : perhaps mine may be ready by that date, but about this I know nothing whatsoever. I have not yet, as you may guess, received my first sheet. . . .

To DANTE ROSSETTI.

[The query whether Dante Gabriel might "recollect" any of the localities about Sevenoaks glances back to a remote year, 1850, when he was there along with Holman Hunt and F. G. Stephens, painting the background of a picture.]

FAYREMEAD, SEVENOAKS.

[26 *July* 1881.]

MY DEAR GABRIEL,

I am glad you are feeling "curious" about my volume, and I hope that now any day your curiosity may be gratified.

Monday (that is, yesterday) was announced to me as the day of publication, but then something was added about getting copies from the binder, which leaves me in doubt how far we are in reality ready for the critical moment. William saw the sonnets before you, merely because calling one day he downright asked to look at book,— a nervous moment for me, though I braved it out. Those he means are *Monna Innominata*, but there is a second set entitled *Later Life*, which I hope may also claim attention. Following your brotherly opinion I have written to Macmillans suggesting the immediate forwarding both of the old and of the new vols. to Mr. Watts, whose address I fortunately have; and, thinking an *early* copy was one main point, I further suggested that if still unbound one should go in sheets. 6 copies are all I claim as my free share, though I have no doubt I may have more when I want them within reasonable limits: but these 6 I supplement at once by a few purchased.

The rent here, all inclusive, is £4. 10. 0 per week : and this, divided among 4 of us, is not overwhelming. On the whole I think these are the very nicest lodgings we ever occupied. Knole Park we have passed by in driving, though we might find it too far for a walk. . . . Another pretty place to drive through—at least, Knole Park is not open to visitors in carriages, only to pedestrians—but one may drive through Wilderness Park, and pretty it is. Then there is a charming wood hereabouts, which recalled those near Hunter's Forestall; and there is a quaint, pretty village named Seal. I wonder if you recollect any of these.

I meant to bring Gamberale's book with me, but in the bustle of preparation I left it behind. So now I must stay my curiosity till I get home again. I entertain the idea of sending him my new volume; though if *Miraggio* is his "chef d'œuvre" I am not quite certain whether *Sing-Song* might not lend itself still better than the other to his hand,—*Sing-Song* containing some of my best songs. Perhaps however it would strike him as too babyish. If his translations from you are inadequate, I am glad that at any rate his article is better. . . .

To Dante Rossetti.

[The reference to "nearly 200 lines added to *Jenny*" applies, not to any addition made by Dante Rossetti, but to the amplification appearing in Gamberale's translation. The article in the *Rassegna* was also by Gamberale; and, by some odd blunder, the name of Christina's prose-volume *Commonplace* had there been given as "Commonplace Cook."—Mr. Horder was editor of a compilation named *The Poets' Bible*.—The phrase "seated by the grave of buried hope" was I think the invention of Dante Gabriel as defining the tone of some of Christina's poems.]

FAYREMEAD, SEVENOAKS.

4 *August* 1881.

My dear Gabriel,

. . . Nearly 200 lines added to *Jenny* is portentous. But, as you imply, what an admirably appreciative article it is in the *Rassegna*. When (as I contemplate) I send Signor Gamberale my new volume, I think I shall put up with it a 1/- *Sing-Song*, and thus he will possess all my poems. How funny it is to see one of my books figuring as "Commonplace cook." Of course I am feeling anxious about the prospects of my *Pageant*, and indeed I am well pleased to be away just now from London. I shall like—or shall I far from *like ? !*—to see Mr. Caine's *Academy* article, and I hope and fear in prospect of Mr. Watts in the *Athenæum*. . . .

Oddly enough I also told Mr. Horder that I doubted whether any one of my pieces would come into his scheme. Besides a few letters between us, he called one day on me, and turns out to be bright and rather agreeable and youngish if not young. I think however that, when my fresh S.P.C.K. volume is actually published, that may perhaps contain a poem or two worth his consideration. . . .

Considering that I was "old and cold and grey" so many years ago, it is (as you suggest) no wonder that nowadays I am "so shrunk and sere."—If only my figure would shrink somewhat! For a fat poetess is incongruous especially when seated by he grave of buried hope.

To DANTE ROSSETTI.

[The *Pageant*, as it turns out, has been performed more than once : once on quite a striking scale, in the Albert Hall, Kensington. —The "courteous tilt in the strong-minded woman lists," between Mrs. Webster and Christina, was merely an interchange of private letters; arising out of an invitation from Mrs. Webster that Christina should give her assent to the granting of female suffrage—which my sister preferred not to do. Two letters of hers on this subject, addressed to Mrs. Webster, are printed in Mr. Mackenzie Bell's work, *Christina Rossetti.*—The reference to a Dante picture and Liverpool arises from the fact that my brother was now negotiating for the sale of his largest picture, *Dante's Dream*, to the Walker Art-gallery in Liverpool; and it had been suggested that the work should be sent to the annual exhibition in that gallery, and should then, if approved, be purchased. He declined to do this, unless there were a positive understanding beforehand that purchased it would be.]

FAYREMEAD, SEVENOAKS.

9 *August* [1881].

MY DEAR GABRIEL,

. . . Indeed I am not "sulking" beside the grave of twice-buried hope because you have not read my book as yet. In fact, there is a certain sense in which delay respites one's nerves, however in the long run one wants to be read: and I am very glad that a glance has certified you of something to be liked. I too am not without hope that the *Pageant* may achieve some success as a drawing-room acting piece. It had its rise in one of the All Saints Sisters asking me whether I could concoct something performable by her sister's family; and, though the result was on too grand a scale for the applicant, yet it was that hint which first set me off. The piece was, in the main, written at Seaford two summers ago. No reviews have reached me as yet. I heard from Boston the other day (enclosing a remittance of £1 - 0 - 7 !) informing me that no early sheets had reached Roberts Brothers: this disappoints me, but now of course they can procure a copy and reprint from it. . . .

This is so lovely a place that I could wish every one to share its charms. One morning we drove to Knole Park, and strolled and sat there to our hearts' content: no wonder you recollect so beautiful a spot. It charmed us along so that our dearest Mother took quite a long walk, rivalling the most active of us.

I am not well versed in George Eliot as a bard, but feel inclined to rate Mrs. Webster decidedly higher. The latter, some of whose poetry I really have admired, has sent me her fresh volume; so I have duly returned mine. Once she and I had a courteous tilt in the strong-minded woman lists, so it became doubly incumbent upon me to fall short in no observance. We think so good a friend as Mr. Watts may well receive even the honour of a Dedication from you, nor am I amazed that he "set his heart" upon it. Thanks for an intelligible clue to "Common place cook:" I had not reasoned it out. . . .

A second visit to you, like the one last April, is something for Mamma and me to look forward to: but in any case "what has been has been," and the one we paid you is good to look back upon.

I should think not, your "Dante" tramp to Liverpool "on approval"!!

To DANTE ROSSETTI.

[Christina's "reference to the *Portuguese Sonnets*" comes in her prose heading to the "Sonnet of Sonnets" named *Monna Innominata*, included in the *Pageant* volume; and is certainly expressed quite clearly enough for a reader's purposes. What she says in her letter—that the speaker in her sonnets was not intended for an "innominata at all"—is curious, and shows (what is every now and then apparent in her utterances) that her mind was conversant with very nice shades of distinction. It is indisputable that the real veritable speaker in those sonnets is Christina herself, giving expression to her love for Charles Cayley: but the prose heading would surely lead any reader to suppose that the *ostensible* speaker is one of those ladies, to whom it adverts, in the days of the troubadours.— The *Ballad of Boding* does clearly bear some substantial resemblance —though a resemblance with much of difference—to *Sleep at Sea*. " The sonnet you hint at" is a double sonnet named *Behold a Shaking*. —" October's remark" is this—

> " Here comes my youngest sister, looking dim
> And grim,
> With dismal ways."]

7

30 TORRINGTON SQUARE, W.C.

[5 *September* 1881.]

MY DEAR GABRIEL,

We are all congratulant over the Dante picture, Mamma heading our family phalanx. I do certainly think it would have been sacrificing real advantage to a mere punctilio if you had held out about its being sold (merely in appearance) from the Exhibition. It looks very friendly of Mr. Caine to have gone off to Liverpool on purpose to see with his own eyes. I am much pleased with his *Academy* article, though sorry that he seems to have misapprehended my reference to the *Portuguese Sonnets*. Surely not only what I meant to say but what I do say is, not that the Lady of those sonnets is surpassable, but that a "Donna innominata" by the same hand might well have been unsurpassable. The Lady in question, as she actually stands, I was not regarding as an "innominata" at all,— because the latter type, according to the traditional figures I had in view, is surrounded by unlike circumstances. I rather wonder that no one (so far as I know) ever hit on my semi-historical argument before for such treatment,—it seems to me so full of poetic suggestiveness. That *you* praise it endorses its worth to me, and I am graced by Mr. Watts's approbation. I do not recall anything in my private [? previous] volume which foreshadows the *Ballad of Boding* : but your memory may well outdo mine. As to the Sonnet you hint at, I cannot joke on that subject. I am desirous of the *Athenæum* critique, and fancied it might be out ere this ; but am not impatient. In a letter from Mrs. Scott Scotus sent me up a warm admiring word on "Monna." . . .

To get back a moment to my book,—I cannot forbear adding how delighted I am at the favourable verdicts on the *Pageant*. *I* fancy it among the best and most wholesome things I have produced, and I have had a quiet grin over October's remark which ushers in November, as connecting it with my own brothers and myself ! Pray appreciate the portrait.—It dawns upon me that *Sleep at Sea* is the piece in your mind : I hope the diversity is sufficient to justify the *Ballad of Boding*.

Surely you need not restrict your affectionate family callers to those moments when there is something "to show " :—but this is merely an observation *en passant*.

With a best of good loves from our Mother, &c.

To DANTE ROSSETTI, *Fisher Place, Cumberland.*

[Dante Rossetti, in company with Mr. Hall Caine, had now gone to a very retired spot in Cumberland to recruit his health—which, however, he did not succeed in doing to any perceptible extent. He had sent to our mother a letter (not addressed to himself) from Sir J. Noel Paton, expressing enthusiastic admiration for the picture of *Dante's Dream.* His "poems" were the volume named *Ballads and Sonnets;* there was also another volume, published about the same time, re-issuing, with some considerable variations, the volume *Poems* of 1870, but I infer that Christina had not as yet seen the re-issue.—The passage about "the snail" is a reply to one in Dante Gabriel's letter to our mother, 22 September : "Christina will be interested to hear that, as I was leaning over a bridge to-day, an old snail came up out of his shell and submitted to be stroked, after which he retired."]

30 TORRINGTON SQUARE, LONDON, W.C.

[1881—? 24 *September.*]

MY DEAR GABRIEL,

Your letters in general and this one in particular charm our Mother. Her dearest love to you, and delight in your delight amid your beautiful new world. Sir Noel Paton (herein returned, but not before I copied the passage for her to keep) gives her keen pleasure; nor, I assure you, in all this am I without my share of sympathetic enjoyment. Mamma is reading your Poems, noting her favourites ; but besides this we are to have the joint treat of my reading them aloud to her, and already I have *dipped* enough to thrill and warm to the much beauty.

The snail—I interpose a space between him and your poems !— soothes and solaces my taste. "Gli voglio bene." . . .

I have not seen any more reviews of my volume, and have failed to procure the severe *Pall Mall* through some mistake in the date.

To DANTE ROSSETTI.

[Christina quotes here an expression of Dante Rossetti in eulogy of Mr. Hall Caine. It may be inferred that she had thereupon, in a letter not now forthcoming, indulged in some reciprocation of this eulogy, including in it more or less Mr. George Hake and Mr. Treffry Dunn; and that Dante had replied (whether reasonably or otherwise) damping down her laudation. He was now returning from Cumberland.]

30 TORRINGTON SQUARE, W.C.

[1881—? 19 *October.*]

MY DEAR GABRIEL,

By the same delivery as your welcome letter came the *Athenæum* review of your poems. I don't know that I ever saw anything so good of Mr. Watts's, and I am happy to see him shine as a planet in conjunction with our family sun. I am wanting (yet dreading?) to see some day the additions to *Sister Helen*:—have even you really found it possible to augment advantageously that terse fierce masterpiece? We usually see the *Athenæum* more or less after date, so the delay of this number was a mere matter of course.

I dare say my "burst" read quite as abruptly as yours! But it had its source simply in your own words to our Mother: "Caine is excessively attentive and friendly, and is really quite an *abnegator of self.*" *Hero-worship* is not the feeling I dedicate to George Hake, much less to Mr. Dunn, though I have a warm liking for the former and a secondary do. for the latter: but I can imagine grave faults in both, and am quite sure you know a great deal about them which must (and is most welcome to) continue unknown to me. Yet I recollect our good Maria once remarking that one never understood a person unless one liked him, and so far I fancy I may have the best chance of grasping our subject. Nevertheless facts are stubborn things, not to be modified by a Quixotic view-point. I fear you are at this moment travelling up in the cold, and proportionately uncomfortable. And the house-hunting is an overhanging dreariness. May you get well through both, but the latter makes me anxious for you.

Our Mother's love to you: she too admires the Watts article, with its felicitous passage about the nightingale singing to the Sahara.

To Dante Rossetti.

30 TORRINGTON SQUARE, W.C.

[1881—? 21 *October.*]

My dear Gabriel,

William tells us you have not seen the *Times* review, and, as he seems to think you may like to look at it, our Mother sends it with love. . . . She and I were reading some more of your Sonnets this morning in a harmony of admiration, and in *Chimes* I revel in *the moth.*

Dear Maria's *Shadow of Dante* has reached a 3rd edition.

From Charles Cayley.

[The reference to "Horace's second Ode" is obscure to me: perhaps Cayley had been translating the poem.—The Howell here mentioned must be Charles Augustus Howell, an Anglo-Portuguese frequently referred to in books about Dante Rossetti. The "Napoleonic discourse" must have been one delivered at the Philological Society by the celebrated linguist of the Bonapi rte family.]

6 *November* 1881.

Dear Christina Rossetti,

For Horace's second ode, in some respects, I won't venture to apologize to you; *conserva pur la speme,* dolce monna. I met quite unexpectedly at the Philol. our old friend Howell: besides that, we were, I won't say enlightened but embrightened, by handsome Mrs. Furnivall. But I and Howell, in succession, both shifted our chairs during the Napoleonic discourse, I to avoid the heat, and H. to listen greedily to the Prince's Portuguese examples, which seem to have been pronounced to his entire satisfaction. Afterwards he introduced himself to the Prince, and they talked away in English, French, and Portuguese, not without very civil references to me, the Prince in regard to my Russian grammar paper and Howell from his points of view. So flowed that hour, but what can I say of Saturday except that the Museum was quite spifflicaiting (I have a cousin in the North country who emphasizes her words by putting as many letters as possible into them, and I suppose would not stick at *creighture* or *Wraddicall*). I saw too on Friday H. Leifchild's bas relief of *Ariadne and Bacchus*. Ariadne sits under a tree, her head drooping though not entirely. Bacchus advances with earnest curiosity, one arm thrown behind him and the hand raised to motion "backward" to his followers; said followers are two Mænads, striding forward and stopped suddenly. . . .

To WILLIAM ROSSETTI.

[This letter is consequent upon an incident which I have recorded in my *Memoir of Dante Rossetti*, as follows :—"By 21 November I observed him to be somewhat less shaken in health, but deeply melancholy. Matters of very old as well as more recent date agitated his mind; even so old as the year 1847 or 1848, when his desultory habits of work, or lack of filial deference, used to annoy our father, and elicit some severe expressions from him." My brother showed on this occasion some inclination to consult a Roman Catholic priest. I mentioned the matter to Christina. Mr. Burrows, whom she names (soon afterwards Canon Burrows of Rochester), was the Anglican incumbent of Christ Church, Albany Street, and well known to my family for many years past. However, my brother did not in fact consult either a Catholic or an Anglican.]

30 TORRINGTON SQUARE, W.C.

[30 *November* 1881.]

MY DEAR WILLIAM,

Thinking about what you said of poor dear Gabriel's distress, I seem to recover a shadowy recollection of the incident, and, if I am right, Mamma used her influence successfully to get the words unsaid. *I* cannot, perhaps, start the subject, as it has never been mentioned to me : but possibly *you* may feel able to do so. No wonder that in weakness and suffering such a reminiscence haunts weary days and sleepless hours of double darkness. How exceedingly I wish Mr. Burrows or one like him had access within the nearly-closed precincts : you must laugh at me if you will, but I really think a noble spiritual influence might do what no common sense, foresight of ruin, affection of friends, could secure. And Mr. Burrows I know he respects.

In much anxiety and sympathy, &c. . . .

To Dante Rossetti.

30 TORRINGTON SQUARE, W.C.

[2 *December* 1881.]

My dearest Gabriel,

I write because I cannot but write, for you are continually in my thoughts and always in my heart, much more in our Mother's who sends you her love and dear blessing.

I want to assure you that, however harassed by memory or by anxiety you may be, I have (more or less) heretofore gone through the same ordeal. I have borne myself till I became unbearable by myself, and then I have found help in confession and absolution and spiritual counsel, and relief inexpressible. Twice in my life I tried to suffice myself with measures short of this, but nothing would do; the first time was of course in my youth before my general confession, the second time was when circumstances had led me (rightly or wrongly) to break off the practice. But now for years past I have resumed the habit, and I hope not to continue it profitlessly.

"' 'Tis like frail man to love to walk on high,
    But to be lowly is to be like God,"

is a couplet (Isaac Williams) I thoroughly assent to.

I ease my own heart by telling you all this, and I hope I do not weary yours. Don't think of me merely as the younger sister whose glaring faults are known to you, but as a devoted friend also.

To Lucy Rossetti.

[It was on 11 December 1881 that my brother had an attack of partial paralysis, the precursor of the form of illness which brought his life to a close on 9 April 1882. This letter, as will be seen, was written soon after the attack.]

30 TORRINGTON SQUARE, W.C.

[21 *December* 1881.]

My dear Lucy,

I dare say you guess what is coming! Mamma sends you love, but has not courage to dine out on Christmas Day : she falls back on her resolution formed after her last such experiment, when

she resolved that that particular effort should really be the last of
its kind. So our party of old ladies will dine (D.V.) peacefully in
company, meanwhile wishing every blessing to yourself and dear
William and *la cara prole*. To-night festivities recede into extra
impossibility, for we have been seeing Gabriel, and have borne the
shock of finding out the state he is in, laid up and partly powerless.
God help us, for human help is but a very helpless thing.

To WILLIAM ROSSETTI.

[I hardly know what was the "little picture" finished by Dante
Gabriel; it may probably have been the latest that he brought to
actual completion.]

30 TORRINGTON SQUARE, W.C.

23 [*January*] 1882.

MY DEAR WILLIAM,

. . . We had the pleasure of a second visit from Gabriel
last week—on Thursday, I think,—when he was more animated
and mentioned having finished a little picture. Our dear Mother
sends you love, and she cheers me by being quite decidedly
better. . . .

To WILLIAM ROSSETTI.

30 TORRINGTON SQUARE, W.C.

[2 *February* 1882.]

MY DEAR WILLIAM,

Mamma thinks you may have heard that she and I were
likely to go down with Gabriel to Birchington next Saturday, and,
if so, she wishes you to know that the plan has failed because Mr.
Stewart absolutely refuses his assent, thinking the risk too great for
her to incur at this season and in conjunction with her recent attack
of illness. We are sorry for poor dear Gabriel, but I can only write
him word of the imperative disappointment. He came here yesterday
seeming quite as well and cheerful as we could expect, and his
leaving town next Saturday seems to be fully fixed. There is a long
review of his book in this week's *Guardian*, in part enthusiastically

laudatory; doubtless we shall recover it from Aunt Charlotte some day, when if you please you can read it.

Dearest Mamma continues satisfactory . . .

To DANTE ROSSETTI.

30 TORRINGTON SQUARE, LONDON, W.C.

8 *February* [1882].

MY DEAR GABRIEL,

Every day you are in our anxious thoughts, most of all in Mamma's. She sends you her dearest love and every good wish she can frame. Mr. Stewart, seeing her yesterday, repeated that a change of weather *must* precede her going out,—so we are awaiting such a change. If it takes place and is of some duration we are still looking forward to the not-impossibility of your liking us to join you at Birchington.

I enclose a review sent me from Macmillan : perhaps, being foreign, it is the less likely to fall in your way. Please, at your convenience, let us have it back, as it belongs to the maternal store of such documents. Roberts (Boston) has sent me £12 4s. 8d. just now : but he is disappointed (and I somewhat) at the sale of the *Pageant*,—under 500 : part of the small sum accrues from the former volume.

From DANTE ROSSETTI.

[Mr. Frederick R. Leyland, the ship-owner of Liverpool, was one of the leading purchasers of Dante Rossetti's paintings. Towards this time he was staying at Ramsgate, and up to the last he was very attentive to Rossetti, to whom he was greatly attached.]

[15 *February* 1882.]

MY DEAR CHRISTINA,

Of course *Monday* was a stupid slip for *Thursday*. But I think the matter must be in abeyance for a little, much as I regret this. It is very stormy here just now,—then there is Leyland's visit probable,—and I should not perhaps refrain from saying that I have been more than usually ill for some days. Indeed I wish L. were not coming, but there has already been delay about his visit. Do not be alarmed, as there is no necessity. I will write again very soon.

To WILLIAM ROSSETTI.

[My "admirably descriptive letter" must have been a letter to my cousin Teodorico giving some sort of description of my father's aspect and habits. He, with a view to a projected monument at Vasto, had asked Dante Gabriel to make some sketches of my father : but my brother's condition of health did not admit of his doing anything efficient, so I wrote down some details instead.— Christina's notes as to my father's appearance will explain themselves pretty well. The final item, "Menacing look connected with removing shade," refers to something I had written as to a somewhat "menacing look" in the oil-portrait of him by my brother painted in 1848 : this (as Christina implies) arose from the very imperfect condition of his eyesight when, in sitting for the portrait, he took off an eye-shade which he then habitually used.]

30 TORRINGTON SQUARE, W.C.

[19 *February* 1882.]

MY DEAR WILLIAM,

Thankyou for budget full of interest. Perhaps the enclosed pencil scrap will show you the points Mamma and I have annotated in your admirably descriptive letter—if you can make it out. I return Theo. and D. G., adding one from the latter to me which can be returned to me any day you come here. . . . Pray do not ascribe all his doings and non-doings to foundationless fidgetiness, poor dear fellow. Don't you think neither you nor I can quite appreciate all he is undergoing at present, what between wrecked health at least in some measure, nerves which appear to falsify facts, and most anxious money-matters? It is trying to have to do with him at times, but what must it be TO BE himself? And he in so many ways the head of our family—it doubles the pity. I have just written answering his (*enclosed*) letter, but Mr. Stewart continues to object to Mamma's risking the Birchington visit. He is no longer in attendance, but happened to-day to see her as a friend.

She sends you love.

It was good Maria's birthday yesterday, and I went to the Home and saw beautiful Sister Eliza.

Height rather 5–7: Throat massive. Adam's apple large. Blue

and black check. Eyes and mouth beautiful. Smile very engaging. Teeth white and regular. Very thin at last, but never slim. Menacing look connected with removing shade.

To Dante Rossetti.

30 TORRINGTON SQUARE, LONDON, W.C.

27 [*February* 1882].

My dear Gabriel,

Our Mother, with much love, responds in kind (as also do I) to your renewed kind invitation, and hopes we shall really be with you in the course of *Wednesday* afternoon . . .

We are sorry for your hindered work, and still more sorry for the failure of galvanism to restore your poor dear arm. If we say little about your health, it is not because we are indifferent on the subject. Thankyou for the chronic good-nature which tells me of 2 mentions of me : I look forward to seeing both *Athenæum* and *Academy* when with you.

The chair is a heretofore unforeseen but now gladly foreseen. haven of rest.

To William Rossetti.

[Mr. (John H.) Ingram had become Editor of the series of memoirs named *Eminent Women.* He wished Christina to write one of the memoirs, and she was not disinclined, but it did not come to pass.—I do not now remember who was the Mr. Nicoll referred to, unless perhaps it was Dr. Robertson Nicoll : the book he spoke of was Christina's privately printed *Verses*, 1847. I possess a later letter from Christina, 1886, showing that her Mr. Nicoll was then a resident at Kelso.]

WESTCLIFF BUNGALOW, BIRCHINGTON-ON-SEA, KENT.

4 *March* 1882.

My dear William,

I cannot give at all a bright account of Gabriel, yet I have seen him by far more depressed and unavailable. He now reads amusing books sedulously, talks about them and draws our attention to them. How much or how little he sleeps I cannot accurately say, —in some degree, I hope; but am not certain. One of the most troublesome and actively distressing points *now* appears to be a terrible defect of digestion . . . The poor left side, the arm and hand especially, continues crippled. I am afraid no sensible improvement takes place. He has not gone out since our arrival, having been but poorly since the attack which delayed our journey; and he thinks it too cold for driving in an open carriage. Very cold it is, but fine and sunny and nothing noticeable as to windiness. I am not sure, but I have some idea that his work is waiting for something or other to be done by some one else: it seems at a stand, but I see a finished (I believe) *Proserpine* and *Jeanne d'Arc* standing in this beautiful drawing-room, one end of which forms the studio with easel and other appliances. I wish you could come down, but I well know you are full of business. Mr. Watts arrived here to-day, and is most welcome to us; Mr. Caine is friendly and pleasant, and so far as I see on comfortable terms with Gabriel; Lily Caine is a nice unobtrusive child of 12,—a real child, not a young person.

I have not yet written to Mr. Ingram, but hope to write on Monday. I had a letter from Mr. Nicoll this morning, and in a P.S. he says:—" I observed a copy of the little volume you refer to (*i. e. Grandpapa's*) in Mr. Pearson's catalogue the other day; the price I think was five guineas "—*5*, I read it, but you know Mr. Nicoll's handwriting is not *pellucid*.

Our mother's love, and mine, to you and yours.

To WILLIAM ROSSETTI.

[Mrs. Abrey was a sick-nurse who remained with Dante Rossetti to the end.—The "ballad of a grotesque-horrid type" was called *The Dutchman's Pipe*, or *Jan van Hunks*. Rossetti took it up on his deathbed, completed it, and presented the MS. as a gift to Mr. Watts-Dunton: the general frame of it, however, belongs to a very early date in his life, perhaps 1847. It has not as yet been published. —The doctor in Birchington who attended Dante from time to time was Dr. Harris. When I was again at Birchington in 1906 I observed that his well-remembered door-plate is still on his housedoor.—Mr. Martin was the tenant or manager of a hotel near the bungalows at Birchington—which was then a less settled residential place than it is now.—The phrase ".I should decline the 2 Georges" means George Sand and George Eliot.—Mrs. Gemmer, a lady well known to Christina (still I think alive), used the fancy-name Gerda Fay for her books.]

WESTCLIFF BUNGALOW, BIRCHINGTON-ON-SEA, KENT.

8 *March* 1882.

MY DEAR WILLIAM,

Thanks for your letter full of interest and brotherly kindness. Our dear Gabriel passed nearly the whole of yesterday in bed, so far as I know; but at any rate in the evening he sat up. This lapse into bed was led to by a touch in one foot of what seems gout; as to its being so Mrs. Abrey and Mr. Watts were unanimous. Happily the rest and safe-keeping of his foot kept him fairly comfortable; and, when Mamma and I sat with him a considerable time in the afternoon, he was chatty and reasonably cheerful, inclined, as so often is the case, to revive old memories, but not under gloomy aspects. . . . I have not seen or heard of him as yet to-day, but hope that he may be tolerable; after swallowing yesterday . . . medicine considered indispensable before grappling with gout as gout: on this point Mr. Watts pronounced imperatively. He left this morning rather early, before we could see him, and a great loss he is from our anxious circle. His kindness is beyond praise, and Mr. Caine co-operates in friendly offices. We find Lily Caine—who by fairness deserves her promotion from Elizabeth to Lily—an agreeable small inmate. One point gained is that Mr. Watts is quite struck with the mental improvement achieved: a ballad of a grotesque-horrid type is in hand, and so far as I observe not a shadow of *delusion* comes to light. I read G. your messages of love and regret for absenteeism, and also the P.S. about Arthur, which charms Mamma who sends you best love. I am much amused at his addiction to *decillions*, which used to figure in my own infant conversation. Pray give our 2 loves to Lucy and all round.

Since writing what precedes I have seen Mrs. Abrey (it is now about noon). . . . By Mr. Watts's advice before starting Mr. Caine has obtained from Mr. Martin a doctor's name in the village who can be called in in case of an emergency . . . I do not know what to think or how much to fear, but at the least I cannot help fearing that more symptoms than one point to a sluggishness or congestion (what is it to be called?) pervading the frame, and of which the arm and left side are but one strongly affected seat. Mr. Watts says, and seems sure, that the arm is really affected by a degree of chloral paralysis. This is all grievous for you to read, but I on the spot must write as I hear. Be sure I will not neglect to let you know of important points; so while I do not write trust that there is nothing special. Mr. Martin came in one evening and seems to be a kind-hearted intelligent man most friendlily disposed, and able to converse on books and intellectual topics. He has lent the bungalow a good large telescope, adequate to displaying Saturn's Rings as I am told. . . .

Now for other matters. Everything you do in the Ingram business has my gratitude. I will remember " Darc," not " d'Arc."—*Mrs. Fry* I would gladly try at, nor do I fancy I should find *Lady Augusta Stanley* insurmountable : I should decline the 2 *Georges*, and prefer leaving Miss Martineau. *Mary Lamb* I should think would be both manageable and well worth writing. Meanwhile it strikes me that the very person to write *A. A. Procter* would be not myself but Anna Mary Watts, who was in the heart of that social set instead of (as I was) on its merest outskirt. I had a long letter from Mr. Ingram this morning, which I must answer before sending it you,— afterwards, it may perhaps interest you to read it. . . . Without counting Anna Mary (whom I think of naming as presumably more to the point than myself for A. A. P.) 3 friends suggest themselves as worth pointing out to Mr. Ingram as perhaps adapted and willing to contribute biographies,—Mrs. Scott, Mrs. Gemmer, and most of all Henrietta Rintoul : these I should *myself* name to him, if you are struck as I am with their merits ; but I should like to have your opinion first. By the by, I must ask Mr. Ingram for Mrs. Procter's address, but he lavishes offers of aid upon me.

Far from being less well, our dear Mother bore the journey with impunity, and now thrives in this fine and not unduly keen air. . . .

I sent my notes of good Maria's life to Mr. Nicoll on Monday, but have not heard from him since. Could you believe that down here I feel over-full of occupation ! ! ! It must, you may say, be a mere morbid sensation ; and very likely so it is in a measure : I must bear in mind the celebrated " There will be eternity to rest in."

To WILLIAM ROSSETTI.

[A passage in this letter, as also in a preceding one, might lead to an inference that I rather doubted the gravity of our brother's illness. This, however, was not the case : I was but too fully alive to it. I may have repeated to Christina, what I knew on medical authority, that some *symptoms* of the illness partook of delusion consequent on the illness itself ; as for instance, when he thought he could not move his arm, he could in fact have done so if only his volition had been in a normally healthy state. But, the volition failing, the ability practically failed as well. The letter of 28 March adverts to this.]

WESTCLIFF BUNGALOW, BIRCHINGTON-ON-SEA, KENT.

14 *March* 1882.

MY DEAR WILLIAM,

With all my wish to send you news, I really cannot say whether Gabriel is gaining or losing ground. In some ways the symptoms appear favourable. The night before last he slept comparatively well without any sedative : last night was much more restless, but not I think at all exceptionally restless. To-day we are expecting to see him enter the sitting-room : till to-day he has, ever since the touch of gout (?) been confined to his own room and in great measure to bed. Wherever he is, Mamma and I sit with him a great deal ; and he reads not novels only, but occasionally he takes up a newspaper. I spoke to Mrs. Abrey this morning, aiming to arrive at her real opinion :—she cannot account for the continued wasting away which goes on in spite of food and in some measure of tonics ; and she considers that he has *retrograded* from the point at which he stood some while ago, when (say) he arrived here. This is sad indeed, but the not saying it is vain. On the other hand we cannot be thankful enough that his head is clear and composed to such a degree that I could not even (judging by appearances) suspect its ever having been otherwise. Mrs. Abrey seems to fear that some deep-seated mischief may exist in the liver or what not, undermining the possibility of returning health. . . . I think there are grounds to fear that some terrible mischief lurks in his constitution, and is (so to say) burrowing about him and checking any return of strength or revival of sensitiveness. Mrs. Abrey we like very much and depend upon thoroughly. Not a word is said about how long or how short a time we may stay here. The weather to-day is delightful, and on the whole has been mild and favourable. Pray do not doubt the *reality* of poor dear Gabriel's illness : do not let any theory or any opinion influence you to entertain such a doubt. Mr. Caine is away at present, for how long I know not. Mr. Martin (I fancied you knew about him) is builder to Mr. John Seddon as concerns this group of variously-constructed bungalows, and is also at the head of a bungalow Hotel and Boarding House close by ; and he is an intelligent man and a most kind neighbour. Mr. Watts, leaving here, was going to see Mr. Marshall the same day : and evidently he did so, illustrated by the fact that he sent down a fresh prescription from Mr. Marshall.

I too have written to Mr. Ingram endorsing your suggestion of Anna Mary, proposing friends, and saying that for the present I find it impossible to set to work. Should a better moment occur later, I can then re-start the subject. . . .

To WILLIAM ROSSETTI.

[Malvern and Wolverhampton are mentioned here because I had to deliver a lecture at Wolverhampton, staying meanwhile at the house at Malvern of Dr. Grindrod, whom I had known for a year past more as the author of some interesting historical dramas than in his medical capacity.]

WESTCLIFF BUNGALOW, BIRCHINGTON-ON-SEA, KENT.

17 March 1882.

MY DEAR WILLIAM,

Very welcome indeed was your good brotherly letter received this morning. Touching on it with Mr. Caine, he asked me to let you know that (as I understand) AFTER seeing you he was assured by Mr. Marshall that no stress whatever need be laid on the extremely trifling quantity of morphia now being taken, as to its tendency in the direction you apprehend. But I am very glad you have told me of such being the result to opium-eaters : I had no knowledge of the fact. Mr. Caine also quoted your notes of a conversation years ago with Mr. Knight, and Mr. Marshall's consequent remark: so you see store is set by what you contribute under the present anxiety. Of course all our talk was carried on not in Gabriel's presence, but when by ourselves: we make a fairly chatty and sociable party at luncheon. On the whole I think I may report Gabriel to have been rather better than worse since Sunday, on the evening of which day Mamma and I felt especially uneasy, though possibly without proportionate grounds. I will not forget about Mr. Ingram, but unless I get home cannot see my way to setting to work,—at the worst, may a worthier than I write. . . .

We are having weather *so* mild and beautiful that I can scarcely define it as beautiful March weather. I hope Malvern will seem to you as delightful as it seems to my memory: Wolverhampton is unknown to me. The Incumbent of Malvern Link—there are a set of Malverns, all contiguous—is a noted Mr. Cosby White, and I met his wife a good while ago—but I do not expect you to encounter either. Maria must have known Mrs. C. W. better than I; and very likely knew the husband too, whom I do not.

Gabriel has read an article on himself in the *World* with satisfaction.

To WILLIAM ROSSETTI.

[Mr. (William) Sharp was a very cordial friend of Dante Rossetti in his closing years. He published a book about him soon after Rossetti's decease; and became himself a well-known author, both in his own name and in that of Fiona Macleod. Mr. John Seddon, the architect who built the bungalows at Birchington, had arranged for placing at my brother's disposal the one from which Christina wrote — now named Rossetti Bungalow.]

WESTCLIFF BUNGALOW, BIRCHINGTON-ON-SEA, KENT.

24 March 1882.

MY DEAR WILLIAM,

I dare say you are at home again, and if so am sure you will like to receive news. Sad to say, there is no very definite news to give. But poor Gabriel is going back apparently rather than going forward, and is so comfortless and sinking and so wasted away that at last this morning I urged him to see a local Dr., who of course can

8

make a thorough bodily examination. He agreed, and in the course of the afternoon we hope Dr. Harris—of whom the Clergyman here, Mr. Alcock, spoke favourably—will call and investigate his case. Gabriel had a restless night last night, and suffered from vomitings : to-day he is restless and depressed. It is a truly pitiable state even if he were not our brother. I will not close this letter yet,—before post-time I may perhaps have something to add. . . .

No one is here now beyond ourselves and Mr. Caine, nor do I know of any one being definitely expected. Mr. Sharp was here for a couple of nights, and Mr. Leyland drove over for an hour or two last Sunday from Ramsgate ; he was longer in Birchington, but at a Hotel part of the time. On Saturday too Mr. John Seddon and his brother Major Seddon called and saw Gabriel. . . .

About 5 p.m. Dr. Harris has just been, intelligent in look and manner. Considers the case very serious, but *not* irremediable. On the nerves, but requiring absolute cessation of Chloral & Co. (as I understand,—of the whole class)—also, if possible to achieve, SELF help in the way of exertion and occupation ; and I think he suggested amusement. This last of course is no easy item. He will communicate with Mr. Marshall, and of course we expect to see him again. Meanwhile it is of imperative necessity that the digestive functions should be adequately attended to. I am not sure whether morphia has been included among the forbidden resources.

To WILLIAM ROSSETTI.

[While I was out of London, at Malvern, and my wife in Manchester, some odd affair happened of a man entering my house without leave : it turned out a trifle.—At Wolverhampton I had had a very scanty auditory for my lecture. The day was a singular specimen of British weather : quite fine and almost summer-like in the morning ; then in early afternoon a wild drive of snow and penetrating cold which lasted into the evening.]

WESTCLIFF BUNGALOW, BIRCHINGTON-ON-SEA, KENT.

28 *March* 1882.

MY DEAR WILLIAM,

Mamma and I are full of concern at what you tell us of the alarming attempt to enter your house. No wonder you feel more than ever the advisability of remaining on the spot to guard all dear and tender persons. Yet, seeing what we do see here, we cannot but rejoice at the prospect of your flying visit. Yesterday I waylaid Dr. Harris as he left the house : and, while he maintains that the impression of failing eyesight and general powerlessness is false in fact, however real to the patient, he showed the gravest apprehension as to mental (he always uses the word *nerves*) despondency, and plainly said that an eye must be kept on G. He is now administering soothing pills, and these seem efficacious. There is irritability at times, habitual depression, yet at the same time a degree of interest in hearing a novel or in conversation ; occasionally a gleam of cheerfulness or of fun. Mr. Marshall has written to Dr. Harris, but of course I did not see the letter: your meaning to see Mr. Marshall yourself is a comfort. I have told Mr. Caine what trains you propose, and he verified them readily in his time-table. . . . I have spoken to Mrs. Abrey, and there are 2 vacant bedrooms at present in the house ; so do not dream of a hotel.

Mamma's love to you. We are quite hurt for you at the 40 auditors, though the snow accounts for lukewarmness. I remember the glorious glimpse into Wales from a drive round the Malvern Hills, and, as I took that drive in summer, I probably saw all to more advantage. On Sunday morning I struggled home from church in what *felt* like danger to my life from a storm of wind which began to rage after I got there: three times I was driven to take refuge in cottages, and at last was most happy in being able to procure a shut-up fly. . . .

I have just been into Gabriel's room for a few minutes: he is in bed and much as usual after a not-noticeable night. I am writing not very long after breakfast. . . .

To WILLIAM ROSSETTI.

[The reference to a cemetery is not now quite clear to me. My brother did not at this time write any story, apart from the ballad of *The Dutchman's Pipe*. He did, however, pay some degree of attention to his old prose-tale *St. Agnes of Intercession*, written towards 1850, and, had the conditions been propitious, he might have completed it.]

30 [*March* 1882].

My dear William,

The " cemetery " is nothing alarming, but (I gather) has to do with a story Gabriel has in hand. He rallied perfectly marvellously under Mr. Watts's influence, bursting once or twice into a scrap of comic song !! and Dr. Harris thought he observed a degree of improvement yesterday. Mr. Watts left us this morning. Mamma's dear love to you and yours.

To William Rossetti.

WESTCLIFF BUNGALOW, BIRCHINGTON-ON-SEA, KENT.

5 *April* 1882.

My dear William,

At last it seems Dr. Harris has formed a more complete opinion of the case,—but it is a *very* serious opinion. The brain is affected in such a way as (from what he says) I understand to be that which is commonly called " softening." But more than this, disease of the kidneys exists ; and, though he gives it no name, he indicates that it is of a fatal (though by no means necessarily of a rapidly fatal) kind. I do not know that so much as a suspicion of this latter disease was entertained even so lately as last Sunday when you were here : but Mrs. Abrey called Dr. Harris's attention to something which now leads him to this sad conclusion. He still tells us that we must not accept as true all Gabriel's views of his own state, though he warmly admits that to the patient himself they are perfectly true ; and he perceives how unmanageable our patient is as to following medical orders : but on all this he may be said to lay no stress while dwelling upon the essential gravity of the case. I fear I shall have greatly shocked you by these details, but obviously I must not keep them back from you. Poor Gabriel this morning was talking affectionately of how affectionate you are and of your good looks, and asked if we had had news of Lucy and Mr. Brown. I hear something of a plan for his taking a drive this afternoon, but it is already past three o'clock and I know not whether it will be managed. If he wished to return home, Dr. Harris says he might do so, nor need Chelsea air be any worse for him than this,—but I do not know that he entertains any such wish. Last night I sat up with him till about one o'clock, talking a little and reading a good deal. In spite of all, Dr. Harris remarks on the acute mind of poor dear Gabriel when he chooses to exert it ; and I am glad to find that he does know something of who he is.

So I write from a saddened house, but I hope I write to a cheerful one. Mamma outstrips me in love to you and yours.

From MADOX BROWN.

CALAIS COTTAGE, CRUMPSALL, MANCHESTER.

30 April 1882.

My dear Christina,

I can scarce thank you sufficiently for thinking of us, and writing to me at a moment when your thoughts must have been so fully taken up, and lassitude might well be supposed to follow on the terrible strain put on you during these last weeks. I was almost about to say discouragement in the stead of lassitude, but the word should have no place in connection with such an ending of such a career. The pain of parting is none the less, I know, but it seems a duty not to repine at a death so like that of a soldier dying for his country; for there is no doubt poor dear Gabriel's life has been consumed the more rapidly owing to the continual outpouring of that poetry in song and picture which he seems to have been sent into the world to produce.

Hoping to see more of you and your dear Mother when our long exile here is over and we may be once again settled in London, &c. . . .

From LADY MOUNT-TEMPLE.

[The *Blessed Damozel* here mentioned was not either of the two oil-paintings, but a study of the head and shoulders of the Damozel, on a gold ground. The Beatrice is the *Beata Beatrix*, which Lady Mount-Temple ultimately presented to the National British Gallery.]

15 GREAT STANHOPE STREET, W.

13 *May* 1882.

DEAR MISS ROSSETTI,

For the love we bore your brother, you will not, I trust, think it intrusive of me to write to you. We have been thinking so much of you—and of your Mother, and of your deep sorrow—and of the blank that the loss of his loving glowing presence must make in your existence. We, who were only on the edge of his life, feel so much gone from us with him. Cheyne House was to me a gate of heaven, and his rich cordial greeting made it glow with heart as well as genius.

How much we owe him!—His *Beatrice* and *Blessed Damozel* daily enrich our lives, and his *being* must always *possess* us; and we may live more than ever in his radiance now that he has passed through all earthly clouds.

If Mrs. Rossetti and you ever feel able to let me come and see you, it would be a great boon to me: but I know how much you love and need seclusion—so do not trouble yourselves about me. I shall always love you—at a distance—for his sake, and for all that you are to us yourself in the books we prize so much.

In deep sympathy &c. . . .

To LUCY ROSSETTI.

30 TORRINGTON SQUARE, LONDON, W.C.

17 *July* [1882].

MY DEAR LUCY,

It would be treating you as a stranger and not as one of ourselves to explain Mamma's answering your welcome letter by proxy. She thanks you for her pleasure in receiving it . . .

You were talking about books the other day,—have you read Wilkie Collins's *Moonstone?* It was the last I read to poor dear Gabriel, and it interested us.

To WILLIAM ROSSETTI, *Southend.*

[I had gone to Southend to rally from an attack of gout.—The poem addressed by Mr. Swinburne to my twin children can only at this time (I think) have been in MS.: it was published later on. His volume issued in 1882 was the noble poem *Tristram of Lyonesse*. It contains a prose dedication to Mr. Watts-Dunton, and a verse-dedication to the same friend, beginning "Spring speaks again and all our woods are stirred." The letter which accompanied Mr. Swinburne's gift to Christina is not now forthcoming.—My "review of Longfellow" was in *The Athenæum*: it was not, I think, depreciatory, but it indicated an estimate of his poetry which would not have satisfied his more thorough-going admirers.—Mr. William Tirebuck appears to have been the very first person in the field with a volume, a small one, relating to Dante Rossetti.—The reference to "not murdering Egyptians" arises from my having said, in a letter to my mother, that my income-tax had been or would be increased "for the valued privilege of murdering Egyptians."—Mr. Craik was a partner in the Macmillan firm, the publishers of Mr. Sharp's book on Dante Rossetti.]

30 TORRINGTON SQUARE, LONDON, W.C.

26 July 1882.

MY DEAR WILLIAM,

Before I say how delighted Mamma was with your letter yesterday, I will beg you to convey her thanks to Lucy for her previous one which was the first to tell us the good news of your being better. . . . You may think how (if possible) our Mother is now more than ever anxious that no imprudence should detract from the well-being of her " Willie wee,"—now that her 4 have dwindled to 2. Everything you narrate or can narrate of your funny little five cheers and interests her warm grandmotherly heart. I wish little Mary may inherit inward virtues even more than outward beauty from our fine-natured and fine-personed Grandmother; of whom, by the by, *I* sometimes reminded Mamma in my early days. . . .

Do you remember how *our* Maria was impressed by the impartiality of your *Lives of Poets*? Now I am so too, as well as by the admirable lucidity of your style. The facts would be interesting under any treatment, but you help instead of hindering readers. Those were interesting notes about Trelawny you lately contributed to the *Athenæum*, and naturally *I* clap hands at your review of Longfellow!

Please give Lucy our 2 loves, and (if you can get through them) our ten kisses to Olive, Arthur, Helen, Mary, Michael. What a prostrate poem does Mr. Swinburne address to the twins! He has kindly presented me with his volume, a valued gift; and I cannot forbear lending you—more especially lending Lucy—the letter which accompanied the book. How much I like the Dedications both prose and verse. This is the fourth book he has sent me, and I not one hitherto to him,—so for lack of aught else I am actually offering him a *Called to be Saints*, merely however drawing his attention to the verses.

Mr. Sharp has paid us two visits, one this afternoon, all about his book. Through Aunt Charlotte he has had access to the "Girlhood" picture, and soon he hopes to see what Miss Heaton has at Leeds. I called his attention to the window and pulpit at Scarborough, of which apparently he had never even heard. He tells us that Mr. Tirebuck is sub-editor of a Yorkshire paper, I forget the name : some of the Memoir of Gabriel I really admire, so I have far from ended in mere laughter at the style. O dear! how willingly would I *incur* Income Tax for the sake of *not* murdering Egyptians or any one else : and our Mother would, I am sure, double or triple hers with the same object. . . .

I was forgetting to tell you that Mamma has lent Mr. Sharp her cherished *Main's Sonnet book*, giving him leave to have the *Sonnet* drawing engraved for his book. Mr. Craik considered that the original could far more advantageously be worked from than could Mr. Sharp's photograph of the same.

To WILLIAM ROSSETTI.

[The Sonnet by Mr. Swinburne on Rossetti, named *A Death on Easter-day*, and published afterwards in his *Century of Roundels*, was as follows :—

"The strong spring sun rejoicingly may rise,
    Rise and make revel, as of old men said,
    Like dancing hearts of lovers newly wed :
A light more bright than ever bathed the skies
Departs for all time out of all men's eyes.
    The crowns that girt last night a living head
    Shine only now, though deathless, on the dead :
Art that mocks death, and song that never dies.

Albeit the bright sweet mothlikè wings be furled,
Hope sees, past all division and defection,
And higher than swims the mist of human breath,
The soul most radiant once in all the world
Requickened to regenerate resurrection
Out of the likeness of the shadow of death."]

30 TORRINGTON SQUARE, LONDON, W.C.

28 *July* 1882.

MY DEAR WILLIAM,

. . . Mr. Swinburne has acknowledged with consummate graciousness *Called to be Saints*, and gives me great pleasure by liking the verses for St. Barnabas, Holy Innocents, SS. Philip and James. I do not think he is at all offended by my offering him the book. And thus he answers something I said about his sonnet for our dear Gabriel: "But I must tell you how very truly glad I am that you should care for my Memorial Sonnet. I wish it were worthier of the subject; but it has at least the one merit of heartfelt (and I venture to hope evident) sincerity."

To LUCY ROSSETTI, *Manchester.*

[I was now preparing for the publication of a book (which did not get actually published until 1895) of Dante Rossetti's Family-letters; and Christina had undertaken to copy out such letters as had been addressed to our mother.—Mr. Dodgson was the "Lewis Carroll" of *Alice in Wonderland*. He was an expert photographer.]

30 TORRINGTON SQUARE, LONDON, W.C.

[*Autumn* 1882.]

MY DEAR LUCY,

We cannot hear from William of your Father's being ill, without my writing to express my Mother's and my own affectionate sympathy . . . I am working away at copying Mamma's contingent of Gabriel's letters—such good old letters some of them, so loving— and some so funny. It is a sad task, though one I like to perform. Mr. Dodgson has not sent me those photographs from Gabriel's drawings I was hoping to receive: but perhaps they may appear yet.

He recollected to send me up a promised ghost-story, and I hope does not doubt which prospect I care most for.

We have been reading Mr. Caine's memoir. Considering the circumstances under which his experiences occurred, I think it may fairly be pronounced neither unkind nor unfriendly; but I hope some day to see the same and a wider field traversed by some friend of older standing and consequently of far warmer affection towards his hero; who, whatever he was or was not, was lovable.

To WILLIAM ROSSETTI.

30 TORRINGTON SQUARE, LONDON, W.C.

[7 *December* 1882.]

MY DEAR WILLIAM,

. . . Our loves to Lucy and to the youngsters. We hope little Mary holds her own, and smaller Michael has regained lost ground. But this cold may try twins, odd babies, and every grade of elder.

I have had a narrow escape of seeing my birthday memorialized in the *Athenæum* by a sonnet from Mr. Sharp. He tells me he can explain the reason of its non-appearance; but in my secret soul I suspect that reason of being the cogent one that it is not a good sonnet. Great however is its good-will, and I feel friendly in proportion.

I heard from Mr. Cayley (this morning) that he has returned with a "sore foot" from Cambridge : gout, I fear; but he does not call it so. However, he seems hopeful of soon getting out again. I hope he will not emerge rashly and prematurely. . . .

From LADY MOUNT-TEMPLE.

[The reference here to Burlington House has to do with the exhibition in that building, the galleries of the Royal Academy, of a large collection of works by Dante Rossetti.—Christina felt very much drawn to Lady Mount-Temple, whom, however, she only saw once or twice. Circumstances did not make it manageable for either herself or our mother to respond to the invitation to go to Broadlands.]

BABBACOMBECLIFF, TORQUAY.

31 *January* [1883].

MY DEAR MISS ROSSETTI,

I often think of you and your grave beautiful mother, as I saw you that evening.

I have gone through much since, of anguish and joy—for my husband has been very ill—and is (D.G.) restored. I hope you both are not suffering much from this very wet season. The only light in London seems, from all I hear, to ray out in Burlington House.

I hope you are satisfied and cheered by the enthusiasm kindled by his unique genius. Of course I have not been there yet. Next month I hope to be among those glories.

Mrs. Sumner is just come to Torquay. She looked in on us this morning, and she was radiant from them—having been there yesterday; and yet sad too, for she felt them all too sacred for ordinary eyes, and shrank for his sake from the publicity, till she remembered that he would not mind it now.

Another friend, fresh from Italy, told us the other day not even the masterpieces of the old world had affected her so solemnly and tenderly, and we rejoiced together in the thought of the triune angels,—the mighty Michael, the beautiful Raphael, and our Messenger of promise. While I write about the impressions made on my friends, I look at a letter written to me by Mrs. Russell Gurney, and I cannot resist sending it to you. It pleased me so much. Do not take the trouble of returning it.

We stay here, all being well, for another fortnight, and then, after a few days in town, return to Broadlands. We shall be there I hope till Easter, and, if you and your mother could come and spend a few quiet Lent days with us, how glad we should be.

Wishing you both (rather late in the day) the blessing of peace and heavenly comfort this year and ever, &c. . . .

To CHARLES CAYLEY.

[I have not any clear knowledge as to the year when this letter was written, but surmise 1883 as not unlikely. It is apparent that Cayley had been writing to Christina, expressing the opinion that he probably

might not live long (in fact he died in December 1883), and offering
to make Christina his literary executrix : this proposal he carried out.
Her statement that, at an earlier date in their intercourse, she
"deserved severity at her own hands," appears to me to imply that
her demeanor to Cayley had tended to encourage him to make her
a proposal of marriage which, when made, she saw fit to decline.
Her rather overstrained feeling of obligation to me, resulting in
a bequest of £2000, was in the fullest sense her own affair, not
mine.   Ultimately she left me her universal legatee, but did not fail
to insert in her will the separate bequest here named.   Her observation that Cayley could probably trace a "train of thought"
guiding her statements means, I take it, that, if she should have
anything further to bequeath, beyond the £2000, a substantial
proportion, if not the whole, would go to Cayley himself.—"My
Dante article" must have been either a paper called *Dante an English
Classic*, relating chiefly to Cayley's translation of the *Commedia*,
or else (less probably) one entitled *Dante illustrated out of his own
Poem :* both of these were published in some magazine or other.—
This letter must have been found by me among Christina's papers
after her death.   It came back into her own hands as shown in
the letter of 7 December 1883 from Miss Sophie Cayley.]

30 TORRINGTON SQUARE, W.C.

26 *February* [? 1883].

MY DEAR OLD FRIEND,

I will not dwell too much on the sad possibility you hint
to me, but rather will put forward—as I sincerely can—the apparently at least equal probability that I may become the leader and
not the follower along that path.   Nor will I care what are the steps
so long as the goal is good.   Nor will I despair of the good goal for
either of us.   Meanwhile I hope you have shaken off the neuralgia,
of which I also well know the pain, and that many happy hours with
the Leifchilds and other valued intimates remain in store for you.

But, all else assumed as inevitable, I should value though I should
not need a memorial.   And three of the translations would be very
dear : watching over them, I might in a measure nurse your name
and fame.   Yet, if you think any of your family could feel hurt, do
not do it : very likely there was a moment when—and no wonder—
those who loved you best thought very severely of me, and indeed

I deserved severity at my own hands,—I never seemed to get much at yours. And some trifle that you had been fond of and perhaps had used would be precious to me.

Now let us suppose the reverse position, and let me explain my own plans. If my dearest Mother outlives me, everything I have (a mere trifle in all) goes to her: perhaps you may recollect my telling you that even now I am not so much as independent, so little indeed have I. Beyond this immediate vista,—William made me a home for so many years that (especially now that he has a young family) I am inclined to rate the money-portion of my debt to him at (say) £100 a year for 20 years: here at once is £2000! and far enough am I from possessing such a sum. Not that William puts forward any such view, but *I* entertain it all by myself. So, to sum up, you see I am an indefinite distance off from having much at my pure disposal. If I live long enough, that is if I survive certain members of my family, I believe I shall be amply provided for: but this is no contingency to count upon. I dare say you will trace, though I certainly have not stated, what sort of train of thought set me upon saying all this.

I hope you will enjoy the Ashburnham MSS. If I had a little more energy I might seek to enjoy them too, but that seems too enterprising a possibility. My Dante article proceeds at the pace of a lag-last snail; perhaps it will reach the printing-office some day. A thousand thanks for the permission I craved.

From ALGERNON SWINBURNE.

[This letter accompanied two copies of Swinburne's volume, *A Century of Roundels.* The dedication, itself a roundel, is to Christina.]

THE PINES, PUTNEY HILL, S.W.

7 June 1883.

DEAR MISS ROSSETTI,

Here is the little book to which you have been so kind. As in duty bound, I send you the first copy I receive of it—or rather the two first copies, as two have been sent together, and I hope your mother will do me the favour to accept one of them for the sake of the dedication.

If the references to Dante and Farinata à propos of caverns in Guernsey seem strange or far-fetched to you, I wish you—as a poetess, and his country-woman—would go and see that wonderful sight for yourself, which I have so faintly tried to indicate. It is amazing to me that so few English folk will trouble themselves to make so short a run to see within their own territory landscapes and prospects to which I really know no parallel—not even in the Highlands, the Apennines, or the Pyrenees—for splendour and variety of sublimity and beauty. Nowhere else, that I ever saw or heard of, is there such a sea for background to such shores—or such land for background to such seas—as in Sark and Guernsey. Watts said of the latter, when we were roaming over it last year—" I did not think there was such an island as this in the world ! " It has literally every kind of loveliness and grandeur packed into it—you step as it were out of the Hebrides into Tuscany in a few miles' walk—or you pass from the valleys of the Spey or the ravine of the Findhorn straight into Valdarno or Valdelsa. And, if you don't believe me on trust, all I can say is, do go and see, and give these almost unknown beauties a word of song—as I have tried to do.

To WILLIAM ROSSETTI, *Hythe.*

[This letter relates to the project that Christina should write, for the *Eminent Women* series, a memoir of Mrs. Radcliffe, the authoress of *The Mysteries of Udolpho*, &c. She was more than willing to do it ; but, after Mr. John Cordy Jeaffreson and other sources of information had been consulted, she judged that the facts known would not fill out a volume, and she abandoned the attempt.—Her allusion to her " girth " indicates that she was at this time not a little fat. So she was often, but not always, in her closing years.]

30 TORRINGTON SQUARE, LONDON, W.C.

29 June 1883.

MY DEAR WILLIAM,

Thankyou both for the letter I return and for the other you forwarded. Mr. Jeaffreson is not encouraging : I am belabouring poor Ingram, and between us all nothing whatsoever have I done. I *Radcliffized* the other day at the Museum, and perceive that the best resource is Talfourd after all, unless it be a *quotation* made by Walter Scott. I doubt if the Memoir is feasible. . . .

To-day is perfect summer here, and I hope is so at Hythe also. May you all thrive, and especially may Lucy hit the happy mean between her actual girth and *mine ! ! !* But I recommend her to stay as she is, rather than the full alternative.

I met Mr. Caine the other day at the Museum, looking all the better for country-quarters. He seems busy, so I hope he gets on.

You may think I have not much news for you when this is a sample.

To WILLIAM ROSSETTI.

CHURCH HILL, BIRCHINGTON-ON-SEA.

16 *July* 1883.

MY DEAR WILLIAM,

I have got so foggy as to your movements that I send this to Endsleigh Gns. Mamma, with all love to you, was very glad to get a letter from you; and now she is wishing to bring matters to some practical issue as concerns the dear grave. If the stone and also 2 windows are contemplated, her preference would be to undertake *the whole* of one window, selecting that one which looks most directly upon the grave, and giving the commission from herself to Mr. Shields. She would like to settle this matter while we are here, and so are at hand to consult with Mr. Alcock. Will you, please, as soon as you conveniently can, let her know that her acting as she proposes will not clash with any scheme of yours, and then without further delay we can open business with Mr. Shields. The more details you can give us the better as to design of gravestone &c.

Going to call on Mrs. Seddon this afternoon, I passed by the old familiar Bungalow and stood gazing into its garden. Dr. and Mrs. Harris have called on us; and Mrs. Seddon reports that Dr. Harris much likes our Mother; and she seems also aware of her being liked more at large, in which impression I confirmed her. I, like you, wish *these doorsteps* could be got rid of,—but, all deductions made from an ideal standard, we yet find ourselves comfortably housed. Mr. Alcock has called on us with his agreeable wife, but not as yet Mr. Martin, whom I should like to shake hands with again.

I send you an article on Gabriel sent me from America. Also a photo. of *Rossetti Bungalow* which pray accept if you have not one already. The Church too has been photographed from a viewpoint which would show the grave but for the outer wall of the church-yard; *this* stands too high to admit of the little mound being seen, though the porch is visible. . . .

From WILLIAM ROSSETTI.

[This letter shows what, in the summer of 1883, was proposed with regard to some memorial to Dante Rossetti at Birchington. The upshot was that Madox Brown designed the tombstone, an Irish cross, for which Christina and I jointly paid; and that Mr. Shields designed the two stained-glass lights of one window, for which our mother paid. Nothing was done beyond this.]

2 SALTWOOD GARDENS, HYTHE.

18 *July* 1883.

DEAR CHRISTINA,

When I was at Birchington I talked a goodish deal to Seddon about the gravestone and windows. The idea then was that I would undertake the whole affair of the gravestone; and that Seddon, along with Shields and other admirers of Gabriel, would raise funds for filling with stained glass the 2 windows of 2 lights each (whole or part thereof) which come near the grave. Shields would undertake to make the design for one light; Brown and Jones would be invited to undertake two others; for the 4th I heard nothing particular suggested. You were to be consulted as to the subjects for all 4 lights. Seddon, as I gathered, would provide for the actual supply of glass &c.

As to the gravestone my idea had from the first been to ask Brown to furnish a design generally resembling (but not identical with) the stone over Nolly's grave. Some uncertainties (not worth detail-ing) have arisen about this. I shall now however get the point settled. If B. should not fall in with my views, I shall ask Seddon to see about making and carrying out a design—which would probably be of a simple but solid and very decorous kind. The B.

project might I fancy cost from £30 to £45 : the S. project from £70 to £100.

You will perceive that the outline of this scheme is that the gravestone should be entirely the affair of myself (or of myself and family, as might be arranged *inter nos*); while the windows would be entirely the affair of admirers of G's genius (personal friends of course included) who would subscribe the needed funds.

Mamma's idea of commissioning one window (or perhaps one light in a window is rather meant) would mar the symmetry of this scheme : but I don't see that that is of the slightest consequence if Mamma prefers this course to any other. It seems however that she should explain to Seddon what she intends, especially as it affects Shields, with whom Seddon himself would otherwise be concerting his plans. . . .

Ellis has sent me £97. 4. as the royalty on G's books (chiefly the *Poems* vol.) for last 6 mos.—Very large this amount, I think.

To WILLIAM ROSSETTI, *Hythe.*

CHURCH HILL, BIRCHINGTON-ON-SEA.

19 *July* 1883.

MY DEAR WILLIAM,

. . . Amongst your all-welcome letters *this* is a very welcome one. Please read first and post afterwards the enclosed to Mr. Shields, which we hope will meet with your sympathetic approval. If our Mother is so fortunate as thus to secure her wish, *I* hope to concur (in a modest degree suited to my resources) in the stone. One window will remain for remoter friends and admirers, and I hope the result of triple effort will be beautiful.

We have been making acquaintance with Mrs. John Seddon and like her very much . . . I have made an ivy-wreath, and we are carrying it to the grave this morning . . .

To WILLIAM ROSSETTI, *Hythe.*

[The term "your *Italian*" means the romance by Mrs. Radcliffe entitled *The Italian*, of which I possess a copy.]

9

CHURCH HILL, BIRCHINGTON-ON-SEA.

23 *July* 1883.

MY DEAR WILLIAM,

Very welcome was your card to Mamma whom it assured of your harmonious accord with her plan. Her love to you. On Saturday Mr. Seddon called with his pretty elder daughter—the younger is beautiful perhaps rather than pretty—and we then talked about all the plans; and he fell in with Mamma's views, and will himself treat with Mr. Shields on that basis. He told us what his own plan for the stone is, and this greatly attracts Mamma: I too admire it, and shall like to concur in a small way: I think I can promise myself to find £10 for the purpose, but fear that will be my humble limit. . . .

A meagre contingent of "Radcliffe" material has reached me through the obliging trouble-taking of a Mr. Sketchley of the South Kensington department—that cannot be right: "Science and Art" perhaps. So my *Athenæum* letter has produced one useful response, besides one or two useless ones: but, all told, I doubt if bulk will anyhow suffice. At present Mr. Ingram and I alike are observing a dignified silence. Of course your *Italian* is safe at your house where I left it. . . .

Of course, whichever design is adopted by you for the gravestone, I hope equally to concur.—That is, as you say, a good "royalty" from Ellis.

To WILLIAM ROSSETTI, *London.*

[Mrs. O'Shaughnessy was the mother of the poet Arthur O'Shaughnessy, who died in 1881. Mr. Deacon was related to him—I think a cousin.—The *Memoir of Emily Brontë* was the work of Miss Robinson (Madame Duclaux) in the *Eminent Women* series.]

CHURCH HILL, BIRCHINGTON-ON-SEA.

30 *July* 1883.

MY DEAR WILLIAM,

. . . Mamma sends you invariable love. She wishes me to express to you her great desire that the monument to Gabriel may include a cross: we do not know what the erection to Nolly is like.

Would it be possible—and would it not, her wish taken into account, be preferable—to substitute for the Nolly design a reproduction of Mr. Brown's beautiful memorial of his first wife? *this* would conciliate both you and our Mother, equally doing honour to Mr. Brown's tried and faithful friendship for Gabriel and near connexion with all of us. If such a plan were hampered by being more costly than the other, I would do my (*very*) little best by contributing £15 instead of £10,—I think I can engage for so much. . . .

A Mr. and Mrs. Deacon made themselves known to me one morning, and yesterday a maternal Mrs. Deacon with Mrs. O'Shaughnessy declared themselves. Mr. Deacon is a clergyman at Milton (?), Oxfordsh. . . .

Saturday was so cold part of the day that we had a fire. Yesterday (Sunday) was sunny summer. To-day warmth continues in moderation. Except perhaps mountain-air, I don't know that I ever was in what seemed to me air more salubrious than this. But we have a great deal of cold weather.

I suspect my *Athenæum* manifesto has borne its last meagre fruit, for no Radcliffeana more come to hand. If this *be* all, I foresee collapse. I am reading with interest the Memoir of Emily Brontë : but does it strike you as being in the main a memoir of *Emily?*

To WILLIAM ROSSETTI.

[The lectures by Ruskin, here referred to, contained some matter derogatory to Dante Rossetti's work as a painter : see Christina's further letter of 15 August.]

CHURCH HILL, BIRCHINGTON-ON-SEA.

6 August 1883.

MY DEAR WILLIAM,

. . . Our dearest Mother sends you her evergreen love. On no account will she supersede you as to the monument design, though you have her maternal thanks for acceding to her wish for a cross,— be the cross Irish or any other, so long as a cross it is, she will rest contented. Mamma and I quite feel for you as to the disagreeable of modifying Mr. Brown's drawing so late in the day. Would it be out of the question to introduce a cross simply in bas relief on the headstone as it stands? in addition to the foliage you speak of, I mean, or perhaps in substitution for some detail of it. But pray believe that in venturing such an ignorant suggestion I am only trying to make matters easy, pleasant, manageable; I am not attempting to meddle where you have and I have not rights. Whatever monument is erected, I hope you will not reject £10 or £15 as my contribution towards honouring our dear brother's memory.

The Shieldses came down last week, and Mr. S. we see daily: he and wife appear better already, but it was gravely desirable for both that they *should* get better. To-day he was in church with Mr. Seddon, going into our business practically. He seems very wishful to select a felicitous subject for the window, but not yet to have lighted upon one—or rather upon *two*, one for each light—quite to his own satisfaction: so as yet I cannot announce all that impends. I put fresh roses on the grave this morning. . . .

Have you seen the 2 Art Lectures lately given by Ruskin at Oxford? Mrs. Seddon has lent them us. Mamma is reading them, and I mean to do so, but already I know enough of their contents to feel not a little wonder and dislike. . . .

From WILLIAM ROSSETTI.

5 ENDSLEIGH GARDENS, N.W.

10 *August* 1883.

DEAREST MAMMA AND CHRISTINA,

This letter is intended more particularly for Mamma's attention, but for convenience sake I shall proceed as if I were simply addressing Christina.

It appears to me that it is not yet quite clear to you that I should WISH Mamma to undertake the work of giving orders for a cross. In deference to her feelings I assent—and *cheerfully* assent—to the idea of introducing a cross into the monument, in whatever form may be agreed upon between Mamma and Brown: but, as my own personal opinion does not go with the cross as the most appropriate device, I entertain a very decided feeling of reluctance to giving the order for it myself; this I should wish Mamma to do (presumably through you), and the entire direction of the monument would then remain with Mamma—my only part in it being the payment of the cost. Please to refer back to my former letter, as to the condition of consulting Brown.

Possibly what I previously said about B. and an Irish cross was a little misapprehended. The fact then is that I did not in any way commission B. to produce a design with a cross: I simply told him that Mamma wants a cross, and that his cross-less design had better therefore be suspended pending a decision—and he replied that a design consisting of an Irish cross might perhaps answer. . . .

I hardly remember whether I did see or not the 2 Art-lectures by Ruskin to which you refer: I think I did at Seddon's glance at a sentence or two of them. I forget details. Dare say there is something more or less unhandsome about Gabriel: R. seems now to be *very* scattered and uncertain, though of course he pretty often hits nails on their heads. . . .

See *Athenæum* of 4 Aug. showing that some of Gabriel's works, bought at the Christie sale, are now in S. Kensington Museum: I rather hope to get round to-morrow and see them. Also something about a musical setting of your " Passing away "—your chef d'œuvre, and the finest sacred poem (me judice) in the language. It is susceptible of an astonishing range and stress of musical expression supposing only the musician to have this at command.

To William Rossetti.

CHURCH HILL, BIRCHINGTON-ON-SEA.

11 *August* 1883.

My dear William,

Thankyou affectionately for the dear . . . letter of this morning. As yours was virtually and primarily to our Mother, so this is to all intents and purposes from her.

There is one superb virtue in which she and you alike shine and in which—at least by comparison—I fear I only glimmer,—justice. She, with unvarying love to you, will not hear of any arrangement which either in fact or appearance displaces you from your proper and dominant position as controller of the monument. She therefore absolutely withdraws her late suggestion; and, enshrining her own pious hope in her own window, awaits the monument under such an aspect as you assign to it. *Therefore* do not ask either of us to write to F. M. B., for direct from you and from you only will he receive instructions. . . . She wrote to you yesterday, and doubtless you already have her letter. And I add, as knowing it positively, that her secession from the monument-question is according to her own absolute and deliberate wish, and creates neither sore nor chill in that glowing maternal heart. . . .

The Shieldses have fairly been hunted out of Birchington by *noise :* we have not, as yet, their address at Margate, but there I hope they are housed in comparative silence. *Here* they were in really distressingly noisy quarters. . . .

Thankyou for telling me what greatly pleases me, that you so much like "Passing away," which also I rate high among the works of that author !

Mamma thinks of our remaining here 7 or 8 weeks in all, unless Aunt Charlotte's coming home (of which there is a prospect) should be so timed as to tempt us back to London a little earlier. The longest period contemplated terminates on Sept. 6. This change and fine air have revived us both ; so there is no reason of health for hastening our return, but rather the contrary.

To WILLIAM ROSSETTI.

[The "accident on the doorstep" had occurred to our mother there were several steps from the street, and at that time no handrail. —The mention of Alma-Tadema in connection with a lecture by Ruskin is an error : the name should be G. F. Watts. It was rather perverse of Ruskin to animadvert upon Dante Rossetti for living "in a garret at Blackfriars." As a youthful painter having his way to make in the profession, he naturally lived in London ; his chambers were not in any sense a garret, but a commodious and rather spacious range of second-floor rooms ; and Ruskin himself used to congratulate him upon having a river-view comparable to most things in Venice.—The *Salterio* was one of our father's principal poems; the MS. about Rome, an account of Roman antiquities drawn up at some length by him when he was in Rome in 1813 during some political complications. I gave this MS. to the Municipality of Vasto, my father's natal city, in connection with a centenary celebration of his birth held there in the spring of 1883. I did not get it translated, and it would not have had any chance with any English magazine.—Giuseppe Marchesani was a relative of our father, of a younger generation: we knew nothing of him until he emerged in connection with the Vastese celebration, after which I corresponded with him not infrequently, and had every reason to regard him with esteem. Filippo Pistrucci produced more than one water-colour head of our father. Christina, as a later letter shows, did not send the "fright" to Marchesani; it is, I believe, a head which I still possess, and which I have had framed along with another portrait, a water-colour by J. W. Wright. Pistrucci's is the better of the two, and does not deserve the epithet "fright."]

CHURCH HILL, BIRCHINGTON-ON-SEA.

15 *August* 1883.

My dear William,

Our Mother sends you her love and regards your letter with mingled admiration and affection. I am glad to trust that no permanent damage results from what might have proved the very serious accident on the doorstep: a degree of bruise remains, but that is the least indeed we could have expected. My only wish now is that we had at once seen about a handrail,—better late than never. Her health is on the whole satisfactory, though naturally subject to *83* drawbacks. This beautiful air and quiet change, in combination with the heart's-ease of being near Gabriel's grave, seem to have revived her. She walks about very well, though certainly the indented cliff-edge is not within her radius. Neither, I foresee, will your sluggish sister foot it. Yesterday we enjoyed a drive through Westgate into Margate. Mr. Shields's move in search of quiet reminds one of Dante's impulse towards a "rovente vetro" for coolness! We have not seen or heard of him since, so can only hope that he feels soothed. It is however quite obvious that his Birchington lodgings must have been distressingly unquiet, thanks to various provable sources of noise. We much wish he could and would so far sit aloof from disturbance as to be able to put pencil to paper in Mamma's service; but perhaps at this moment he is hard at work, so I need not wax ill-natured.

The Ruskin Lectures are no longer here, so to my regret I cannot refer to them for the exact title. I think they were named in some such way as this: "Art Lectures: 1. Dante Rossetti and Holman Hunt; 2. Burne Jones and Alma Tadema." Each lecture formed one pamphlet. The copy Mrs. Seddon lent us was not her own but was lent by some friend. Though the 1st alone professes to treat of Gabriel, the wind-up of the second re-introduces his name in a more agreeable manner than most or perhaps than any of the preceding portions. Part is really irritatingly depreciatory, but I can well imagine that the lecturer is not now altogether his pristine self. From internal evidence it suggests itself that Holman Hunt and Burne Jones are certain to possess copies of utterances so gratifying to each. But, if for any reason you do not feel disposed to slake your curiosity at either source and have none better at hand, I will (if you please) try whether I could borrow for you . . . The most irritating sentence perhaps of all is one in which Ruskin speaks of Gabriel's having cut himself off from the possibility of studying outdoor nature by living in a "garret" at Blackfriars; but even this utterance should not, I admit, perturb Christian patience! He also particularizes "Chinese puzzle" details, and foliage (?) like the contents of a Noah's Ark. Yet the opening of Lecture 1. and the close of Lecture 2. are affectionate and admiring. . . .

The old original edition of the *Salterio* is exhausted. But of the later edition, if I am not mistaken, you will find several copies in one or other of the boxes or paper-parcels which (at least used to) inhabit the same garret as the box of correspondence. At the worst, however, doubtless one can be found in our quarters in case of need: I feel certain that some do exist. What a dear old M.S. you have unearthed about Rome! Mamma surmises that it was probably a ministerial production while Papa headed "Public Instruction" under Murat. Would it be worth while translating it into English (before it vanishes to Vasto) and trying its fortune somewhere as a magazine-article?—this occurred, this question of the translation, to Mamma.

She and I may perhaps make our way to South Kensington to see the beautiful drawings.

As to Marchesani, Mamma does not feel inclined to enrich him with her photograph, and I (chronically) do not possess mine. Yet I like his letter, poor man, and wish him well. I wonder if he would greatly value a fright by Pistrucci of our Father: *possibly* I might bestow it in such a case upon him, but I do not promise. . . .

Yesterday we drove to Margate, and found it superior to at least *my* expectations. Westgate, on the way, rather pleased me, but did not attract Mamma.

The enclosed represents, and does in some sort misrepresent, "love in a mist," a white blossom with green centre and green thready widespreading calyx (?), an annual which I do not recollect ever to have seen elsewhere. Do you know it? it charms us both. My powers do not suffice to exhibit the free in-all-directions growth of the calyx "mist," which instead of lying down like a frill often rather envelopes the blossom like a cloud. . . .

I see I have TWICE told you we went to Margate—pardon!

To LUCY ROSSETTI, *Hythe.*

["Cathy" (Mrs. Francis Hueffer, half-sister of my wife) had some musical training, and it would appear that she was endeavouring—but with no eventual success—to impart some of it to our daughter Olivia.]

BIRCHINGTON-ON-SEA.

22 August 1883.

MY DEAR LUCY,

Your long and interesting letter is very welcome to Mamma who thanks you for it with love. .ı. . If ever she hears Olive warble forth a sweet soprano melody, it may do something towards supplying the defects of her own unmusical daughters. So Cathy cultivates graces while you train intellects among your young people: a capital exchange. . . .

I have been seeing more of the Seddon family down here than perhaps I ever saw before; and I incline to like them much, as well as to esteem them. In different styles what beautiful girls both the daughters are . . .

I am not fretting over the Ruskiniana, though at the moment I plead guilty to having felt annoyed. Yet my resumed philosophic calm is not based on a contempt for the writer, as I cannot help admiring

much of his work. I hope it is based on something more permanent
and less discreditable. The Shieldses have vanished from our
ken. . . .

To Lucy Rossetti, *Hythe.*

[Christina's scrupulosity re-appears in this letter. Apart from
mere casual fractiousness in days of quasi-infancy, she had really
never been ill-tempered or exasperating with me, that I can remember, and I had no "tale to unfold." Any "irritability" which she
may have shown while housed along with my wife (summer of 1874
to autumn of 1876) was hardly to be called irritability : it all depended upon differences of view as to matters of religion and the
obligations of life. But Christina was of that self-abnegating temper
which might have said with King David after he had danced before
the ark, to the disgust of Queen Michal—"And I will yet be more
vile than thus, and will be base in mine own sight."]

CHURCH HILL, BIRCHINGTON-ON-SEA.

24 [*August* 1883].

MY DEAR LUCY,

. . . It is such a triumph for ME to attain to philosophic calm
that, even if that subdued temper is applied by me without common
sense, "color che sanno" may still congratulate me on some sort of
improvement ! Ask William, who knew me in my early stormy days :
he could a tale unfold—though indeed I am sorry to recollect how
much you yourself have undergone from my irritability, and how
much there is for you to bury in kind oblivion. I fear you may
detect me in many an inconsistency, yet I assure you that in theory
you do not deem consistency more essential than do I. I did not
discuss Ruskin with the Seddons : it was with Mr. Shields that our
conversation on that subject took place ; and he, generously on fire,
thought me (I fear perhaps) a little tepid.

We have just begun our seventh week here, and entertain no idea
of exceeding eight weeks in all. I wonder whether you or we will be
at home first. . . .

From Miss Sophie Cayley.

[Christina already knew of Charles Cayley's death before this letter
reached her. As suggested in the postscript, I wrote a notice

regarding him for *The Athenæum*, referred to in Christina's letter of 15 December.]

4 SOUTH CRESCENT.

7 December 1883.

DEAR MISS ROSSETTI,

I do not know whether you will have heard—I received a telegram yesterday, at 12, from Dr. Pope in this house, saying I had better come at once to my brother,—there was little hope. I came by the next train; but found, as I had dreaded all the way, it was only a preparation, as people kindly think. They found him dead in his bed, and the Doctor says he must have passed away, hours before, in his sleep. He looks beautifully calm and peaceful, and he is [in] God's all merciful and holy keeping. But it has been a terrible shock. Some time ago we were very uneasy about his health, and tried to get him to come for a little change and nursing; but latterly we thought him better again, especially while my sister was in town. He has left you all his own works that are now at his Publishers', and a large writing-desk, in which is an envelope with a letter of yours to him, and a ring: there is also a large packet of your letters. Would you like them returned? You were I know *the* friend he valued most.

We intend to have him buried near my mother, at Hastings—the day is not quite settled. . . .

Do you think your brother would write a short notice of Charles in any paper he thinks most fitting?

From PROFESSOR CAYLEY.

CAMBRIDGE.

9 December 1883.

DEAR MISS ROSSETTI,

I enclose an extract from my brother's will: I am very sorry that I did not when I was in London take out from the desk the packet addressed to you. The letters are all separated and tied up in parcels: I understood from my sister that you wished them to be destroyed, and I will of course see this done.

And, in the event of my dying before my dear and kind friend Miss Christina Georgiana Rossetti, of 30 Torrington Square, London, I bequeath her the remainder of such books as have been published for me by Messrs. Longmans & Co. and which they are in the habit of selling on commission for me, and all sums actually payable to me on account of such sales, and all books I shall have in warehouses or at the binders of the editions so sold on commission. And the said Christina Rossetti is also to have my best writing-desk, and any packet that may be lying therein addressed to her, and she shall be entitled to reclaim or order to be destroyed any letters of hers which may be found among my papers or effects.

Will dated 3 May 1883.

To FREDERIC J. SHIELDS.

30 TORRINGTON SQUARE, W.C.

11 *December* 1883.

DEAR MR. SHIELDS,

I enclose the inscription as my mother will like it inscribed on the window, if there is room for it in full.

It really is her wish to begin paying the money-part of her debt: the friendly part she accepts and owns as priceless. Shall she send you £50 or £100? Whichever you prefer at this particular moment, she having no choice one way or the other. Anything beyond the £100 you will draw upon her for when you know the entire sum needed. Please let us know which sum she shall send you : a degree of delay will occur in her getting it actually into hand, but no great delay we trust.

We hope you will approve of the inscription: both she and I favour simple prose rather than rhyme; and she wants to express that it is his Mother who erects the memorial, this being sufficiently conveyed by "my dear son."

Pray remember us warmly to your wife, to whom with yourself we wish all blessings of the approaching Christmas Feast; nor will we shut your *stray lamb* out of our good will and good auguries. . . .

Don't fancy *the delay* will be long—perhaps a week or so, but we never quite know ourselves from the nature of the temporary investment.

To WILLIAM ROSSETTI.

[15 *December* 1883.]

MY DEAR WILLIAM,

Please tell Lucy with my love how gratefully I am feeling her sisterly kindness.

Mamma and I are delighting—what a word!—in your article. She thinks it one of the best of the kind, if not *the* best, she ever read. *I* cannot write about it.

You said of old how mistakes beset these records :—the date was the 5–6th.

From FREDERIC SHIELDS.

[In the first instance Mr. Shields intended to use, as the subject of one of the lights in the stained-glass window at Birchington, the design by Dante Rossetti of *The Magdalene at the door of Simon the Pharisee :* hence his allusion to "the Magdalen's dress." The Vicar of Birchington did not wholly like this selection : and another of Rossetti's designs, *The Passover in the Holy Family*, was substituted.]

7 LODGE PLACE, N.W.

16 *December* 1883.

DEAR MISS ROSSETTI,

I have been steadily working at the window since seeing you last—and the ornamental border of the whole, with the monogram and its rose-supports, are now designed. The Magdalen's dress has received its pattern, and all seems now filling up into complete harmony.

Moreover the inscription, which I feared too long when it arrived, has actually found full insertion, and this will please Mrs. Rossetti to know. I have prepared the lead-lines also, and all is in readiness to set the stained-glass people at work, if they would now begin—which they will not till the Christmas holidays are past.

I will not longer put restraint on your dear Mother's good will to send so much as the smaller sum of £50—but it is premature to think of sending more till much further advanced, and I am very anxious to keep the cost within the original estimate.

Opening yesterday's *Athenæum*, I was startled into sudden distress by the obituary notice, from your brother's pen, of Mr. Cayley's unexpected death. His gentleness and harmless absent manners had won my love, as much as his work had my admiration.

Truly does William say—"We shall not look upon his like."

His face was always beautiful to me—one I liked to dwell upon. Here I shall see it no more.

From you, good wishes are prayers and blessings, and we thank you both for them, reciprocating them affectionately for your own happiness at Christmas . . .

To WILLIAM ROSSETTI.

[It would appear, but I do not recollect any details, that I had proposed to Christina that a subscription might be got up for re-issuing some portion of Cayley's writings or translations. This was not actually done.]

30 TORRINGTON SQUARE, W.C.

17 *December* 1883.

MY DEAR WILLIAM,

Having to write, I return Mr. Shields's letter which I like truly. It happens I heard from him this morning about the window, and then he expressed himself to me as sympathetically : the meeting he alludes to I had been told of by my dearest Friend.

As to the books, be sure I shall subscribe if that comes to pass. But at this moment I think you had better wait, for (*not* the copyrights but) the remainders of the translation-editions on sale have been left to me, and I suppose Longmans will communicate with me some day. . . .

You certainly ought to know this now ; as, if you write on the subject of your scheme to Profr. Cayley—evidently, though I have not been actually told so, the executor—all might get into a confusion between you, unless you are aware of this circumstance. Don't think I have been keeping it to myself of unkind purpose,— but all is what it is, and no other aspect is of much moment.

CHARLES BAGOT CAYLEY.

From a Photograph, c. 1866.

To face p. 142.

Thankyou for the offered *Athenæum*, and still more for the aimed-at correction : I am sorry I was the misleader. . . .

A beautiful desk has been left me too, and Arthur Cayley brought it me himself the other evening.

To WILLIAM ROSSETTI.

[" Not an *aquila* " (eagle): this was a wonted expression of our father when he meant to imply that some one was the reverse of sharp-witted.—" Mr. something Ford " must have been Mr. Onslow Ford: I am not aware that his acquaintanceship with Christina proceeded any further.—Mr. John Walker, then quite a young man, has written various works in verse and prose under the name of Roland Thirlmere: he was a strong admirer of Christina's poetry.— Mrs. Isabella Pietrocola-Rossetti was now about to re-marry with Mr. Lionel Cole, a connection of Lord Congleton.—The " ivory of a nestling " was a choice trifle of Japanese art which I (or possibly my brother) had given to Christina years previously.]

6 STATION ROAD, BIRCHINGTON-ON-SEA.

28 *August* 1884.

MY DEAR WILLIAM,

Our Mother sends you her old-established love : as you are *en garçon* we do not salute wife and children. We think we may be very fairly comfortable here, and hope to remain where we are until our return home. Mrs. Gardner, our landlady, seems an obliging well-meaning young woman, although not an *aquila*. No children, and a judicious husband who makes no show: a small farmer and carrier, I am told.

Think of our feelings at the station,—Mamma tired, and no cab ! Happily on the platform was a clergyman, a Mr. Deacon whose acquaintance we made last year down here: he came forward, took us in tow, helped Mamma along, carried our 5 umbrellas and parasols, and, having got us to our lodgings, crowned courtesy by not coming in. Next morning he reappeared, before quitting Birchington the same day: and a little later re-appeared with his wife and 2 nice little baby boys to say how do you do and good-bye. Utilizing the flying moment he (I permitting) introduced to

me a Mr. something Ford, a sculptor, who with his family lodges
I believe next door, or at any rate close by. Do you know aught
of a Mr. anything Ford? Mr. Deacon profoundly believes in his
talent; and I hope it exists, as he has promised me a photo.
from a work of his representing a dirge (?) tributary to the talent
of Englishmen, and I dare say including in intention Gabriel, of
whom he is an outspoken admirer.

We have seen the Cross, very fine in our Mother's eyes and in
mine; and I see that Mr. Alcock, with whom we fell in, perceives
its beauty. This I am glad of. The grave is not covered with
roses or trellis or aught else, but I see with pleasure one of the
original little shrubs (doubtless) standing where it stood. Also that
unaccounted-for cross of artificial white flowers remains lying as t
lay. The afternoon brought me a boxfull of heather from Mr. John
Walker, so this I made up partly in a cross, strewing other spra s
of blossom; and then the whole grave looked cared for and pretty
for the moment.

Full of other subjects when you called, we quite forgot to speak
of Isabella. Amazed we were! If you can, please tell something
about "Lord Congleton," whom I fail to find in an *antiquated*
Peerage where I rummaged. . . . I wrote to her . . . hearty
good wishes to her and hers; and I sent her as a little wedding-
gift a charming ivory of a nestling I had kept these many
years. . . .

We have a pretty sitting-room paper which Mamma pronounces a
" Morris."

To WILLIAM ROSSETTI.

[My daughter Helen, then in her fifth year, had written a letter to
me, found acceptable by my mother in virtue of its *naïveté :* it will
be seen quoted in my Appendix, Diary of Frances Rossetti. Mr.
Bristow was the custodian of the churchyard at Birchington.—Achille
Pietrocola, a maternal relative of my father, and one of our then
Vastese correspondents, had had an idea of publishing some uncul-
tured verses, not destitute of native humour and faculty, by an elder
brother of my father, Antonio Rossetti : he had consulted myself
and some others, and now acquiesced in the opinion that it would be
better to drop the project.]

HERE SLEEPS
GABRIEL CHARLES DANTE ROSSETTI
HONOURED UNDER THE NAME OF
DANTE GABRIEL ROSSETTI
AMONG PAINTERS AS A PAINTER
AND AMONG POETS AS A POET
BORN IN LONDON
OF PARENTAGE MAINLY ITALIAN 12 MAY 1828
DIED AT BIRCHINGTON 9 APRIL 1882

THE GRAVE-CROSS OF DANTE ROSSETTI.

Designed by Ford Madox Brown, 1883.

[*To face p.* 144.

6 STATION ROAD, BIRCHINGTON-ON-SEA.

2 September 1884.

MY DEAR WILLIAM,

Helen's letter is charming,—our Mother does not think so more genuinely than do I : *the kitten* is inimitable. Here it is back again, but not without my first copying it into the maternal diary. Thank you too for Isabella : . . . I quite see that the marriage is under all circumstances a brilliant one.

I propose to call on Mr. Bristow this afternoon and (if I can) put him into direct communication with you, first of all explaining why at the time your orders could not be carried out. It seems that just then the long-continued drought rendered the ground intractable for your purpose. Now that rain has fallen in some quantity and in repeated downcomes perhaps something may be feasible. Supposing the roses and trellis for some reason relinquished, I think *violets* would have this plea, that a golden violet was (was it not ?) a Provençal prize for poetry. Perhaps, though, you would think this arrogant : *I* surmise that no one besides ourselves might scent the allusion. . . .

Achille tells me in so many words that he will suppress Uncle Antonio's poems. I send you his letter, which you need not return hither. . . .

Mamma sends you much love. Her positive wish is that the beloved grave should be completed as *you* think best. How fine the Cross looks : I wrote to Mr. Brown yesterday on purpose to express Mamma's and my own admiration and satisfaction. . . .

I have just received the letter I enclose from Isabella. I like it very much. . . .

To WILLIAM ROSSETTI.

[The observation, " I cannot remember that my portrait ever was engraved," arises out of some question which had been raised as to a portrait in an American edition of Christina's poems. The " little early water-colour " now belongs to my daughter Olivia Agresti in Rome. " The amazing object achieved later," also by Filippo Pistrucci, is in my possession, representing—or rather totally misrepresenting—Christina at some such age as eleven.]

10

6 STATION ROAD, BIRCHINGTON-ON-SEA.

3 *September* 1884.

MY DEAR WILLIAM,

. . . I called on Bristow, who will write straight to yourself. He is quite prepared to do what you require, and seems fully to understand your order : only it appears that not till November can we count upon setting roses. I think the effect, at the blooming season, will be charming indeed if all prospers. Have you mentally selected the sort of rose ? I recollect Gabriel's paramount love of the wild rose, and fancy that either this, or else the exquisite sweet brier which bears a very similar flower, could not be excelled for the purpose. . . .

The Fords have left Birchington : I find they frequent the Gosses. . . .

I cannot remember that *my* portrait ever was engraved, unless one reckons Scotus's etching (?) from Pistrucci's pretty little early watercolour,—the one Gabriel liked, not the amazing object achieved later.

Bristow told us of the amount of visiting dear G's grave which has taken place, one lady " fainting." He seemed quite impressed by the attention shown.

To WILLIAM ROSSETTI.

[This letter (as may readily be perceived) was consequent upon my having announced that my youngest daughter Mary was attacked by scarlet fever; and that, in order to avoid infection for the other children, I was proposing to stay for a while with some of them at No. 30 Torrington Square. I did so, along with Olivia and Helen— not Arthur.—" *Avrà più spirito di tutti* " (she will be the cleverest of the set) is what our grandfather Polidori had said of Christina herself in very early days.]

6 STATION ROAD, BIRCHINGTON-ON-SEA.

23 *September* 1884.

MY DEAR WILLIAM,

. . . It is only your letter of this morning which tells us that darling little Mary positively *has* scarlet fever, but happily adding the good news that the crisis has passed favourably. I hope Lucy's throat will recover without further mischief, as also Arthur's. We are finding Birchington air as suitable as heretofore.

About your staying with Olive, Arthur, and Helen, in Torrington Square, nothing would in itself please US anything like so well. The sole (and this merely contingent) difficulty seems to us to be whether your and my very advanced Aunts may find the charge too anxious and too much for them altogether. If this is not the case, surely the maternal roof is the natural refuge for you and yours. . . . I shall be much disappointed if you vacate 30.

Olive has written 2 agreeable notes of thanks to us. Helen (I augur in the style of our Grandfather) "avrà più spirito di tutti," —allowing, that is, for the inborn preponderance of man over woman ! . . .

From ALGERNON SWINBURNE.

[This letter accompanied a copy of Mr. Swinburne's volume *A Midsummer Holiday and other Poems*. The piece to which he calls particular attention is entitled *A Ballad of Appeal, to Christina G. Rossetti*. It begins "Song wakes with every wakening year," and craves that Christina would again give "Sweet water from the well of song."]

THE PINES, PUTNEY HILL, S.W.

17 *November* 1884.

DEAR MISS ROSSETTI,

I hope you will not think I have taken a liberty in addressing you publicly without so much as "*with* your leave" or "*by* your leave." Your kind acceptance of a previous little offering in metre emboldened me to express a wish which all your readers must share, and to which I trust you will not always turn a deaf ear—long as it seems since you have given us any fresh cause to thank you for a fresh gift of such verse as you only can give. It is but very little, of all that one would like to say, that can be expressed in so short and simple an appeal as that which you will find addressed to you at page 112 of the little volume which accompanies this little note : but you must allow its sincerity and earnestness to atone for its brevity and inadequacy. I wonder if I may venture to hope that you will like the seven baby-songs which immediately follow it.

With kind regards to Mrs. Rossetti, &c. . . .

To WILLIAM ROSSETTI.

[This letter marks a beginning in the decline of vital energy which affected our mother's closing year. After returning to London from Birchington, in 1884, she did not again leave town for any holiday-recruiting.—The notice which I wrote in the *Athenæum* was on Mr. Cordy Jeaffreson's book, *The Real Shelley.*]

30 TORRINGTON SQUARE.

[10 *June* 1885.]

MY DEAR WILLIAM,

I do not think we can have told you that we have quite given up going to Brighton : the prospect proved to be too upsetting, so now we are substituting drives (our first taken to-day) for the more ambitious outing.   To-day we utilized our fly by calling at the Scotts' where I had the pleasure of seeing W. B. looking very fair all considered ; he now takes and enjoys drives, and speaks cheerfully of his own health.   Alice Boyd appeared, but Mrs. Scotus was out. Mamma—her dear love to you—and I have read with admiration your first notice of the "real". Shelley : I wish I were as fair-minded as you are, but I must not despair of acquiring as a grace what you have as a gift.

I wanted you to know that here we are lest you should get off coming to see us ! !

To LUCY ROSSETTI, *Ventnor.*

[The illness, bronchial pneumonia, which gradually led on to phthisis and its fatal termination, had begun with my wife in February 1885 : thereafter she often had to go to some health-resort or other—in the present instance, Ventnor.   Miss Tynan is the admired authoress in verse and prose, now Mrs. Hinkson. Shortly before this date she had begun corresponding with me about her first poetic volume, in which I found abundant charm : she also called upon Christina.   The latter was frequently beset by budding bards (not of like rank with Miss Tynan) and their first volumes.   To make her believe that poetry is good when in fact it is only mediocre was by no means an easy task.   She had a habit of acknowledging with thanks a book as soon as received and before reading it, so as to save herself the disagreeable alternative of either "damning with faint praise" or else attempting a strain of eulogy beyond her real belief.]

30 TORRINGTON SQUARE, W.C.

11 [*January*] 1886.

MY DEAR LUCY,

I felt an impulse to write to you on Saturday, but "Time flew" and it remained undone. Now I sit down to respond to your last delightful letter. We get fairly good news of you from William, whom last we saw on Friday : I hope when he has joined you— as he was then planning to do one day this week—you will rejoice his heart by coming into fuller bloom before his eyes. I wonder whether Miss Tynan told him what she told me, that she preferred your portrait to Lizzie's,—and I wonder whether you will think this worth telling you ! (I should appreciate it, were it I.) Miss Tynan is an agreeable young woman enough, and deferential enough to puff me up like puff-paste. She has given me a volume of *Vagrant Verse* by her friend Miss Rosa Mulholland, but I rate higher K. T.'s own muse. Sad to say, another unknown has presented me with a volume of Sonnets of which (so far as I have waded) the less said the better *as poetry ;* my note of thanks turned out jejune, though the spirit is admirable and I found one point to praise. Don't you ever publish a volume unless you are quite sure you can excel (say) Mr. W. Shakespear ; or if not, at least don't bestow it on poor disconcerted me ! a warning to be early and with absolute impartiality brought home to Olive, Arthur, Helen, Mary, who exhibit alarming tendencies.

News is not my forte. We potter contentedly on with no very marked vicissitudes even of health. We have just read the *Memoir and Letters of Sara Coleridge* (I reading aloud to Mamma), and perhaps, if you were at a loss for a book, you might find some of it interesting.

Besides the warning (*see ante*) please give my love to your four, and much more my Mother's with a share for yourself. Aunts Charlotte and Eliza send love. . . .

To WILLIAM ROSSETTI, *Ventnor.*

[My article upon Butler's prose-translation of Dante's *Paradiso* was in *The Athenæum :* I need not enter on any of the details referred to by Christina.—The "old nurse Stevens" was the mother of a female servant in our house in Endsleigh Gardens. She had acted as an assistant (not a regular servant) in the house towards 1871 &c., more especially in looking after Christina in her then formidable illness.]

30 TORRINGTON SQUARE, LONDON, W.C.

19 [*January*] 1886.

MY DEAR WILLIAM,

It was a distinct pleasure to get your letter this morning, and a second distinct pleasure this afternoon to read aloud to Mamma your admirable review of Butler's *Paradiso*, lucid, interesting, and delightfully written. I was perfectly charmed when I came upon your reason for reading "Dante" rather than "da te": how Maria would have enjoyed the suggestion. Good too is the "Marsyas" subtilty ; and perhaps it tones down somewhat the disgust of the myth, by inviting us to think of the catastrophe not as a vengeance after the contest but as a strong way of announcing that M. was fairly rapt out of himself and surrendered all insane rivalry. For I do think the original myth very horrid. . . .

The weather you describe is glorious for January. Here we are less flourishing, though to-day I took a good cold dry and for me rather long walk. My errand was to see my dear old nurse Stevens who is ill and very aged and weak now, and to take her a present from Mamma. Of course, she was much besides being my nurse ; but she is always *that* to me because she was so kind in my great illness. . . .

Our dearest Mother continues on the whole much as when last I wrote. Day after day the cold detains her indoors, but we trot a little about the drawing-room, which is better than nothing. . . .

It is getting towards 10 o'clock, my latest ordinary bedtime. . .

To LUCY ROSSETTI, *Ventnor.*

30 TORRINGTON SQUARE, W.C.

[1886—? *January.*]

MY DEAR LUCY,

I hope when this reaches you my dear Olive and Mary will be better or well, and Arthur and Helen quite off the sick list. . . .

Mamma and our Aunts unite with me in love to you and the children, and especially to our *old crony* William. I wonder whether he will bring home any marine trophies from what I fancy a good shore for object-hunting. Do any of his children inherit his and my taste for such quests? To this day I think I could plod indefinitely along shingle with my eyes pretty well glued to the ground. . . .

To LUCY ROSSETTI, *Ventnor.*

[The opening of this letter refers to a raffle which was being got up by Madox Brown for the benefit of the widow and daughter of an old friend of his, Daniel Casey. This was a painter whom Brown had known in Paris at some such remote date as 1843—a Frenchman of Irish extraction.]

30 TORRINGTON SQUARE, LONDON, W.C.

[16 *February* 1886.]

MY DEAR LUCY,

Thank you very truly for sending me a notice which has set me hankering after a guinea ticket,—but sad and sober sense dictates that such expensive luxuries are not for me just now. Much more important than the chance of Mr. Casey's or even of your Father's work would be the putting myself into sympathy with that same kind Father of yours and securing a share in his good deed: but pray believe in my bodiless sympathy and good will for the widow and daughter. We poets (!) judging by myself are not an opulent race. . . .

I am heartily glad you have not been in London this winter, which has been severe and trying, though for the present frost has vanished.

It is just as well too that you escaped the alarm of the riots, which were serious enough as they were, and alarmed one lest they should become yet more so. But, however one may deplore lawlessness, it is heart-sickening to think of the terrible want of work and want of all things at our very doors,—we so comfortable. Emigration is the only adequate remedy which presents itself to my imagination : and that, of course, may leave the mother country to die of inanition a stage further on : yet no one can call upon people to starve to-day lest England should prove powerless to hold her own to-morrow. You see, my politics are not very intricate. . . .

I like much the pretty photograph William brought me, and I like the looks of your independent and well-placed residence. How fine a storm would be from your windows : yet one has no heart to wish for a storm whilst " men must work and women must weep."

To-morrow is our dear Maria's birthday,—my irreplaceable sister and friend.

To LUCY ROSSETTI, *Ventnor*.

[Christina here refers to the accident—a fall in her room—which began the final illness of our Mother.—" Olive's *Theseus* " was a small drama (of a kind) written by our small Olive, then aged ten.— " Your father's labour of love " is the bust-medallion of Dante Rossetti now erected, in connection with a drinking-fountain, in front of his house, 16 Cheyne Walk.]

30 TORRINGTON SQUARE, LONDON, W.C.

4 *March* [1886].

MY DEAR LUCY,

Your kind letter would have been answered yesterday, but you don't know—or you can very well believe—how hurried and engrossed I am. Dearest Mamma suffers much from the prolonged pain of her fall, and is very weak : I am full of anxiety, yet Mr. Stewart has said nothing to extinguish hope. What I most dread is the exhaustion of her strength, so frail at 85 : but all my dread is for myself, not (thank God) for her. She sends love to you and to *all four* in which I join : dear Olive's *Theseus* has reached us safely, but I am not sure when I can read it aloud to my patient,—

yet very likely she will enjoy listening to it this very day. Ah will she ever see your Father's labour of love erected at Chelsea? William drops in daily, and is very good and dear and welcome. . . .

To LUCY ROSSETTI, *Ventnor.*

30 TORRINGTON SQUARE, LONDON, W.C.

[1886—? 5 *March.*]

MY DEAR LUCY,

Love responds to love: accept my dear Mother's and mine, and pray pass on their full share to your dear four.

I am scarcely daring to be hopeful, yet what change has taken place appears to be in the direction of recovery. But weakness at 85,—you can well imagine what are my fears and my feelings. And indeed I am not venturing to fix my wishes on either result: I see my dearest Mother suffer much, though very patiently; I could not wish her to suffer on indefinitely for my own selfish sake. God's Will be done.

We do hope the painful attack of indisposition you were suffering from when you wrote will not be of long duration. . . .

I had one pleasant glimpse of your Father.

To LUCY ROSSETTI, *Ventnor.*

30 TORRINGTON SQUARE, LONDON, W.C.

2 *April* [1886].

MY DEAR LUCY,

I have no news about dearest Mamma for you,—doubtless William tells you of what little gradual change appears. She does not cease to hear about *your* health with interest, and to think of you with every earnest good wish for you and yours. . . .

Our Nurse Annie Jackson is a perfect friend and treasure in our sore need. . . .

Cathy is truly kind in calling and sending to enquire, and to-day in offering help—but alas! help is not in question: Mrs. Brown joins her in kind interest. This morning I received a very pleasant letter from your Father in answer to my expression of admiration of his "DGR" photograph.

Mamma's love to you, for I have just spoken to her. Opposite her bed stands a fine bunch of daffodils looking quite cheerful.

P.S. I was forgetting to tell you that poor Aunt Charlotte is very unwell again, and is pretty well laid up. I suppose she took cold, colds being so prevalent; and now her strength is at so low an ebb that she too must have a nurse:—and only think! I have just engaged Mrs. Abrey who nursed Gabriel, to come to her this evening. I tried in vain for an All Saints nurse, but we are particularly fortunate in securing our good Mrs. Abrey. Aunt Eliza bears up well.

To LUCY ROSSETTI, *Ventnor*.

[Our Mother died peacefully on 8 April 1886, in the presence of Christina and myself. As Dante Gabriel had died on 9 April 1882, the interval between the two deaths was exactly four years.]

30 TORRINGTON SQUARE, LONDON, W.C.

19 *April* [1886].

MY DEAR LUCY,

It has become a different world since last I wrote to you. Yet I rejoice that it is I who am left in the grief of this separation, and not my dearest Mother.

Please thank your dear children one by one for each instance of their love towards either of us. And my thanks and love to yourself, dear Lucy. Grateful thanks too for the pretty wreaths you and they sent. Some Italian flowers, sent by one who cannot have known of my loss, arrived just in time to strew in the coffin before it was closed. I am glad Cathy and Mr. Hueffer were with us in church and at the grave. . . .

To LUCY ROSSETTI, *Ventnor*.

30 TORRINGTON SQUARE, LONDON, W.C.

21 *April* 1886.

MY DEAR LUCY,

I am glad to believe that a letter of mine crossed your sisterly one, for this is the last moment at which I could wish to loosen the ties which remain to me. Love and thanks to you, my dear Sister, for all you have felt and expressed for us : I can still say " us " and look forward to the end of our separation. But please do not fancy me bearing this bitter trial so much better than I really am bearing it. It has been a comfort to see William, though now I rejoice that he is going to have a reviving time at Ventnor. Most brotherly he has been, taking trouble in my stead and helping me along. I am of course still in the midst of business, as even a very small executorship involves anxious effort. As yet I do not know exactly what my means are likely to amount to, but I am sure they will amply suffice : soon, of course, I expect to have all made out. Did William tell you of a conversation we had ?—when I said that I hoped finally to leave at least as much as £2000 to him. I have long felt in his debt for all those years when his munificent affection provided me with a most ungrudged home, and he and we all think that, if we loosely compute this debt as for 20 years at £100 a year, I shall pay back the *money* in full ; the *love* can only be repaid in kind,—he, moreover, never till I talked to him viewed it 'as money-indebtedness. Now I particularly want you to know all this, because, if I were so unhappy as to lose my dear William, I should (so far as I foresee at present) feel that his claim lapses in full to yourself or to the children. Please be sure of this, according to my present power of foreseeing. Altogether I expect to have a good deal more than £2000, but this is the special sum I propose for the given purpose.

Sympathy has flowed in from very different quarters, and I like to see the love and high honour in which my dearest Mother was held. High and low have shown kindness. After speaking separately to each of my Aunts I find it is the preference of both that I should continue to make my home with them, and thus it is settled.

Pray give my love to Olive, Arthur, Helen, Mary, with joy to dear Arthur on his recovery, and a birthday kiss to *aged* Mary : what a beautiful thing to be no more than 5 years old ! . . .

To WILLIAM ROSSETTI.

[I have forgotten the details about All Saints Home and the £500. The affair was evidently connected with my mother's will, and probably, more or less, with Maria, though deceased as far back as 1876. My mother and I had been joint legatees under Dante Gabriel's will: therefore my mother had a half share in his drawings &c. left unsold—though these remained with me as being *practically* mine. As Christina inherited from my mother, the half share had now become hers, and she hereby relinquishes it.]

30 TORRINGTON SQUARE, W.C.

[18 *May* 1886.]

MY DEAR WILLIAM,

. . . On Saturday I attended by appointment at Mr. Turner's Office, took the required affidavit, and understood that now all is well forward for the actual proving of the will and rendering available of the property: so ere long I hope both to pay you your £100 legacy and to transfer to you, Lucy, Olive, what appertains to each,—besides honouring the claims of the few other claimants. After very careful consideration and discussion with Mr. Turner I have sworn the property under £6000, and to meet expenses I am going to sell out Bank stock 3 per cents: these at the moment of valuation stood, I think, at about 99½. Yesterday I called at the All Saints Home to reconnoitre, but found that the Revd. Mother is not expected there before next Monday or Tuesday: so if *we* act at once I shall leave £500 untouched for her to decide about; it can be either transferred or sold out afterwards as she shall decide.

I take this opportunity of relinquishing to you any possible share I may have in the things left over from Gabriel's sale, including pictures, drawings &c., if there are any. You know the class of goods I mean. . . .

To WILLIAM ROSSETTI.

[Christina had gone to stay awhile at Brighton, and she had offered to take our daughter Olivia with her—to which we gladly assented. I don't think that Olivia was at this time, or has ever become, of "a jealous disposition." Jealousy did not run in the Rossetti race—except indeed in Maria in her merely childish years.]

17 BRUNSWICK ROAD, BRIGHTON.

20 *August* 1886.

MY DEAR WILLIAM,

How very kindly you think of me. There have been no more fits of choking, and I hope there may be no more. My headaches are very much relieved. What you report of Olive's cheerfulness inspirits me, I do assure you, and at present I see no reason why (you and Lucy permitting) we should not stay out 4 weeks here together as I mentally proposed before starting. Olive looks very well, and even my anxious eye is satisfied. I think her a very nice child, docile and independent, which is a very fine combination of qualities. In face I think her a good deal like Lucy. She is full of intelligence. I cannot give any adequate reason for the doubt, yet I feel in doubt whether she has not some tendency towards a jealous disposition. So far as I know, every one here likes her ; one or two do, certainly. . . .

To WILLIAM ROSSETTI.

[My "graphic prefix" was the preface which I wrote to the *Collected Works of Dante Rossetti*. Christina was right as to the point she adverted to, and I altered my text.]

30 TORRINGTON SQUARE, W.C.

[6 *October* 1886.]

MY DEAR WILLIAM,

Musing on your graphic prefix, a point strikes me which I suggest with a suspicion that either—or both—of two weak points will annul it. Either you will not agree with me, or I shall bring my wares too late to market.

In recording Gabriel's *steady* but *undemonstrative* affection for his family, don't you think it would be just to except Mamma from the "undemonstrative" ness? I am well aware (as I believe) that long periods of silence and non-appearance took place : yet on the whole I should say that beyond all possibility of dispute he petted and worshipped our Mother with exuberant fondness.

But, dropping this detail, what an interesting prefix it is: I hope it will rank as one of the attractions of the new edition.

Nothing and nobody has occurred since we met. If the weather holds up, perhaps I may achieve my call "de rigueur" on Lucy this morning.

To WILLIAM ROSSETTI.

[The dedication which I prefixed to Dante Rossetti's *Collected Works* was to the memory of our mother.]

30 TORRINGTON SQUARE, W.C.
[13 *January* 1887.]

MY DEAR WILLIAM,

Thank you for the handsome D.G.R. I have returned to your delightful prefix with a renewal of pleasure, and recognize the *blue-grey eyes* and the *fondness* for our Mother. Your Dedication took me by surprise and charms me. Amongst the notes too there are points of particular interest.

Mr. Turner was here this morning, and at last I am going to remake my will. Perhaps you may like to know about it when we meet: you are to be my sole legatee, but with some temporarily modifying memoranda, subject however to your convenience. We can talk it all over if you like in a few minutes.

There are various trifles waiting to be shown you.

To LUCY ROSSETTI, *San Remo.*

[My wife, with the two elder children, had now gone to San Remo for health's sake: I after a while joined them.—Mr. W. J. Knewstub had studied painting under my brother's guidance towards 1863, and produced several good works, praiseworthy more especially for colour. He was now in Manchester, assisting Madox Brown in extensive cartoons &c. for the decoration of an exhibition-building in celebration of Queen Victoria's jubilee. He became the father-in-law of two fine artists, Mr. William Rothenstein and Mr. William Orpen, and died in 1906.]

30 TORRINGTON SQUARE, LONDON, W.C.

25 *January* [1887].

MY DEAR LUCY,

I have a letter and a card and a pretty little plant "for thought" to thank you for. The little heath looks charming planted, and promises I hope to live some time in spite of having exchanged Italy for England. You I trust thrive through having exchanged England for Italy. And I fancy this letter may not be long in your hands before William himself is with you, for I saw him yesterday and he proposes starting to-morrow. A great slice of my heart travels about with him now, he being the only one of his own standing left to me. . . .

Since the new edition came out (*D.G.R.*) I have re-read *Poor Henry.* What a fine thing it is, well worthy of publication ; poor Gabriel mentioned it when we were together at Birchington : I am glad it at last has seen the light. William's preface too and his notes abound in interest, especially perhaps the former.

The news that Mr. Knewstub has been working under your Father is superexcellent.

To WILLIAM ROSSETTI, *San Remo.*

[The phrase "Are you still *vagheggiando* Vasto" means "Are you still thinking with pleasure of going to Vasto," our father's native city. I had some such vague intention when I left London for San Remo : but neither then nor at any subsequent date did it get fulfilled.]

30 TORRINGTON SQUARE, LONDON, W.C.

5 *February* 1887.

MY DEAR WILLIAM,

Gracious was the moment when I discovered your P.S. at foot of Olive's letter. To her and to Arthur thanks, and to Lucy at their head love. It sounds earthly-paradise-like, your sketch of San Remo : but even there it would behove me to feel, " Arise ye and depart, for this is not your rest." I am glad you have more happy and endeared ties than I have,—I am glad, as so it is: otherwise I should be afraid of wishing it for you any more than for myself, and for myself I do not wish it. . . .

And now, if an old sister is worth triumphing over, you may triumph over me. For, after declining your company to San Remo which might I dare say have answered far better, I find myself despatched to Torquay! A month there is laid down, and perhaps in the course of the coming week I may betake myself thither. My doctor finds me very weak, and I see no way of evading his dicta (let us hope that termination is correct: I mean *plural*). Of course I will send you my address when I have one. Except general standing impediments and distaste, there is nothing now to keep me here as my will was finished off yesterday.

I hope by the time you are returning that neither snow nor floods will impede your path. Are you still *vagheggiando* Vasto? *No*, I suspect.

To WILLIAM ROSSETTI, *San Remo*.

["Una specolazione da pezzente" means "a pauper-like specula-tion."]

30 TORRINGTON SQUARE, LONDON, W.C.

10 *February* 1887.

MY DEAR WILLIAM,

Share my warm thanks and love with Lucy for the great kindness of your telegram received yesterday afternoon. I was then not sure of my Torquay prospects, but this morning brings me word that I have secured for next Tuesday 2 rooms at Mrs. Harvey's—

2 Beechwood

Abbey Road

Torquay—

by which arrangement I judge it prudent to abide despite the engaging charms of San Remo. I heard of these rooms through two persons, and they woo me to try them by being only a guinea a week: if uncomfortable I can shift quarters, but I am assured of their respectability. I think of taking a month's return ticket, as I am desired by my doctor to stay a month,—not longer, I hope, yet at the

worst one can get an extension of ticket. So you see I am armed
at all points with reasons and resolutions. For one thing, I regret
leaving behind me the rather amusing oversight of your correspondence : *English* postage costing a minimum, if you did not mind the
delay the whole batch might follow me to Torquay where I would
deal with it as heretofore : but this I foresee you will brand as "una
specolazione da pezzente !"

Perhaps my mirthful style has already suggested to you that your
"youngest sister looking dim and grim with dismal ways" is feeling
better.   Indeed I am : the last prescription, which I continue taking
diligently, seems quite to the point, and fortifies my adherence to Sir
William Jenner. . . .

Mr. Niles (Roberts, Boston) tells me that 17/9 due to *me* is
appended to his cheque to *you* : I dare say you see that so it is.
Poor *Time Flies* has failed in their hands, but perhaps it is doing
something at the S.P.C.K.'s New York depôt. Aunt Eliza's love
to all, and I invent Aunt Charlotte's who is upstairs : both tolerably
well.

To WILLIAM ROSSETTI, *San Remo.*

[It seems that Christina had been sending some snowdrops to my
wife.   The "never-to-be-forgotten drawing" was one which the latter
had made in 1883 of our infant Michael in death.—Harriett was a
servant in the Torrington Square house.]

2 BEECHWOOD, ABBEY ROAD, TORQUAY.

21 February 1887.

MY DEAR WILLIAM,

Our last letters crossed, as I hope you perceived : otherwise
what could possess me not to respond to such expression of affectionate
kindness from Lucy and you? My love to her, flowing downward
to Olive and Arthur.   As to my precious health, I am now at a very
tolerable level, against which if aught is to be alleged it is that I
may perhaps be further defined as at a standstill.   But I continue
medicine, diet, prudence, and am not aware of any great outrage
I am perpetrating against (that modernism) hygiene. . . . The
weather is cold, but encouraged by sunshine I sat out a long time

11

to-day mostly reading. I don't know whether you have been at
Torquay; it is a noble mass of hill, rock, vegetation; but the sea
is so land-locked and pier-locked (though the piers are quite small)
as to look very like a lake, while my delight is a boundless expanse.
However, the beauty is very great.

Alas! my snowdrops were merely some given me by Harriett,
though in the course of the transaction I recollected Lucy's in one
never-to-be-forgotten drawing.

Very fair news reaches me from home, and I have the gratification
of believing myself missed.

I like you revelling in lizard-like laziness! Never break the spell
for me. . . .

So even San Remo has had severe cold. I may doubly content
myself and be thankful here; but I hope you are again warm and
comfortable, or at least comparatively so. "Cold hand, warm
heart," is not very far from my plight at this moment.

To WILLIAM ROSSETTI, *San Remo.*

[This letter was consequent on the very severe and wide-extended
earthquake which took place on the Riviera, including San Remo,
on 25 February 1887. Christina had telegraphed to me as soon as
she saw a newspaper-notice of the earthquake, and I telegraphed and
wrote to her in return.]

2 BEECHWOOD, ABBEY ROAD, TORQUAY.
[28 *February* 1887.]

MY DEAREST WILLIAM,

Your blessed telegram yesterday afternoon between 5 and
6 o'clock, and your (and Olivia's) letter to breakfast this morning,
have eased me of a burden. I gave in my telegram at the P.O.
before 10 a.m. on Friday, and it seemed long indeed before the
reply set me at rest. My love to Lucy who I hope is not suffering
from shock and makeshift quarters, and to Olivia, and to Arthur
whose attack of pain and illness I hear of with regret,—I wonder
whether he is half such a coward as I am at the dentist's. . . .

What an awful awestriking experience an earthquake must be. . . .

I cannot help wishing that you and yours may already be on the homeward road. Of course, no more shocks may ensue, but who can feel even ordinarily secure at San Remo after what has happened? . . .

Please tell Olive that I look forward with wonder and admiration to the Trap-door Spider's nest, but that I only guess "a molla" to signify *with a spring:* she must instruct me when I see her treasure.

I am doing very well in health, not at all retrograding. Yet perhaps I may claim to have made a 10 years' stride both as to looks and feelings in these last weeks. If so, not by any means to be regretted. To-day I enjoyed a drive, the morning being sunny and lovely though not (barring sunshine) warm. I fully contemplate returning home at the completion of my 4 weeks (March 15), as I know I am wanted and shall be welcomed there.

To Lucy Rossetti, *Dijon.*

[Isabella (Mrs. Cole) was at this time residing at or near Bordighera.—The P.S. about "la Turquie" may call for a word of comment. Some one—it may have been our ex-nursery governess Madame Laffey—hearing lately that Christina was going to Torquay, supposed that she was going to la Turquie, and the rumour had got round to Lucy at Dijon.]

30 TORRINGTON SQUARE, LONDON, W.C.

21 *March* 1887.

My dear Lucy,

So *I* was in your kind thoughts at such a moment! I hope never to forget it with sisterly love and gratitude. I fully agree with you that it is impossible to pass through so awful an experience without deep impressions: the suspense I was in on all your accounts made its impression on me and sent me to prayer. . . . What alarming prognostics till the end of this year are published about earthquakes on the Riviera: I hope Isabella and her husband will be preserved.

I have had the pleasure of seeing William looking well, for he has

called here since my return last Tuesday.   Torquay and all that went
with it have greatly revived me, so that now I feel better able to bear
the wear and tear of daily life.   And really I am glad to be settled
at home again (though the break was refreshing), for I feel that here
is my proper place.   It will be a bright day when *you* can settle at
home too, but anything but bright would it be if a premature return
were to undo the good so anxiously wrought out.   No,—better that
we should know you are well at Dijon or at Bournemouth than ill
and suffering in London. . . .

I am much amused at the rumour that I was starting for "la
Turquie."

To Lucy Rossetti.

[As I have said elsewhere, the opinions of my wife and myself on
matters of religion were not such as to induce us to have any of our
children baptized.   In one instance—that of the infant Michael who
died in 1883—Christina, when he was visibly in danger, besought
and obtained my permission to baptize him with her own hand—
which she did.]

30 TORRINGTON SQUARE, W.C.
[*Summer* 1887 ?]

My dear Lucy,

I have been thinking over something that passed yesterday,
and, as I am sure of my own affectionate feeling, I confidently appeal
to yours.

We were talking about your "happy" children.   And so I think
them in the daily home-matters.   But I cannot pointedly use that
word *happy* without meaning something beyond the present life.
And baptism (where attainable) is the sole door I know of whereby
entrance is promised into the happiness which eye has not seen nor
ear heard neither hath heart of man conceived.   I now live so
much in the other world—or at least I ought to do so, having
my chief Treasure there—that please do not take offence at what I
say. . . .

I constantly pray for you and William and my dear nephew and
nieces.   Yet I feel and acknowledge that every one of you is setting
or has set me an example.

To WILLIAM ROSSETTI.

[At this time Eliza Polidori possessed a pencil-head of my brother done by himself, and I suppose some other drawings of his not of any leading importance. I was not so flush of money as to try to secure any of them. The head of Rossetti, done when he was about nineteen with a mass of long hair, was later on sold by Eliza to the National Portrait Gallery.]

30 TORRINGTON SQUARE, W.C.

8 *May* 1888.

MY DEAR WILLIAM,

. . . Our Aunts go on nicely from day to day. If ever you should feel disposed to make a bid for any of the Gabriel portraits which belong to Aunt Eliza, I THINK you would have a chance of success. But this I merely remark on my own account, without any authority: and please bury the hint in your own unshared inner consciousness. . . .

Perhaps you do so already,—but if not, and if you would not think it wrong, I wish you would sometimes pray for me that I may not, after having (in a sense) preached to others, be myself a castaway. Of course you and yours are very much in my prayers. It seems unnatural to love you so much and yet never say one word about matters which colour my life.

To LUCY ROSSETTI, *Worthing.*

30 TORRINGTON SQUARE, LONDON, W.C.

[1888—? *June.*]

MY DEAR LUCY,

I am shocked and pained to know what you are suffering. For though I never myself endured a carbuncle I have seen my dearest Mother more than once ill with one, and so I know the keen pain and exhaustion which ensue. Dear Sister, I would help and ease you if I could. . . . Meanwhile I hope our dear Olive's recovery is cordial and balm to you. . . .

At last I have seen Sir William Jenner, and, whilst he admits the impossibility of my leaving home, he insists on my taking what care

I can. He did not that I recollect use the word, yet I think what he detects is a tendency to *exhaustion* threatening some distinct result. "What then? the sweeter after this stripped earth Will be the shady rest of Paradise". Not that I arrogate to myself so blessed an end: but God's Mercy to sinners is infinite. On the other hand, I fancy that with reasonable prudence I may do very well. In fact I am very much as when last you saw me, so do not fancy me "dim and grim" beyond my wont. . . .

What funny proposals meet one! I have just been asked to go to Weston-super-Mare next month and take part in distributing the prizes to a large girls' school,—of course, the mistress is an acquaintance. My answer was an unflinching No. . . .

To WILLIAM ROSSETTI, *Worthing.*

[Mr. Stewart, who constantly attended female members of my family, was the father of Dr. Edward Stewart, who had now, owing to an interesting train of circumstances, become engaged to Lady Philippa Howard, daughter of a Duke of Norfolk.—After Christina's death I took possession of the "priceless *Singsong,*" and am not likely to offer it to any one for any level of price.]

30 TORRINGTON SQUARE, LONDON, W.C.

[5 *July* 1888.]

MY DEAR WILLIAM,

I hope your own health and those other healths so dear to you are thriving. . . .

Do you recollect encountering Dr. Edward Stewart one day at our door,—one disastrous day when no one heard your knock? He is engaged to a sister of the Duke of Norfolk, with apparent satisfaction to both families. Lady Philippa is the bride elect, and the marriage is talked of for November. The only regret, so far as I know, on *our* Mr. Stewart's part, is for the difference of religion,—wherein I quite agree with him. Dr. Stewart will continue his medical practice, which intention accords with his fiancée's wishes, and they want a house near his father's. "Edward and Philippa" match well. . . .

Poor old Aunt Charlotte, she is very patient,—and truly it needs patience to lie peacefully day after day on a helpless bed. . . .

In some trepidation I lately balanced my ½ year's expenses against the corresponding receipts, and found a small overplus on the right side. So I hope I have turned over a new leaf, for I do not think it at all satisfactory to draw habitually on a reserve. . . .

With an eye to its future I have concocted a *priceless Singsong* with marginal additions. Indeed, I advise you not to disperse my library to the four winds without careful inspection of copies, lest you should squander unsuspected treasures here and there.

To WILLIAM ROSSETTI.

[This letter relates to some articles I wrote for *The Magazine of Art* on Portraits of Dante Rossetti.—The affair of Mr. Frederick Sandys was this. He produced towards 1858 a caricature of a picture by Millais, representing the three leading Præraphaelite painters riding upon Ruskin as a donkey. I had said in my article that this was done before Sandys had ever seen Dante Rossetti : but no doubt Christina's rectification was correct.—Mr. Shields made a drawing of my brother lying in death, and two replicas of it followed.]

30 TORRINGTON SQUARE, W.C.

[1 *October* 1888.]

MY DEAR WILLIAM,

I have been with great interest and pleasure through your "Portraits." You told me you thought *Part 2* might still be accessible to afterthought : therefore I deferentially submit a note or two.

1. I feel sure Gabriel spoke of a *random visit* of Sandys, then a perfect stranger to him, in connexion with his getting-up a likeness for the caricature. Of course the *motive* of the call was inferred : its ostensible aim was something trivial, say to ask for an address.

2. The larger Downey photo. (my framed copy) is endorsed in your handwriting "taken Dec. 1862."

3. Of " male portraits " I remind you of George Gordon Hake, of

which a mention would I suspect give pleasure. A pen-and-ink of Uncle Henry will not, I dare say, count.

4. Don't you think, both because of Gabriel's affectionate feelings and ways and because of the grave protracted nature of his last illness, it would be judicious to add his trained nurse Mrs. Abrey to the list of those present at the last?

5. A *third* posthumous portrait (drawing) by Shields was given (?) by him to Mr. Leyland.

To WILLIAM ROSSETTI, *Pau.*

30 TORRINGTON SQUARE, LONDON, W.C.

10 *December* 1888.

MY DEAR WILLIAM,

I am sure Lucy will accept my love and sanction my writing to you this time, as I have written once to her and to you not at all. How kindly you both think of me: and I like my little pet Mary's interest in St. Christina; years and years ago I was disconcerted by a particular some one's announcing it as doubtful whether that Saint ever existed in reality. . . .

Please do not say "The grapes are sour"! Beautiful, delightful, noble, memorable, as is the world you and yours frequent,—*I* yet am well content in my shady crevice: which crevice enjoys the unique advantage of being to my certain knowledge the place assigned me. And in my small way I have my small interests and small pleasures. To-day I presented Mr. Stewart with a *Shadow of Dante*, and believe it was received with real gratification. . . .

Not long ago I visited our good Maria's grave and found all well. Later I have been to our dearest Mother's, taking a few chrysanthemums and pretty greenery: how she loved flowers! The one bush, and otherwise blank little bed, are kept nice and trim, and little Michael's was in good order beside it. . . .

Tell Mary from me that I have heard of a brandy-drinking cat. Poor puss was taken ill and milk and brandy was tried. It rallied. When afterwards plain milk was offered it, it declined it till brandy was added! I believe it is a long-haired pussy.

Here I break off, and this will probably wait till the next enclosure as assuredly it can well afford to wait.

To LUCY ROSSETTI, *Pau.*

[The earlier part of this letter contains a reference to Christina's habit of destroying letters as soon as answered. Had not this been her constant practice, something considerable might have been added to the bulk of this volume.—The affair of Birchington is not wholly present to my mind : I suppose some one had said (and not in this instance only) that Dante Gabriel's grave was not properly attended to. I made inquiries more than once, and could never find that any solid ground of complaint had arisen. However, I heedfully attended to whatever could be needed in a minor way.—"Olive's play" was named *Le Jeune Bara:* it applied to a boy-hero of the great French revolution, and was acted in our hotel just about Christmas-time—Arthur personating Robespierre (!) whom the youthful authoress had not treated in the "raw head and bloody bones" style of some annalists.]

30 TORRINGTON SQUARE, LONDON, W.C.

13 *December* 1888.

MY DEAR LUCY,

I got a charming letter from William this morning, so charming that I felt tempted to swerve from my propriety and write to him twice running ! But your prior and welcome claim I deliberately honour, and indeed I should be very short-sighted to forfeit by neglect a continuance of "your esteemed favours." So please give him my love, and tell him that at present I am reprieving letters from that summary injustice which executes them forthwith,— his are really too nice. Also he must know that I have at once written to Dr. Maccoll explanatorily, and to Birchington enquiringly —Mr. Alcock has moved to a different Kentish Incumbency, but I feel no difficulty in addressing his successor : I hope the affair is on its way to a satisfactory issue.

How lovely Pau must be, with delicious climate, leisure, rest. . . . Although I had heard two or three times of Olive's play, never till this morning did I understand that it was written in French ! Still more impressive is the German journal ! ! My love to my polyglot niece and the juniors. I hope the four will not leave Italian out of their "curriculum" (which learned word I further hope runs on all fours in this my sentence). . . .

Yesterday two ladies called to ask if I was at home, would not come in, retired without leaving name or message, returned with a few very beautiful flowers; and vanished anonymously as they arrived: a funny, pretty little incident. . . .

To HELEN ROSSETTI (Angeli), *Pau.*

[*December* 1888.]

MY DEAR HELEN,

I recollect how pretty Olive's play of *Theseus* was, and how well the dresses were managed : so I dare say this second drama will go off nicely too. I wonder what part the daughter of the " femme Bara" has to play,—for I do not know the plot of the piece. I hope virtue triumphs.

My love and best wishes to you accompany *Dodo.* There is a disagreeable little girl, sister of the hero, whom I recommend you not to be like ! Dodo himself I like, and the ugly Colonel; and I think perhaps even the disagreeable girl improved. Have you ever noticed how portraits sometimes seem to look at one? I have. When you read the story through, you will see what I allude to.

I like to think of you in dear Aunt Charlotte's necklace to-day, and still better I like that you do not need it to remind you of her who loves you. She likes to listen to the letters from Pau.

To MARY ROSSETTI, *Pau.*

December 1888.

MY DEAR LITTLE MARY,

I have had at least 2 of your nice little letters, and only now do I answer them straight to yourself. But I am a busy aunt in a small way. I am working away at a heap of cards and letters this very day. Be sure, dear, of my true love and very best wishes. I hope you like the "Zoo": I dare say you will recognize some of the beasts, and I hope there are some amusing anecdotes of one or other of them. The spectacled kitten and the tabby kitten are old enough now to be sent away, but I do not know when they will be fetched : soon I hope. I now like the spectacled one better than the other, which is pretty but not uncommon. They might be called Beauty and the Beast.

I dare say your kind Papa is sorry to leave you, just as you are sorry to lose him : but then how delightful it will be to see him again !

To OLIVIA ROSSETTI (Agresti), *Pau.*

30 TORRINGTON SQUARE, LONDON, W.C.

14 *February* 1889.

MY DEAR OLIVIA,

I am very glad you like the *Shadow of Dante*. It is indeed a work written from a fund of knowledge far wider and deeper than could be compressed into its pages, eloquent and elegant, the fruit of a fine mind and a noble soul. And to me, though not to you, it is graced with the endearing charm of resembling its beloved author by being full of goodness and with no insignificant touch of greatness. I do not think that it is sisterly partiality which thus draws her portrait. . . .

To ARTHUR ROSSETTI, *Biarritz.*

[I have only a vague recollection as to Christina's " game " (of cards). My children used to play it a little, but I suppose it is now totally defunct.]

30 TORRINGTON SQUARE, LONDON, W.C.

26 *February* 1889.

MY DEAR ARTHUR,

I have taken quite an extra-large sheet of paper ; and how it is to be filled who knows ? Not I, your affectionate aunt.

However, my birthday love and my earnest wishes for every blessing upon you supply quality if not quantity. I write to-day on purpose that this may reach you not later than Thursday, and not knowing exactly how much time I should allow. Your last letter pleased me much, and enables me to enjoy with you that wonderful prismatic foam which is denied to my bodily eye, and that noble rocky sea which I hope is helping to fortify all my dear exiles for a happy return home some day. . . .

If you are not tired of feline literature it may please you to know that the spectacled kitten was pronounced pretty (!) in its new home, and that it touches, and I believe takes in its mouth, some white mice (its fellow citizens) without injuring them.   I hope instinct will not suddenly assert itself to the dire detriment of mousey.

I dare say you never suspected your sober old aunt of having invented a game.   Years ago, however, I did : and I send it you in case you may like to try it some evening when even sunny Biarritz may be dim and chilly.   I don't know whether any one else will think it amusing, but I entertain a weakness for it. . . .

We in London are wintry at present.

To WILLIAM ROSSETTI.

[This letter refers to the proofs of my book entitled *Dante Gabriel Rossetti as Designer and Writer*, which (as indicated in the letter) was not, and was not intended to be, a "biography" of him.   A very few explanations must here suffice.   Christina's remark numbered 18 refers to James Collinson's picture of *St. Elizabeth of Hungary*.   19, H.H.H. were the initials used by Dante Rossetti when he first printed *Sister Helen*.   25, The volume was Main's *Treasury of English Sonnets* presented to our mother on her eightieth birthday, with my brother's sonnet on *The Sonnet* inserted.   27 refers to his sonnet *The Monochord*.   30 refers to the sonnet *A Superscription*. 31, The "boyish and youthful work" consists of sketches &c. by Dante Gabriel.   32, *Sorrentino* was a romantic tale of his begun (not completed) towards 1842.   37 relates to an oil-portrait of Eliza Polidori.]

30 TORRINGTON SQUARE, W.C.

[20 *June* 1889.]

MY DEAR WILLIAM,

. . . I fully concur in your negative as to yourself writing any biography of poor dear Gabriel : such a suggestion has once or twice been made to me, but I hold inflexibly aloof. . . .

18. Gabriel spoke (at Herne Bay, 1877) with considerable esteem of the "St. Elizabeth," thinking in whose hands it might be.

19. At the Howitts' one evening Allingham suggested "Hear, hear, hear," for "H. H. H."

20. Teodorico was consulted about some of Gabriel's Italian verse. . . .

24. Do you recollect the ready wit with which Gabriel suggested "viperous" as rhyme to "Cyprus" when the matter was mooted?

25. Literally, *I* was donor of the volume, and my hands inserted the Sonnet. . . .

27. Abandoning verbal particulars—don't you think the point may be the common essence (so to say) of all these outward and inward matters?—as if one thread (the musical "monochord," but not in the sense of any weight or measure) ran through all, vibrated through all? Thus we should get the sort of truth which the blind man so neatly conveyed who likened *scarlet* to the sound of the trumpet. . . .

30. I think "Dead Sea" suggests much more than your note recognizes; and I conjecture that so it did to Gabriel.

31. I have our dear Mother's old hoard of boyish and youthful work: do look at it some day,—perhaps a lost treasure or two may come to light.

32. — for instance, I think the 2 sketches (duplicates) I send are a last lingering trace of *Sorrentino*. Keep them if you care for them; if not, some day please send them back. I fear I do not possess what I seem clearly to remember, a drawing from S. in which an evil spirit crouches down by a balustrade. . . .

37. *Charlotte* P. originally, and so far as I know still. This portrait was done, I believe, as a substitute for a water-colour (*Kate the Queen?*) first given Aunt C., and then with her consent (possibly after the fact) sold.

Here, such as they are, are my annotations: some, you see, are friendly remarks not relevant to the particular text.

What a lovely day. Love all round your circle.

To LUCY ROSSETTI, *London.*

[I have mentioned elsewhere this affair of the corks—*i. e.* slabs of virgin cork. Christina, in the autumn of 1889, showed my wife a printed leaflet recommending the depositing of such slabs in a room as a remedy against bronchial or pneumonial troubles; and Christina gave her some of those slabs. My wife used them for many months together, with apparent benefit.]

[TORRINGTON SQUARE.
C. 1 *October* 1889.

MY DEAR LUCY,

Buoyed up by corks I invoke your notice! Pray try my corks,—not that I pin faith to them, but that I trust they cannot do harm. And please reject them not after *one* night, but try them for at least *2* consecutive nights, such being the suggestion of my document.

I saw my dear delightful William yesterday, and we "vagheggiammo" corks together.

To WILLIAM ROSSETTI.

30 TORRINGTON SQUARE, W.C.

[15 *November* 1889.]

MY DEAR WILLIAM,

I enclose A LEGIBLE letter from Lady Mount-Temple. . . . I am heartily glad (are not you?) at the *Beata Beatrix* being presented to the nation, hoping meanwhile that the Clifford replica is not quite unworthy.

Now let me *pavoneggiare* a surface scrap of history. You once scorned the idea of an extern King of Spain. But, considering that at the outset of the War of the Succession the then Duke of Savoy alleged a fourth contingent title to that crown, I do think that el Rey Don Amadeo had something to say for himself. [N.B. I am aware of the theory that vanity piques itself on one's weak point rather than on one's strong point: which may account for my ostentatious bit of history.] I have just finished three volumes of Marlborough memoirs and correspondence, nominally *Duchess* but involving much *Duke:* the latter, in spite of Thackeray's verdict, seems to me to have a very attractive side to his character. . . .

I have heard nothing of the dear old Scotts this long time.—My love to Lucy and the four.

To WILLIAM ROSSETTI.

[The text quoted was for the tombstone of Charlotte Polidori, who had died on 8 January.—I do not now distinctly recollect what was

Mr. Gladstone's "list of poetesses," nor how Christina came to know anything about it—perhaps through Lady Mount-Temple. As to Mrs. Webster, I have more than once had occasion to record Christina's very high admiration (fully shared by myself) of that poetess's tragedy *The Sentence*: this more especially, and some other works in fair proportion.]

30 TORRINGTON SQUARE.

[22 *January* 1890.]

My dear William,

. . . In case of your proceeding to give orders, I remind you that you approved of the text "I waited patiently for the Lord," Ps. 40. 1.

My love to dear Lucy, who I hope was better when you got home than my croak suggested.

By-the-by, did not Mr. Gladstone omit from his list of poetesses the one name which *I* incline to feel as by far the most formidable of those known to me, Augusta Webster? I did not notice the omission at the moment, but suspect it in retrospect. . . .

I am writing with cold hands and a cold nose !

To William Rossetti.

["A Kemble" (mentioned at the close of this letter) is, I suppose, an autograph letter from the celebrated actor John Philip Kemble to my grandfather. This must have been discovered among Charlotte Polidori's small hoards ; and I at a later date found half-a-dozen or so of similar letters in the Torrington Square house. They were all slight casual missives.]

30 TORRINGTON SQUARE, W.C.

[26 *March* 1890.]

My dear William,

Thankyou for " cemetery " news and powers, on which I hope to act to-morrow morning by going to Highgate if the day favours. . . .

I want to correct a mis-statement I made some time ago. Something you said led me to answer in a general way that morning prayer took me (about ?) half an hour,—but it did not and does not take me so long.   This has justly worried me, as the inaccuracy told in my own favour. . . .

I am looking through Aunt C.'s journals, and have found a small —very small—proportion of sentences to preserve : amongst these some which it would have been a pity to destroy.

Yesterday came to me a rather pretty book from " Lewis Carroll," the *Nursery Alice.*—I have settled with Mr. Greenwood who accepts me as tenant, but of course Aunt Eliza and I go shares in rent &c. She, poor thing, without perhaps being very ill, endures a good deal of distressing sensation.   I hope I shall succeed in keeping her money-matters as well as my own under my administration, for if not I know not how we shall be able to go on.   However, I should beware of being (as indeed I am) " careful and troubled."

I have seen various friends lately, but not so as to supply much news.   Have you heard of a *Dante Map* projected by a Miss Hensman, who wanted my good word to help her towards a publisher ?   I wrote accordingly.   Lately I contributed a " Kemble " to the Wisbech Museum, and received formal thanks.

To WILLIAM ROSSETTI.

[The term "the idiotic I " applies to a certain photograph of my sister, taken in 1877, which she used to term "the Idiot," as the expression of the face is not a little vacant.]

30 TORRINGTON SQUARE, W.C.

[6 *December* 1890.]

MY DEAR WILLIAM,

I enclose 3 photographs; the *idiotic I* for contempt and cremation, the other 2 for your American.   Please hand to Lucy and Helen their respective notes.

I forgot yesterday that I lately saw the George Hakes, and heard that Dr. Hake versifies as ardently and vigorously as ever.   Henry Hake's marriage seems a very happy one.

There is a book too I might have shown you, if I had remembered : Poems by Emily Dickinson, lately sent me from America—but perhaps you know it.   She *had* (for she is dead) a wonderfully

Blakean gift, but therewithal a startling recklessness of poetic ways and means.

I am feeling at 60 very much as I did at 59!! though not quite as relieved and exhilarated by the circumstance as when at 30 I gazed in the looking-glass, and discerned no marked change from 29.

To WILLIAM ROSSETTI.

30 TORRINGTON SQUARE, W.C.

[8 *December* 1890.]

MY DEAR WILLIAM,

Thinking of the National Portraits desideratum, a scheme occurred to me. I mentioned the affair to Aunt Eliza, and find her inclined to SELL her long-haired portrait of Gabriel. If no bid ensues, I dare say she will *give* it: but the first overture is commercial. Are you disposed to negotiate the business? or will you kindly furnish me with an apposite name and address? To own the truth, I am heartily glad of the present prospect, because at one time she seemed to take a dislike to the work, and proposed giving it to Mr. Turner!! but do not mention this, as I do not want to spread so queer an incident. . . .

Please expedite matters as much as you can, all delays being harassing to our poor old Aunt.

Loves.

To WILLIAM ROSSETTI.

[The reference to my "picture-valuing" applies to my having undertaken for the Board of Inland Revenue, without any remuneration, the work of estimating the value of pictures and drawings falling liable to estate-duty. As Christina hoped, I did, after retiring from Somerset House, continue this work, receiving some fees.—My *Adonais* was the edition of Shelley's poem, with my notes &c., which had recently been published by the Clarendon Press, Oxford. My "Phantasm remark" had to do with a cancelled passage of *Adonais*, generally supposed to apply to Coleridge: I will not here quote my remark, not being sure that other people would find it so amusing as Christina did.—"The condensed DGR" must have been a recent re-edition (from the *Collected Works*) of Dante Rossetti's original poems.—Christina expected to see me on "the 2nd Wednesday in April" because this was one of the evenings

12

when the Shelley Society, to which I belonged, met in University College; and, since my removal to distant St. Edmund's Terrace, I always took my meal with Christina on those evenings.—" *Il Tempo, Salterio* " (which has been previously referred to), is one of our father's leading poetic volumes, published in 1843. There had been an earlier and not identical edition, under the title of *Iddio e l' Uomo, Salterio*, 1833.]

30 TORRINGTON SQUARE, W.C.

[9 *March* 1891.]

MY DEAR WILLIAM,

I am so glad you are better and comparatively well that I must not mind any minor matter. I am glad too in itself that you are picture-valuing, and I secretly indulge a hope, short of despair, that you may have a snug little berth awaiting you at the moment of superannuation. . . .

When you do come you will find that I have been reading your *Adonais* with much interest. Indeed I have gone the length of a scrapfull of notes which I hope to pour out on your devoted head. I fairly laughed all by myself at your " Phantasm " remark. I have read too the condensed DGR, but am inclined to doubt whether his fatal chloral propensity can have dated so early as you suggest : had he then come in contact with Mr Stillman ? to whom I understood the introduction of chloral was innocently owing. . . .

Aunt Eliza is not much amiss except as to brain which at present is very untrustworthy . . .

I dare say, if not before, we shall have the pleasure of seeing you on the 2nd Wednesday in April. . . .

For the first time (!) I am reading *Il Tempo, Salterio*—much that is fine.

To WILLIAM ROSSETTI.

30 TORRINGTON SQUARE, W.C.

[16 *March* 1891.]

MY DEAR WILLIAM,

We have just received from Mr. Scharf the good news that "the Trustees of this Gallery unanimously agreed upon the purchase of your Brother's . beautiful drawing at the price named £20."— This, I think, is a very gratifying evidence of dear G.'s standing. . . .

To WILLIAM ROSSETTI.

[Luigi Polidori, residing in Florence, was a relative (first cousin first remove) of Charlotte Polidori, who had constantly assisted him, as succeeding to other relatives in that line, with money. He persecuted her not a little. Since the death of Charlotte, Mr. Turner, as solicitor for the estate, had consented to deal to some extent with Luigi's importunities. In consequence of the present letter from Christina I undertook to do what she wanted—*i. e.* (as I understood it) to receive and read *future* letters from Luigi, and to advise Christina concerning them. As a preliminary, I began by destroying all the past letters. Christina, whose squeezableness in such matters exceeded mine, was startled when I told her of this ; and she receded from the arrangement proposed, and henceforward dealt direct with all Luigi's missives, sending him no doubt a good deal more money than she ought to have allowed him to wring out of her. His letters must still have been sent to Mr. Turner's address : for Christina had at least the prudence not to let Luigi know the name or address of his benefactress. Thus did things continue until my sister's death, when I wrote to Luigi to explain.]

30 TORRINGTON SQUARE, W.C.

23 April 1891.

MY DEAR WILLIAM,

I am prepared to be viewed by you as more or less obnoxious.

Last night I received the enclosed letter from Mr. Turner, which was followed by his visit this morning. Within that letter you will find an accumulation of *Luigis*, and the card of the gentleman, A. Galzini, who called on Mr. T. This Galzini lives it seems in London, but happily Mr. Turner with-held from him our names and addresses. However, come what may, it is high time to relieve poor Mr. Turner (who really has now nothing to do with it all) of further trouble and besetment. Talking with him, I struck out this plan, for which I beseech your toleration and concurrence. I now and he henceforward are to send all *Luigis* to you, to be judged according to your own judgment : whenever (if ever) you think a remittance advisable, *I* will find the cash if you will take the trouble. I invoke your aid both as Aunt Charlotte's quondam

executor and as my one brother.   If however you reject this
overture, please return the painful packet: if the contrary, bestow
a card to calm my mind.

Please give my love to Lucy; and explain that I was on my way
to say good-bye when the door at which I was presenting myself shut,
and shut me out: I dare say she detects that I am still sufficiently
shy to lose heart under such a rebuff.   The "at home" seemed to
me very successful, and I only regret not having had a glimpse of
your library.   What a beautiful stair carpet.

Love to any who love me—but really that is quite unChristian!—
to all who do and to any who don't!

To WILLIAM ROSSETTI.

[Two Italian phrases here may perhaps deserve translation:
"Nemico" &c., "*Better* is inimical to *good;*" "pegni," pledges.—
Olivia and Arthur went in for the Oxford local examination of 1891;
and the rest of us accompanied them to Oxford.—The "stump of a
tree" was the remains of a tree, in the back yard of Christina's
house or visible therefrom, which had been lopped down almost to
extinction in 1890.]

30 TORRINGTON SQUARE, W.C.

[4 *July* 1891.]

MY DEAR WILLIAM,

Lucy and you are brotherly and sisterly in this matter, and
both have my love and thanks.   But really and truly so long as
conscience does not urge me to start, and so long as I go on as
tolerably as at present, I feel unenergetic and loth to come out of
my hole.

Nemico del bene è il meglio.   Your company would in itself
be a lure, and if not precisely in dulness I dare say I could beat
you hollow in dismalness!   Only would that game repay us for our
candle?   Let us leave that Yarrow unvisited.   So long as I have
you I have one very dear person left, and I trust you will not
misinterpret my apathy towards myself into indifference to you.
Just now too I am much more comfortable again, for Mr. Stewart
has stopped all physic and my throat has gained greatly.

I wonder where you and yours will take your holiday: I hope it will cheer you, strengthen Lucy, and foster the four "pegni," to whom my love. I hope soon—or at least in due course—to hear the result to Olive and Arthur of the Oxford examination. . . .

Did you not despise our stump of a tree at the catastrophe of last year? I on the contrary am very glad of it (since better may not be) for it is leafy and pretty as far as it goes, and its taller neighbour does something towards veiling its shortcomings. Turn a blind eye towards those of &c.

To LUCY ROSSETTI, *Bournemouth.*

[Mr. Joseph Skipsey, the coal-miner poet, was at this time custodian of Shakespear's birth-house in Stratford-on-Avon: I had had some little part in procuring him this post. My wife, on leaving Oxford, had gone to Stratford for a day or two: and she then made acquaintance with Mr. Skipsey, whom she particularly liked. He told her that he was likely to resign his post, finding that the majority of visitors to the birth-house took next to no interest in the serious and exalted associations of the place, but rather in silly stories about a pipe which Shakespear had (or had *not*) smoked, or a neighbouring locality where he had got drunk, or something of the kind. This is what Christina adverts to. I understood soon afterwards that the more essential reason why Skipsey resigned was that his wife, who had to be constantly showing visitors about, was in a condition of health which rendered this highly unsuitable, and even unsafe.—Mrs. William Bell Scott was now a widow, her husband having died in November 1890.]

30 TORRINGTON SQUARE, LONDON, W.C.

26 August [1891].

MY DEAR LUCY,

I hope, I do hope, Bournemouth is doing you more good than Oxford appears to have done . . . I did not know Mr. Skipsey was installed as custodian: such is my sordid mind that I might scarcely venture on discharging myself without an alternative berth, if *taste* alone is outraged. . . .

Here is a message to you from Mrs. Scott :—"Will you tell Lucy I should be so happy to see her. I dare say she is not in town, but will be available in some autumn day perhaps." This dear old friend has been ill and very weak, but is better now, and is I hope comfortably settled in her new home at Lancaster Hall,

133 Lancaster Road
Notting Hill—W.

Looking up I see sunshine and some blue sky: I hope you see the same and are cheered by it.

William came last Friday, welcome as usual.   He showed me one or two interesting letters, and was his own agreeable self,—for you know of old I believe in William !

My love to your and my four.

To WILLIAM ROSSETTI.

["Signor Mayo," or properly the Conte Adelfo Mayo, was one of my Vastese correspondents, the one whose letters I received with most pleasure : he still continues to correspond with me.   The proposal then pending was that of purchasing for the city of Vasto the house in which my father had been born.   The project was much agitated, but has never, I fancy, been fully effected.]

30 TORRINGTON SQUARE, W.C.
[28 December 1891.]

MY DEAR WILLIAM,

I am glad to have dined with you and yours on Christmas Day, though to me the meeting had a sad side.   The last time we dined thus together, it was you with our dearest Mother on the last Christmas Day she kept on earth.   "I will lift up mine eyes unto the hills from whence cometh my help."

Thankyou for Sr. Mayo's letter re-enclosed.   It is a more cheerful document.   If it comes to a general subscription for purchase of house, very likely I shall be able to contribute; but at the end of the year is not one's most opulent moment, and I express myself cautiously. . . .

To WILLIAM ROSSETTI.

[This letter relates to a volume of poems written by Mr. Morley Roberts.   This gentleman became personally known to me at a later date; but for the present I had only some acquaintance with his father, an official at Somerset House.   The latter had presented me

with a copy of the *Poems of Energy*, and had informed me that the
author was particularly inclined to learn what view my sister would
take of them.   Hence her pronouncement.   " I think him clever" is
(apart from whatever else) an opinion in which thousands of readers
have vigorously concurred since then.]

30 TORRINGTON SQUARE, W.C.

18 *February* [1892].

MY DEAR WILLIAM,

I am glad indeed that nothing has involved me in writing
straight to our poet, whose book I return.   I think him clever,—but
what is the use of *cleverness* in matters poetic ?   A number of lines
strike me as I go along, but at last I feel myself stranded on a not
high level.   Is he a Scotchman ? possibly, I should think.   " Poems
of Energy " they are, but of judicious energy ?   The goodness of his
actual work gives me the idea that he could if he would work *well* in
a different field.   *Grotesquerie* seems to me woven of good points
and relative come-downs.   I do admire some, yet on the whole I
must not rank myself as an admirer.   The little man on the cover
seems not quite to have seized his bull by the horns, and the great
man within the cover may have done much the same.   I regret my
opinion, but being mine it has to be given : consign me to discreet
oblivion.

What a mercy that the influenza has abated ; I hope yours will not
return. . . .

Aunt Eliza goes on very fairly, and people in bed are not the
worst off in such weather.   I go on, if not friskily, doggedly. . . .

I am open to a hope that I am wrong about our poet : time will
show.

To LUCY ROSSETTI.

30 TORRINGTON SQUARE, W.C.

20 *March* 1892.

MY DEAR LUCY,

. . . Mr. Stewart is keeping guard over me at present, and
the other day suggested that he does not see why (like others of us)
I should not live to be 80 !   Time will show, and I only wish what

God wills; but I do not run up like quicksilver at the announcement. . . .

I quite enjoyed some Dante conversation with William when last we met; please hand him the enclosed *P.S.* to our talk. Perhaps it is enough to be half an Italian, but certainly it is enough to be a Rossetti, to render Dante a fascinating centre of thought; moreover, I am not sure that my dear old Grandfather did not outrun my Father in admiration for the poet *as* a poet.

To WILLIAM ROSSETTI.

[This must be the "P.S. to our talk" named in the preceding letter. Christina's remarks go into details which will be understood by readers of the *Inferno*. Once launched upon an *ingenious* train of thought, she had considerable mental *finesse* in pursuing it.—I have not any recollection about the affair of "Wynifred Rawlinson": possibly, however, a member of a family of which I knew something, the father being a gentleman of means who collected pictures by Whistler and others.]

MY DEAR WILLIAM,

After flourishing over *Alchemists* and their allies, I recollected *Sorcerers* who also seem exempt from sustained external infliction though the original wrench seems to have been given them; I fear this weakens my theory as to substance-deterioration of Alchemists. My enthusiasm actually sent me to the *Penny Cyclopædia*, and a glance confirms my surmise that *transmutation* was in question before Dante's date; but I confess it was a glance, and not a careful reading. Don't you think something (additional to your exposition) might be made of Mastro Adamo's dropsy? His crime was to debase coin; his punishment to have his blood debased; that by alloy, this by water. And, if (as I think I saw somewhere) the circulation of the blood was not unsurmised as long ago as would be required, would or would not a play upon words suggest itself between the circulating vital fluid and the circulating medium? or would our own who "il gran comento fece" repudiate the triviality? As to *Usurers* who (I see) are considered to correspond with

Alchemists,—if so (in addition to points already established or suggested) might not some stress be laid upon their in a sense requiring money to "be fruitful and multiply" contrary to its natural constitution? May my remarks not bore you!

I think I have recovered the name of the person who wanted *Sing-Songs* about flowers to illustrate: Wynifred Rawlinson.

To WILLIAM ROSSETTI.

[The beginning of this letter refers to *The Face of the Deep*, and to a copy of it which was to be sent to Mr. Theodore Watts-Dunton. —The latter part of the letter relates to the alarming condition of Christina's health, which directly afterwards necessitated an operation for cancer. This was the first intimation which reached me on that precise subject.]

30 TORRINGTON SQUARE, W.C.

20 May 1892.

MY DEAR WILLIAM,

Thanks for all brotherliness. No! I send on your note to Theodore Watts *un*read, thinking it wiser on this occasion to peruse neither my own praises nor dispraises. Of course I am ordering the copy, and I hope it will be one with a sadly-needed slip of "errata," for at the end of an investigation I sent a list to Mr. McClure, and he wrote back that already the list was given in hand. The list, alas! was so long that I omitted trivial printers' errors. . . .

At last it seems that something brooding in my health has reached a point demanding sharp treatment, but I cannot be quite sure till a second opinion has been sought which (D.V.) will be obtained to-morrow. I will write again if I can, and if there is anything more definite to say: as yet the point is not decided, and so it may even remain, though I do not expect this. I beg prayers of every one who will pray for me. And, dear William, do not worry yourself about me: you see this is not an avowed certainty as yet, and come what will I am in Better Hands than either yours or my own; I desire to realize and to rest in this.

To LUCY ROSSETTI, *Bournemouth.*

30 TORRINGTON SQUARE, LONDON, W.C.

23 [*May* 1892].

MY DEAR LUCY,

I know our dearest William has written to you about me, and I think you may conceive too gloomy an idea of my position. As to pain, I have felt none worth speaking of, but it seems that it would not be prudent so to trust to this merciful circumstance as to neglect the step now to be taken, and about which I expect to know nothing under influence of ether. I dare say a cheerful view of me will be entertained by the time you return home, but I earnestly hope you will not leave the delightful seaside whilst it promises to do you good. We are keeping this anxiety from Aunt Eliza, who sends you love, and whom I join in love to Helen and Mary. Various kind souls will remember me in prayer, and each one who joins the praying band confers on me a favour beyond money and beyond price. I have asked the prayers of the congregation at my Church, but without my name being given out, as I deprecate getting into "paragraphs," and these are so in vogue nowadays.

To LUCY ROSSETTI, *London.*

[As soon as she had rallied a little from the surgical operation my sister went to Brighton with a professional nurse; I joined her there in a day or two.]

17 BRUNSWICK ROAD, BRIGHTON.

30 *June* 1892.

MY DEAR LUCY,

What a truly kind letter yours is, and how long I have delayed answering it. And how shall I excuse myself to you by pleading *weakness* when you are suffering from the same cause, or *occupations* when my one must be set against your dozen? But you are accustomed to overlook my shortcomings, and once more I beg you to do so and to reserve a nook in your heart for me. . . .

I am making steady progress, and look forward to returning home next Tuesday comparatively well. Thank you for the invaluable loan of William; he transforms our enforced expedition into quite a holiday. He is everything that is kind and tolerant—but you know him at least as well as I do!

One of my "occupations" is to lie down! Another is to write letters. Another is to go out in a chair. Shall I reckon breakfasting in bed as an occupation? You see I am not over-exacting towards myself.

To LUCY ROSSETTI.

30 TORRINGTON SQUARE, W.C.

13 [*July* 1892].

MY DEAR LUCY,

I want to hear all about you all when this anxious week is over. I hope Olive and Arthur are not overstraining their excellent wits; if only they could share their old aunt's philosophy, and realize that not one triumph at a particular moment but the treasure amassed of useful and delightful knowledge must prove the permanent boon! Meanwhile despite philosophy I wish them success. . . .

Now that I am at home again it is satisfactory to resume my quiet round of not difficult duties. Strong I cannot as yet profess to feel, and I am still being fed up and breakfasting luxuriously in bed, against which self-indulgence may be set a daily walk of more or less brevity. . . .

To WILLIAM ROSSETTI.

[The book referred to at the opening of this letter is that capital volume by Canon Moore, *Dante and his Early Biographers.*]

30 TORRINGTON SQUARE, W.C.

[19 *July* 1892.]

MY DEAR WILLIAM,

At length with thanks for pleasure I return Dr. Moore's little book, which instead of being dreary is even sparkling at proper moments. My frivolous mind dwells delighted on the note on the

authorship of the *Iliad* and *Odyssey*, also on the remark that happy
was it that Dante taught (?) Greek before the epoch of examinations.
Filelfo too is treated amusingly.   Abandoning such gems,—does any
one dispute the *existence* of Beatrice Bardi, nata Portinari?   I
should fancy the point of any such controversy might be limited to
the question of her identity or otherwise with the surnameless
Beatrice of Dante's immortalization : and if so Boccaccio's Lectures
would appear explicable, whether or not he simply meant what he on
the surface said.   You see, all too late I am being sucked into the
Dantesque vortex.

Now abandoning my *voci alte* however *fioche* I turn to matters of
to-day.   I am wanting news of you all; especially I want to know
that your entire caravan is going somewhere, and further where that
somewhere is. . . .   It is a comfort to reflect that the Oxford Senior
Exam. is at last over : I hope Olive and Arthur are justly sanguine
of results, and I congratulate them on not having had Dante for
Greek tutor. . . .

What unexpected money do you think has accrued to me ?
£12. 6. 6. from Maria's *Exercises* and *Aneddoti*.   When in 1886 I
wrote to ascertain (for probate) value of copyright, I was informed
no value : but I think it was in that very year—see " statement "
from Williams and Norgate— that the works cleared themselves and
began to yield a profit. . . .

To LUCY ROSSETTI, *Malvern Wells.*

30 TORRINGTON SQUARE, LONDON, W.C.

[1892—? 17 *August.*]

MY DEAR LUCY,

. . . Aunt Eliza quite enjoyed William's conversation
yesterday, and you will know whether I appreciated a sight of him.
He tells me of Olive's and Arthur's success in chemistry, which I
hope will be followed up by success in the wider Examination.   The
babies of yesterday are the sages of to-day !   I wonder if Helen has
been reading some of my old favourite Turguenieffs : I fancy the
first of his which I read was *Lisa* translated by our old friend Mr.
Ralston.   *Le Roi Léar de la Steppe* I greatly admired, but Gabriel

did not quite agree with me. *Moue-moue* was consummate, but so fearfully painful. I hope dear Helen will not appraise life quite according to any such pessimistic standard, but will use her great gifts to better purpose. . . .

I am still decidedly weak,—but no wonder. Nurse gives me her arm, and so I manage a little air and exercise. To-day is a superb summer day.

To WILLIAM ROSSETTI.

[The request made by *The Graphic* must evidently have been that Christina would sit for, or would supply, a portrait of herself, to be published in that paper. With this note Christina sent me also a full-sized review, extracted from the *Rock*, of *The Face of the Deep*. The suggestion in that review, that she advisedly abstained from making her verses good ones in the executive sense, was certainly funny. Two answers, both of them true, could have been returned by her to that suggestion :—1. The verses *are* good ; 2. If they were bad, the only reason would be that I could do them no better.]

30 TORRINGTON SQUARE, W.C.

[9 *November* 1892.]

MY DEAR WILLIAM,

All my enclosures alike are not wanted back. . . . The note from *The Graphic* (name of Editor I could not make out) I have negatived, but referred him to an Elliot and Fry of '77.—The review is a pleasing one, laudatory to a high degree,—yet I am surprised to see the suggestion that (perhaps as a devout self-denial) I forbore to make my verse as good as I could : neither as praise nor as blame do I deserve the imputation.

Love to Lucy who I wish may be facing these foglets scatheless. And love all round.

To WILLIAM ROSSETTI.

[Mr. Lawson was the surgeon who in May 1892 performed the operation for cancer on Christina. He now gave a reassuring opinion, but it had to be set aside all too soon.—" Mr. Scott's book " is the *Autobiographical Notes* of W. B. Scott. As is well known, that book contains some harsh, and not always accurate, remarks about Dante Rossetti : Christina, through my information, was aware of this fact, and she preferred to leave the book unread.—" The verse-vol. scheme," referred to in Christina's postscript, was the scheme, which I had proposed to her, that the poems contained in her various books published by the Society for Promoting Christian Knowledge should all be collected together into one volume. This was done, in the volume entitled *Verses*, 1893.]

30 TORRINGTON SQUARE, W.C.

[29 *November* 1892.]

MY DEAR WILLIAM,

Please go shares with my kind Lucy. Mr. Lawson has just been (apparently of his own accord, and simply as a friendly call I accepted it) and, at his own request of course, made an examination. With a joyful result. He inclines to think that there is nothing but what is otherwise and quite satisfactorily explicable at the suspected point, and even on the contrary supposition impresses upon most willing me that in his opinion nothing is to be done—now ; perhaps he means *ever*, but of this I am not sure. He will himself see Mr. Stewart to-night, and was altogether as amiable as possible. Knowing how affectionately Lucy and you feel for me, I write at once so that this may reach you before you start for Somerset House.

In last night's *St. James's Gazette* there was a rather long article on Mr. Scott's book, pleasant and laudatory and containing nothing obnoxious.

Love all round. . . .

Writing to Mr. McClure I mentioned the verse-vol. scheme, and referred to you.

To WILLIAM ROSSETTI.

[The " illustrated *Goblin Market*" must be the one designed by Mr. Laurence Housman. The other, proposed by Mr. Kegan Paul, cannot have come to anything. Mr. Housman's designs are the work of a very clever artist : but they did not correspond to Christina's notions, and I remember that, in sending me a copy of the book, she wrote on the wrapper the single word " Alas."]

30 TORRINGTON SQUARE, W.C.

30 [*December* 1892].

MY DEAREST WILLIAM,

Your *card* received this morning brightens a foggy world !
My love to dear Lucy, with my earnest wishes for her recovery, and
especially for that first stage of recovery which may enable her to exchange London for some promising spot, perhaps Bournemouth
which is not so very far to reach.   I fully believe in Olive's nursing-
powers, and I know what you yourself are in a sick room.   Our
nurse tells me that there is an admirable doctor at Bournemouth
who succeeded in a case of the same kind after I know not how many
London doctors had failed. . . .   *I* am quite shut up again, though
with all precautions fairly well: but it happened that (supposing it
the right thing) I went out a few steps on the 24th, and after getting
back was taken with such a fit of gasping breathlessness that Mr.
Stewart ordered me not to attempt another sally till this severe cold
has abated. . . .

How oddly things happen ! I told you of an illustrated *Goblin
Market* sent me not very long ago with an eye to permission to
publish it : now I have had a letter from Mr. Kegan Paul with the
same or a similar scheme, and proposing to issue it for next Christmas, I to go shares in profits : but I fear my having to refer him to
Macmillans for joint-sanction has put an end to the plan.

A friend has sent me *Tennyson Land* which possibly you may like
to look at.

Love to our dear four. . . .

You know *Goblin Market* has been out these 30 years ! !

To WILLIAM ROSSETTI.

[Christina's acquaintance with Madox Brown must have begun
not only before she was twenty (as she here says) but soon before she
was eighteen.—The kitten who "made the Y of our childhood"
was probably one (a semi-Persian) dubbed Muff, whom I was glad to
house between the date of Christina's death and that of Muff's own:
or else it was an offspring of Muff.   The "Y" was a pose, with

outstretched fore-paws, of which (as assumed by a tabby of my very early recollection) I made some passing mention in my *Memoir of Dante Rossetti.*]

30 TORRINGTON SQUARE, W.C.

2 [*January*] 1893.

MY DEAR WILLIAM,

This is my first letter this year, and is charged with deepest and widest good wishes to Lucy, yourself, and your four. Keen as the cold is, I yet hope that the vanishing of fog may favour our dear patient. . . .

Thankyou for your dear little card received on new year's eve : so much of my heart is yours that you may be sure of my sympathy. The "gasping" seems to have been brought on simply by my having gone out at an ill-chosen moment, and nothing of the sort has recurred. You know how glad I shall be to see you, but I do not even wish it before all circumstances favour my indulgence : it is a treat to talk over things with you, the head of my house and my natural adviser.

Some days ago I received 6 copies of my 2nd ed. *Face of the Deep*, a *corrected* ed. much to my satisfaction.

A card of kind remembrance came on Saturday from Mr. Madox Brown. What a steady old friend he is : to me a *very* old friend as I knew him before I was 20.

I am turned doctor myself ! rubbing a kitten who appears weak (to say the least) in the hind legs with camphorated oil. Yesterday I flattered myself that the treatment afforded some promise of amendment. Such a pretty kitten, with such a rich fur. And it stood up yesterday at the fender and made the Y of our childhood !

To WILLIAM ROSSETTI, *Boscombe.*

[Mr. McClure was (and I think still is) the Secretary of the Christian Knowledge Society. Christina was now performing a "slavish copying" of her various poems scattered throughout publications of this Society, with a view to compiling her book, published in 1893, entitled *Verses.*]

30 TORRINGTON SQUARE, LONDON, W.C.

8 *February* 1893.

My dear William,

I am heartily glad to hear from you, but not at all discontented at not having heard sooner. . . .

I was approved of by Mr. Stewart yesterday: to my discomfiture he has added a daily glass of port wine to all my eats and drinks. As I am always seeing him I am defenceless against these enactments. . . .

One afternoon came Mr. McClure with his wife. He tells me that my last book sold beyond what was anticipated, so that the second ed. was not out quite in time to meet the demand. Very grand. I am getting on with my slavish copying of the verses for the S.P.C.K. . . .

To William Rossetti, *London.*

[Christina had in conversation proposed to dedicate to me her forthcoming volume, *Verses.* I had expressed some doubt as to whether this could be deemed appropriate : a doubt essentially based on the consideration that her intensely devotional Christian poems ought hardly to be dedicated to any one who did not share the same beliefs in full.]

30 TORRINGTON SQUARE, W.C.

[10 *March* 1893.]

My dear William,

. . . Since we talked about it I have come to the conclusion that very likely you were right in hesitating to accept the dedication of my reprint. But, if so, I shall leave it undedicated ; and you and I will know that in my heart thus it stands :—

To my dearest Brother
William Michael Rossetti
I commend these verses.

I have not yet completed the printers' copy, but am far on with it. . . .

13

To WILLIAM ROSSETTI.

[About this time my wife had a frightful attack of illness with blood-spitting &c. : for three or four days, each day seemed likely to be her last. "Drizzarsi in sullo stelo" means "to straighten on the stem."—Sir Robert Micks was the Secretary (Excise Branch) in the Inland Revenue Office. I did not succeed him as Secretary, but continued for a short while to be Assistant Secretary.—The 8th and 9th April were the anniversaries of my mother's and my brother's death.—Mrs. R[ussell] Gurney's book related to Dante.]

30 TORRINGTON SQUARE, W.C.

13 *April* 1893.

MY DEAR WILLIAM,

I assure you I am sharing your anxiety for our dear Lucy. My love to her and every best wish I can form. This return of wintry cold—though tempered by such warming sunshine—makes me hope that we are now in "blackthorn winter"; and that before so very long these trying winds may cease, allowing flowers in general, and especially our own Flower de Luce, to drizzarsi in sullo stelo. . . .

What a burden double work at Somerset House must just now be upon you. I noticed in the paper that Sir Robert Micks is about retiring. I fear it is a phantom hope to foresee you as his successor : but of course I wish it, were it merely to augment your superannuation.

How nice of you to recollect me in the midst of such engrossing thoughts. Mr. Stewart wished me to see Mr. Lawson again, and to-day they held consultation. The result is that the state of my heart would render an operation too hazardous : but for this bar, I suppose one might have been judged advisable, as some mischief is going on, but happily slowly. So you see there is nothing to debate about at present, "and underneath are the Everlasting Arms." I continue to like Mr. Lawson, and am glad to escape the heavy expense of an operation and its context.

Did you remember the 8th and 9th of this month? The 10th also was the anniversary of our parents' wedding day.—I have begun the Memoir of James Smetham and like it, also I like Mrs. R. Gurney's book so far.

To WILLIAM ROSSETTI.

[Mr. G. Somes Layard was at this time preparing a book named *Tennyson and his Præraphaelite Illustrators.* I do not recollect ever seeing Mr. Kitton's article.]

30 TORRINGTON SQUARE, W.C.

[19 April 1893.]

MY DEAR WILLIAM,

. . . Please if possible give my love and very best wishes to Lucy. If ever it would give her the slightest pleasure to see me pray let me know: I should be afraid of startling her were I to present myself unexpectedly, as I am such an exceptional phenomenon; but under encouragement I dare say I could manage the transit in a cab. . . .

Of course the serious point remains unchanged, and I do not expect any more investigation for an undefined period. The *only occasional* pain continues so trifling that if I called it discomfort instead of pain it might give you a more accurate impression; and in other ways I am quite tolerable.

I have heard from a Mr. Layard about Gabriel's Tennyson illustrations; but, as he tells me he has already heard from you who are so much better an authority, my customary ignorance will not signify. Also from a Mr. Kitton who is concocting an article on the pets of "celebrities": but here again I had sadly little to say beyond the cat who made a Y.

To WILLIAM ROSSETTI.

[Eliza Polidori, the last stage of whose illness is announced in this note, died on 4 June, aged eighty-three. This left Christina the sole tenant in the Torrington Square house.]

[2 June.1893.]

MY DEAR WILLIAM,

A thousand thanks for your brotherliness. . . .

I am glad to write this afternoon, as I must tell you that good Aunt Eliza is lying in a very precarious state. Should my next letter even bear a black border you must not be surprised. She is insensible, which Mr. Stewart attributes to an access of brain-mischief: so far as appears the case at this time, she would neither see you nor know of your presence even were you at her bedside,—so it was when I was in her room half-an-hour or. so ago. Happily Mr. Stewart spoke positively this morning of her being free from suffering, and please understand that he has not given her over in talking to me.

To WILLIAM ROSSETTI.

[As a last (and fruitless) effort for health, my wife, with our three daughters, left London for Pallanza on 3 October.—Madox Brown was too truly "a frequent sufferer": but he had not much oftener to suffer, for on 6 October he died. His pictures sent to Chicago did not come in for a prize.]

30 TORRINGTON SQUARE, W.C.

4 *October* 1893.

MY DEAR WILLIAM,

Thank you warmly for letting me know. Anxious and painful as is the step, I cannot but be glad that poor Lucy has at last set off with her flock. I hope the journey will be accomplished safely, and Pallanza prove a suitable sojourn. You know I called and saw Lucy last week? I did not like her to leave England without my at least trying to see her once more, and when I got to your, house she consented to admit me. As to looks she quite surpassed my expectation, but I know that looks are not always to be depended upon. I am glad also to have seen all your children. . . .

After all I have sent Mr. Swinburne a "reprint" avowedly from myself. The S.P.C.K. bestowed on me a 2nd half-dozen, so I set aside manœuvring.

Will you be quite sick of my begging a Gabriel autograph? It is now one of Mrs. Bull's (Bessie Read that was) daughters who desiderates one.

I have just been reading the *Epic of Hades*, and do not care about it. Do you know that this month's *Magazine of Art* contains Gabriel's *Veronica Veronese* in photogravure? So I saw announced.

Poor Mr. Brown, what a frequent sufferer he is. When I see you I want to know whether his pictures received one of the Chicago prizes. I saw "Fred Brown" in a list of prizemen, and thought it might possibly misrepresent him.

To WILLIAM ROSSETTI.

[The "handsome cheque" must have been money due to Christina from the copyrights &c. of Dante Gabriel. The rest of her note refers to Madox Brown: he, however, had died on the preceding day.]

30 TORRINGTON SQUARE, W.C.

7 October 1893.

MY DEAR WILLIAM,

I head with that startling stamp because I once understood that, even to acknowledge receipt of a present or of one's own money, such was the intention of the revenue—or perhaps I should rather say such was its theoretic ideal. Thank you for the handsome cheque, which of course shall lie by for the present. I well know the run on ready money at such moments, and would gladly act banker up to £100 for that most kind old friend: please remember this in case of need, although of course ostensibly you would supply the funds. Even if my advance were lost it would not half repay the kindnesses of other days.

Your last letter shows that you had abandoned hope. I have seen such amazing rallies that I do not yet feel certain, but that is all I can say. I am hoping for a word of news again to-night. Your report of Lucy so far ought to cheer us and make us thankful, but I fear what effect this shock may have upon her.

To WILLIAM ROSSETTI.

[In consequence of Madox Brown's death, and of my great un- certainty as to the demands which might be made on his survivors (principally Mrs. Cathy Hueffer), I thought it would be desirable to have some cash in hand to meet *their* requirements—I was not under any personal responsibility. Christina (as her last letter shows) had already volunteered to advance £100. I, probably before receiving that letter, had started a query as to £200, and she produced that amount.—Miss Lisa Wilson, a very accomplished lady, was one of Christina's most intimate friends in her closing years, and my daughters and I continue to enjoy her acquaintance.]

30 TORRINGTON SQUARE, W.C.
7 *October* 1893.

MY DEAR WILLIAM,

  I do not think your letter sounds unfeeling. Do not fancy it.

Perhaps you already have mine of this afternoon in which I volunteered a loan (or in case of ultimate need a gift) of £100. But I can instantly and without the slightest inconvenience send you a cheque for *£200* out of my current account. Beyond this I have just laid by £200 in the Freehold, which is an investment on which I constantly draw on occasion ; not like my other investments supposed to be permanent. So let me feel that one point of your harass is allayed. I would send you the cheque in this letter if I knew you wanted it at once, and I only wait to hear exactly what you wish done. I quite agree with you as to the probable lack of funds for some time to come, and I feel that I am the proper person to look some up.

But about poor Lucy is alas a difficulty utterly beyond my power to cope with. I feel with you the incalculability of what effect such painful news may take upon her, frail as she is. I hope she is at Pallanza ere this, and so may have caught the alarm from your letters before the final blow falls on her. My poor dear William, I wish I could comfort you. . . .

Already a friend (Lisa Wilson) has seen the death announced in the *Standard*, and expresses herself very feelingly, for she knows how delicate our Lucy is. . . .

To WILLIAM ROSSETTI.

[This was written on the day of Madox Brown's funeral—to which the opening sentence refers. By " No. 1 " Christina meant " No. 1 St. Edmund's Terrace," the house in which Brown had died : it was separated from my own house by only one intervening dwelling.]

30 TORRINGTON SQUARE, W.C.

11 *October* 1893.

MY DEAR WILLIAM,

It is nearly noon and you may be sure I am not unmindful of all to-day brings with it. I am often thinking about Lucy. When you can, I dare say I shall be told how she bears what by this time I assume her to know. Poor Lucy, I well remember in old days her great affection for her Father. I hope the will has come to light and put an end to one complication of trouble. Your negativing any idea of my attending the funeral truly obliges me: I am glad not to have to decline, although I could not have accepted an invitation. My love to Cathy if worth giving.

What you suggest about my becoming tenant of No. 1 had occurred to my own mind, but, unless some special reason leads me thither, I do not think it altogether advisable. The house which would suit my infirmities would have sitting-rooms on ground-floor, bedrooms on 1st floor, thus saving me many stairs; so that such a cottage as our Grandparents occupied in Park Village East would meet my requirements better than a superior house. A number of empty rooms too are not merely useless but depressing. However, were there a strong motive the other way these drawbacks might be overruled, and *annual* tenancy is very attractive. But common sense forbids my scheming for a remote future. You ask about my health: there is nothing very particular to report, but the heart still occasionally makes itself felt, and the other weak point is I suppose gaining rather than losing ground. Even now the pain is trifling. Mr. Stewart often comes to see me. . . .

I dare not write to Lucy before being quite sure that she knows all. This secured, I should like to send her a word of sympathy if you see no objection.

Love to Arthur.

To WILLIAM ROSSETTI.

[Dante Rossetti's "burlesque drama" is entitled *The Death of Topsy* (*i.e.* William Morris). It is amusing, but must, I suppose, remain perdu in my hands, not being intended nor yet suitable for

publication.—The *Inferno* which Christina returned was the translation by Mr. Musgrave in the Spenserian stanza.]

30 TORRINGTON SQUARE, W.C.

[4 *December* 1893.]

MY DEAR WILLIAM,

Thank you for errata, which I am sending on to Mr.
McClure in case they may still be in time. . . .

Perhaps you have seen . . . a further reference to a burlesque
drama (?) of Gabriel's which he once read us. This was alluded to
in the *St. James's Gazette ;* how known of, who knows? . . .

Is any book ever absolutely accurate? Kegan Paul says in his
Preface that he has added 17 new poets to his re-issue, whereas on
careful examination I find (and fail to see any other explanation) 18.
I should like to know which is correct. . . .

I return the *Inferno* with considerable admiration.

To WILLIAM ROSSETTI.

[Christina's health at this time was in such a condition as to make
it totally unfitting that she should go to Pallanza. I must no doubt
have replied to her to this effect, and her doctor, if she consulted
him, must necessarily and imperatively have forbidden her.—Mr.
Aldrich was then, and still is, Curator of the Historical Department
of the State of Iowa, in its capital, Des Moines : a highly estimable
gentleman well known to me, keen in collecting for his institution
documents, autographs, and other relics.]

30 TORRINGTON SQUARE, W.C.

[24 *December* 1893.]

MY DEAR WILLIAM,

I receive your news into a somewhat heavy heart. That
you have been ill is in a measure balanced by the joyful announcement of your being better,—but poor Lucy, I cannot but feel grave
apprehension. Is it imaginable that my going over could be of any
use or help or comfort? If so, I would try to get leave to start

(accompanied of course by a nurse) from Mr. Stewart. By the beginning of next year I should be in sufficient funds. Yet it seems almost mere words to speak of such a plan under actual circumstances, my health considered: still, I would certainly ask Mr. S. were there an opening. Of course I would not be an expense to my family, and perhaps the girls might find some sort of support in the presence of one who might be their grandmother. Without Mr. Stewart's permission however I should not feel at liberty to go.

As to the pleasures of Christmas I say nothing. I wish you and Arthur (to whom my thanks) and all yours its overflow of blessings. Flowers have come to me in profusion, amongst them a box from Pallanza.

I wonder what brought on this fit of gout; you had been so long comparatively free from it: I hope it has not been one of the most painful attacks. I too am not at my very best at present, although very tolerable and able to get to church to-day. . . .

I sent Mr. Aldrich 2 specimens of Gabriel's hair: one in the early fair stage, the other dark; both dated. I hope that by this time my earlier letters have reached him.

To WILLIAM ROSSETTI.

30 TORRINGTON SQUARE, W.C.

[29 *December* 1893.]

MY DEAR WILLIAM,

. . . Don't let expense be the insurmountable difficulty if you wish to go to Pallanza: of course, if I could have managed my own journey thither, I could be your banker as well or better. . . .

Mrs. Garnett called one day and told me that by Christmas there was no meeting the demand for *Verses*: at one considerable shop she tried at she heard that twenty or thirty applications had had to be negatived for the moment. I wish the new edition may now be out, but I have not heard.

I wrote to Lucy at Christmas, merely a sisterly letter, not I hope one in any way to try her. . . .

To WILLIAM ROSSETTI, *San Remo.*

[From Pallanza my wife went to Genoa, and then to San Remo. On 19 March I received a telegram showing her to be almost at the last gasp; so on the following day, accompanied by my son, I started for San Remo. Lucy, though she had once more rallied in a certain sense, was at that time far past any hope of recovery or improvement: she continued alive and suffering up to 12 April. It was a kind thought of Christina to commission our family-doctor, Mr. Gill, to go over to San Remo, if wanted by the patient. But there was truly nothing to be done, beyond what a young Italian physician, Dr. Ansaldi, supplied by his daily and judicious attendance. My wife and all of us appreciated this gentleman highly.]

30 TORRINGTON SQUARE, LONDON, W.C.

[26 *March* 1894.]

MY DEAR WILLIAM,

Cathy very kindly brought me round your and Olive's letters to-day, so now I know how you all are suffering and in suspense. Be sure you are in my heart and thoughts. May I send love to Lucy? as well as to the rest.

Is it possible that you (or that dear Lucy herself in any degree) are wishing you could see Mr. Gill? If so and if you would allow me, I could and would help as far as £100. But if there is no feeling of the sort do not trouble yourself to allude to this. I am very tolerable to-day.

To WILLIAM ROSSETTI, *San Remo.*

30 TORRINGTON SQUARE, LONDON, W.C.

2 *April* 1894.

MY DEAR WILLIAM,

Welcome was your card last Saturday morning. I think the account to the full as good as could be looked for after what has passed, although of course with the limitation you indicate. . . .

Longmans have written to me on the subject of a 3/6 *Shadow of Dante*, and I suppose they will issue one in their Silver Library series as I left the decision to them : they would keep on also the current ed. but foresee that its sale would be diminished by the cheaper volume. I hear also of a third ed. of my *Verses*, S.P.C.K. I have had a visit this morning from Mary Cayley (Arthur Cayley's daughter) and was glad to hear news of the family. Sophie and Henrietta Cayley (her aunts whom you may remember) died some years ago within no very prolonged period of each other. Profr. Cayley himself is a good deal of an invalid, at least for the present : his wife sent me some pretty daffodils which now adorn my table. Henry Cayley, the son, looked in and fetched his sister and is very tall : I understand that he is studying architecture. . . .

To WILLIAM ROSSETTI, *San Remo.*

[I cannot remember about the "little papers" which Christina was "trying to write" : one might surmise, something for publication, but I question this. Neither have I any knowledge of the affair of Mr. John Shelley ; nor of the name of Rosamond Martin.]

30 TORRINGTON SQUARE, LONDON, W.C.
9 *April* 1894.

MY DEAREST WILLIAM,
You may think how much my thoughts are with you all. My love to dear Lucy, and thanks for love sent me by you. . . . They have been doing up this Square really prettily just now, and I have been remembering the pleasant days when you and yours were all staying here, and Helen and Mary frequented the enclosure, and we used to muster cheerfully round *a ham !* I hope Lucy will be equal to accepting my love and to knowing how often I think of her. . .

I forgot in my last to thank my nieces for a box of flowers, and I do so now with my love. Here is a dried heartsease : I wish I could send you its sentiment as well as itself. That the girls are not quite downcast is really to be rejoiced at ; but I can fancy its effect on you.

I have just finished certain little papers I told you I was trying to write, and to-day I hope to have them posted. It is a good thing really to do what I have to do *now*. I go on extremely tolerably, yet I think with a gradual downward tendency.

Not long ago a Mr. John Shelley sent me a little Latin book with an amiable letter. Would he be one of *the* Shelleys? He wrote from Plymouth. . . .

" Rosamond Martin " writes from Chesham that a performance of my *Pageant* is preparing for a charitable purpose. She mentions her mother as authoress of several novels, but I do not recognize the name. . . .

To WILLIAM ROSSETTI, *London.*

[This is a reply to a brief letter which I wrote to Christina immediately after returning to London, consequent upon my wife's death at San Remo. Her will had left her separate property, including the house 3 St. Edmund's Terrace, to our children under trusteeship.]

30 TORRINGTON SQUARE, W.C.

[18 *April* 1894.]

MY DEAR WILLIAM,

At least it is a comfort and great matter for thankfulness that you are all safely back again. Be sure my heart is with you in your grief, desolation, and general harass and anxiety. Every word of your letter is full of interest to me: I am glad that poor Lucy's last day was of diminished rather than of increased suffering. I already knew from Mr. Stewart how costly an undertaking the removal from San Remo to London would have been, but I can understand the pang it cost you to leave so beloved a person behind. . . .

I will not venture to say that I regret anything in Lucy's will, and I will not suppose it possible that any trouble can arise about the house. If for any reason you should wish entirely to recast your plans, I remind you that mine are wholly unsettled, and that, if any combination with me would help towards an arrangement, it seems probable that I should be available—available, that is, if life lasts so long. But, if not, I have the comfort of knowing that your income would be increased.

Do not suppose by this that I have fresh reason to anticipate a speedy end, but you and I know how precarious is all life and how doubly precarious mine has become.   Mr. Stewart detects progress of the mischief, but I understand slow progress.   And now put me out of your dear old thoughts so far as to feel that I can contentedly wait till you have heart and leisure to look me up: you will not, I think, distort this sentence into meaning that I do not care to see you!

My love to my nieces and nephew.   I recollect that Mary's birthday is next Sunday, but perhaps you might come before then; otherwise I may get a P.O.

To WILLIAM ROSSETTI.

[This note is of interest to me as being the last that I received from my sister, written with her own hand.   The next following (and final) one was dictated to her nurse Harriett Read.   "*The Portfolio*" must be the monograph on Dante Rossetti written by our old friend Frederic G. Stephens.   The present note is an observably good specimen of Christina's always good handwriting.]

30 TORRINGTON SQUARE, LONDON, W.C.

[21 *June* 1894.]

MY DEAR WILLIAM,

I have just finished reading with much interest the *Portfolio* you lent me.   I have made a few notes on points here and there which I hope to submit to you when next we meet: after that, I shall be ready to return the N?.

This lovely summer day revives the world,—I hope it revives you. I am not very bright, but quite tolerable all considered.   Eczema much better if not almost gone.

Love all round your circle.

To WILLIAM ROSSETTI.

[The details in this note were sent for the purpose of keeping me correct in the *Memoir of D. G. Rossetti*, which I was then writing.

Christina's recollection of old family-facts was more precise than mine, and was noticeably accurate. Her last sentence, however, is a little jumbled, as she and our mother (not as yet our father) had gone down to Frome *before* 27 April 1853.]

30 TORRINGTON SQUARE.

10 *August* [1894].

MY DEAR WILLIAM,

You and Maria stayed in Arlington Street some time after we had left—till I believe Christmas 1853. I think you were only one quarter at Burcham's, and certainly we all rejoined company about Lady-day in Upper Albany Street. Our parents and I settled at Frome not long after the 27th of April 1853, at which date our Grandmother died. Glad to be of use.

The End of the Year.

New Year met me somewhat sad;
    Old Year leaves me tired,
Stripped of favourite things I had.
    Baulked of much desired:—
Yet farther on my road today
God willing, farther on my way.

New Year coming on apace
    What have you to give me?
Bring you scathe, or bring you grace
Face me with an honest face,
    You shall not deceive me:—
Be it good or ill, be it what you will,
It needs shall help me on my road,
My rugged way to heaven, please God.

13th December 1856.

FACSIMILE OF A POEM BY CHRISTINA ROSSETTI.

[*To face p.* 206.

APPENDIX

1. *Extracts from the Diary of William M. Rossetti,* 1871–95.

1871. February 18. Locker and Cincinnatus Miller, a Californian whom Locker made known to me, also Stillman, came to Euston Square : the former two were introduced to Christina, whom they more especially wished to know.

,, April 25. Christina has for some days past been suffering from neuralgia (so her doctor says), and looking very much out of condition. Dr. Jenner advises her to get change of air.

,, May 5. Christina's illness still extremely serious ; I feel more alarmed about it to-day than heretofore. Sir William Jenner says there is " no immediate danger," and at his late visit to-day reassured Mamma a little—but only a little. He orders Christina to keep her bed strictly, which I have thought for several days would be the best thing ; hitherto she has got up regularly, but done little or nothing more, save lying on the sofa.

,, May 15. Obtained some specimens of the wood-designs of F. A. Fraser, whom Dalziels propose for illustrating Christina's book [*Singsong*]. I don't think him, from the evidence of these designs, at all a desirable man. Wrote to Dalziels to say so, and strongly recommended that Hughes should be invited.

,, June 6. To-day, at last, Christina was sufficiently convalescent to be moved off to Hampstead—17 Christ Church Road; the doctor wishes her to go on to the sea-side pretty soon.

,, July 20. Mamma and Christina returned to-day from Hampstead. Christina has certainly made some degree of progress, though still far from set-up in health.

,, October 19. Brown called. I showed him the proofs of Christina's *Singsong*, with Hughes's illustrations. He was singularly pleased with both ; going so far as to say that the poems are about Christina's finest things, and Hughes the first of living book-illustrators.

1871. October 26. Christina (whose health continues unsatisfactory, though much less bad than during the spring and summer) consulted Dr. Fox to-day. He says that the circulation is out of order, and prescribes digitalis.

„   November 5. Dr. Wilson Fox called to see Christina, who has been particularly unwell these two days. He does not seem to consider her state different from what it was before, but has made some modification in the digitalis medicine. He says that the external swelling in her throat (he does not define it by any particular name) is a sort of thing prevalent in some parts of England—as for instance Derbyshire; also that it has nothing to do with the difficulty in swallowing, which is now one of the most troublesome details of Christina's illness. This, he says, depends upon spasmodic nervous action. He says nothing as to the probable duration of the swelling.

„   November 13. Brown's family and Hughes dined at Cheyne Walk. . . . Hughes says that the illustrating of Christina's book took up his whole time for a while. At first he worked tolerably leisurely, but after a certain time Dalziels asked him to furnish ten designs per week : he furnished twenty the first time.

„   November 16. Poor Christina continues in a very deplorable state. Besides her two standing maladies, both of which seem for the time to be kept tolerably in abeyance, she has the external lump on the throat, which shows no signs of going, and of late a sort of fluttering at the heart (*not*, it would seem, regular palpitation of the heart, or other definite heart-disease) which incommodes her, producing a kind of stifling or fainting tendency from time to time, compelling her to desist from any occupation, and lie down. She often passes bad nights, which seldom befell her heretofore. Frequent headaches of a very aggravated kind are another trouble : these she thinks are mitigated by the early tea with brandy which the doctor makes her take. He calls the heart-symptoms "accelerated circulation." As regard appearance, she is a total wreck for the present, and I greatly fear this change may prove permanent; her hair also comes off in a distressing way, and she expects to have to take to caps almost immediately. . . . With all these disasters—and she is fully alive to every one of them—her spirits are not so bad as might have been expected; she shows a really admirable constancy, and the worst shafts of Fate find her their equal. Another of Christina's troubles now is the continual shaking of her hands. This has quite spoiled her handwriting, which is so shaky now that it might be the work of a woman of 75.

1871. November 18. Christina's book, *Singsong*, was sent to her to-day. The general publication of it will take place, I understand, within two or three days. It *ought* to be a great selling success, and even perhaps *may* be. She is to get 10 per cent. on every copy sold; it seems there is no stipulation as to any conjuncture at which this arrangement would terminate.

„   November 24. Dr. Fox, having called again to see Mamma, entered into some details regarding Christina's illness. The thing that is essentially the matter with her now is connected with the heart (as previously indicated), though not amounting strictly to heart-disease. The swelling outside the throat and other symptoms depend on this same malady. It is a very rare one: so rare that Dr. Fox has seen only two cases of it (one of which he treated successfully), and Sir William Jenner, I understand, has also only seen two cases. Sir William has concurred in the treatment of Christina as conducted as yet by Dr. Fox.

„   November 25. Sir William Jenner (just back from Balmoral) visited Christina, and gave minute attention to her case. He confirms what Dr. Fox said about the complaint, and adds that there is a change in the colour of the skin-pigment; this indeed is sufficiently evident, though I had not noticed it as going beyond what might be ascribed to Christina's extreme thinness now, and depressed condition of health. Jenner clearly regards the case as a serious one, and says Christina ought not to go up and down stairs, in the present state of her heart, but should be confined to one floor. She has for this fortnight or more been sleeping in the same room as Mamma, the back drawing-room. She will now therefore restrict herself to the back and front drawing-rooms.

„   December 11. Swinburne complimented Maria very warmly on her book upon Dante, and is (as a letter of his had shown us some days ago) most enthusiastic about Christina's book.

„   December 14. Dr. Fox saw Christina again to-day, and pronounces her progressively and even considerably improving. To-day, indeed—for the first time to any serious extent—she strikes me as looking decidedly not quite so miserable in the face. There seems some little diminution of the thinness, starting eyes, &c.

1872. March 16. Christina is miserably exhausted now, as to all such matters as appetite, strength, &c., causing us all grave anxiety; yet it seems that the lump outside the throat has

14

diminished, and the spasmodic difficulty in swallowing is also less.

1872. March 21. Sir William Jenner called again. He told Maria that the disease Christina suffers from, exophthalmic broncho-cele, is one from which the patient more generally recovers: the chief danger is exhaustion. Of this, unfortunately, there have been of late very distressing symptoms in Christina— almost total want of appetite, prostration of strength, and very frequent vomiting. The last was particularly bad yesterday.

„   April 16. Maria says that, having to-day seen Christina's throat uncovered, she was agreeably surprised to find how very much the external swelling (once so large) has diminished. One might now almost take the throat for its natural shape; the discolouration is also less marked.

„   April 21. The doctors recommend Christina to keep her bed (which, indeed, I have frequently thought and said would be the better course); and, as she can't take natural nourishment at ordinary times, they direct that every two hours, day and night, unless she is asleep, she shall take some small modicum of food.

„   May 1. Christina's illness seems to have taken rather a peculiar effect on her mind. It necessarily diminishes her powers of continuous attention, but appears to have disposed her in some increased degree to reading books conveying some sort of positive knowledge, such as history—all of which class of reading has been almost wholly neglected by her all her lifetime. She has just got Mamma to read through to her Southey's *Life of Nelson*, and is herself reading Goldsmith's *History of Greece*—neither of them certainly a work of arid or profound learning, but still the sort of thing that Christina has mostly steered clear of as yet. She thinks of reading Herodotus.

„   May 15. We felt very uneasy about Christina all the earlier part of the day, as, although she had slept well in the night, she was in a terribly low condition, accompanied with frequent vomitings. Sir William Jenner called again, without saying anything very particular. In the later part of the evening Christina had revived to some extent, and seemed pretty much at her usual level, and she again passed a good night. I have great apprehensions as to the result, however—perhaps at no distant date—for there seems to be no real rally of physical energy now for months past, and the process of exhaustion proceeds with fatal and frightful steadiness. What shows least trace of disease in Christina now is her voice (which had indeed altered some while ago, but that passed off). She speaks with much the same tone, animation, and general manner, as of old, and with equal readiness on any subject that is uppermost, and her strength of mind continues to maintain an admirable triumph over all physical suffering and prostration.

1873. January 26. One of the most annoying outward symptoms of Christina's illness, the enormous protrusion of the eyes, is now very sensibly diminished; this diminution has been going on for some while past, but I am more particularly struck with the stage it has reached just now. The swelling at the throat is also so far subdued as to excite no particular attention when Christina is dressed.

„ March 19. Joaquin Miller looked me up at Somerset House, and left with me the remaining proofs of his forthcoming volume. He showed me the dedication, "To the Rossettis." I strongly recommended him to write direct to Gabriel as to the matter before anything further is done. I mentioned the dedication to Christina. She feels some hesitation in sanctioning it, not knowing what the book may contain. If she makes up her mind to object, she is to write to Miller. I looked through the proofs and noted down some remarks on them. They include a series of poems about Christ, named *Olive Leaves*, implying a sort of religious, or at least personal, enthusiasm, mixed up with a good deal that has more relation to a sense of the picturesque than of the devotional. These poems, though far from worthless from their own point of view, are very defective, and would, I think, be highly obnoxious to many readers and reviewers. I have suggested to Miller the expediency of omitting them altogether.—Christina, I find, has already read these particular poems, and to some considerable extent likes them, which is so far in their favour as affecting religious readers.

1876. October 1. My mother and Christina removed from our house, 56 Euston Square, and went to live along with my two aunts at 30 Torrington Square.

1881. December 15. Christina called on Gabriel to-day. She found him passive and inclined to doze.[1] Marshall has not yet appeared, but seemed certain to do so in the course of the day.

[1] This was consequent upon that seizure of a quasi-paralytic kind which was one of the later stages of Gabriel's fatal illness.

1882. February 8.   Mamma seems now as well as usual : would like, with Christina, to join Gabriel at Birchington, but her doctor, Stewart, will not allow her to do this until the weather becomes milder.

„   February 28.   Mamma and Christina expect to go down on Thursday to Birchington, to stay awhile with Gabriel. I mentioned to Christina the proposal made by Ingram—that she should contribute to a series of Biographies of Women of which he is to be editor, and more especially that she should write a life of Adelaide Procter : sum to be paid in each instance, £50. She is quite willing to enter into this arrangement : does not particularly want to do Adelaide Procter, but has no real objection either. Would like to do Mrs. Browning,[1] which would indeed be highly suitable. Both she and I will now write to Ingram to settle matters.

„   September 6.   Christina handed me some eight or nine letters of Gabriel's addressed to herself [2]—all of them belonging to his last few months—which she would not mind having published if wanted : all others, except perhaps some few handed over to Mamma, she destroyed (as I knew must have been the case).

„   October 11.   Christina showed me, in a halfpenny magazine published by the Society for the Promotion of Christian Knowledge, two little sketches she wrote lately narrating facts regarding two poor families of her acquaintance, the Meaders and Bakers. She completed not long ago a book on The Commandments, and it now lies with the same Society for consideration, and one may surmise publication.

1883. December 7.   Another death to which some of us are far from indifferent. Christina came to Somerset House, and informed me that—as she was told this morning by his brother and sister-in-law—Cayley was on Wednesday found dead from heart-disease : I would not press her to dwell upon details, so I know little of the facts beyond this. I had not been aware that Cayley suffered at all from heart-disease, although the settled and rather hard high colour in his cheeks may have been symptomatic. The family, it appears, would like some mention of Cayley to appear in print. I will most willingly write a paragraph for *The Athenæum*, and Lucy seems rather disposed to

---

[1] This project lapsed.   Christina would not write about Mrs. Browning unless with the sanction of Robert Browning : and this sanction was not forthcoming—I think never asked for.

[2] These letters were handed over with a view to my including them in a volume of Gabriel's family-letters.

forward one for *The Times* through Hueffer. Cayley was a rare model of a retiring, single-minded scholar; cheerfully absorbed in literary, especially semi-philological, studies, and sociable too in a shy way—little concerned in anything else. I saw him last on this day week, when, on going to Torrington Square, I found him taking the fourth hand in a game of whist with the family. Had also seen him the preceding day at Somerset House, when he called to inquire whether I possessed a certain dialogue by Galileo.

1883. December 8. Lucy went round to Torrington Square, and heard from Christina some more details about Cayley. On 5 December he retired to rest as usual: on the 6th he was found dead in his bed, without the slightest trace of any struggle or agitation. He is to be buried at Hastings, by his mother's side.

„ December 12. Lucy took round to Christina three notices of Cayley which have appeared in newspapers—*Times*, *Daily News*, and *Manchester Guardian*. It is curious that a large proportion of the notices of Cayley (in fact, *all* that I know of) derive from one or other member of our own families. *The Times* was done by Hueffer, at Lucy's suggestion; *Daily News* from *Times*; *Manchester Guardian* by, or at the instance of, Brown; and the comparatively long notice which I expect *The Athenæum* to contain will be mine.

„ December 18. Christina writes me that Cayley left her by will the extant remainders of his published books.

1886. March 1. My mother seems to me a little worse to-day: voice less natural and less under control. The doctor (Stewart) speaks of a shock to the spine, such as one hears of in railway-accidents. Christina bears up with great fortitude and exterior cheerfulness.

„ April 11. My dearest mother, the pattern to me of everything that is simple, sweet, kind, and noble, died on 8 April at 25 minutes past noon. She had been unconscious for a couple of days or more, and expired in great peace, without any strain or agitation. Present—Christina, myself, Stewart the doctor (who came in at the very last moment), and the nurse Annie Jackson, whom Christina found exceedingly attentive and agreeable.

„ April 12. The funeral: the first portion (and most of the second) conducted by Rev. Mr. Nash at Christ Church, Woburn Square; second portion repeated at Highgate Cemetery by him. My mother lies in the same grave with my father and Gabriel's wife. Present in the church—Christina, Eliza,

Hueffer, Cathy, and myself; also four or five servants &c., including old Sarah Catchpole. In the cemetery, the same except Eliza: she returned home to keep company with Charlotte, who is utterly weak and ill in bed—I think at death's door. In the afternoon Christina produced the will, of which she is executrix: it leaves (practically) everything to her, save for £100 to me. This I consider right. Christina says she wishes to compensate me, when her means allow, for her maintenance during the many years when she was substantially dependent on me—say 1854 to 1876. She fixes a sum of £2000, which is certainly more than the actual amount. I have no serious *wish* that she should do this—also certainly no objection: I therefore expressed my assent. But I don't understand that Christina contemplates giving any effect to this arrangement at *present*. She will inherit, I understand, something less than £4000 from our mother, and this sum could not be cut down in any such way.

1886. October 4. Christina dined with us—an incident perhaps unprecedented these four years. Christina looked through my preface to Gabriel's *Collected Works*, and told me that she considers I have given an accurate and telling sketch of his character &c.

1887. January 17. Called on Christina, who wrote me a few days ago to the effect that she is about to re-make her will, and means me to be sole legatee, subject to some temporary conditions. She explained to me what these conditions would be —not onerous. I can see that she regards her tenure of life as very fragile: she even speaks of our aged and infirm aunts being probably her survivors. What the precise illness is I don't gather: it is connected with the heart (as of old), but does not at present involve those suffocating-fits which used to be so alarming. She has seen Jenner several times of late: were she unable to call on him, his attendance upon her would cease, and she would consult either Gill or Stewart. Of course it may well be that she yet takes a decided turn for the better. The prospect of death is not, I think, in the least alarming to her—on the contrary, consolatory.

„   April 2. I saw Christina who, since returning from Torquay, seems to have remained nearly stationary in point of health— perhaps a trifle less well. She says that her income this year has amounted to about £300—more than she had reckoned upon.

„   April 24. Olive has now finished turning into blank verse her little drama of *Theseus:* Christina coached her up somewhat while at Brighton last autumn, and I have set some lines right, but only to a moderate extent.

1887. July 3. I called in the evening to inquire after my Aunt Charlotte, and I saw her for a minute or two. She seems to have again taken a turn for the worse, and, to judge by appearances, might be accounted very near her end: however, the reserve of vitality and strength has evidently been very great, and possibly it so continues. Christina tells me Charlotte has left to her an amount of money about double what she has left to Eliza. This, however, is on the understanding that Christina will continue keeping up certain benefactions &c. which Charlotte had at heart, especially to the Polidori family in Florence: insomuch that Christina regards about half of the money left to her as being practically trust-money, and to be still applied as such (more or less) even after Christina's own decease. I recommended her to carry out (of course) with strict faithfulness whatever is really incumbent upon her in this regard; but not to indulge in mere fancies and wire-drawings, such as mere voluntary largesses to the Polidoris, or continuance of this full allowance (some £40 p.a.) after the widow (Amalia) of Filippo Polidori shall have ceased to live. In especial, I dissuaded her from trenching on the capital sum—a course which she seemed inclined to adopt without much reluctance should it serve some ostensible convenience.

1890. January 8. My venerable Aunt Charlotte died this afternoon: she was 87 last May. For uniform placid sweetness of temper and manner, complaisance, and pleasing moderation of character and feeling, I certainly never knew her superior—indeed not her equal. Her abilities were of an ordinary stamp—no marked degree or tendency of faculty in any direction. The news of my aunt's death reached me from Christina. . . . The last day when I saw Charlotte may have been towards 15 December. She then presented an appearance of more ill-health and depression than usual, and her memory was infirm and treacherous. For the most part, although almost wholly bed-ridden since about May 1887, she has looked surprisingly well—placid, and even cheerful in countenance (though I have constantly understood from Christina that Charlotte was very wishful for death), clear in complexion, and firm in flesh: one could hardly believe her arm and hand to be those of a more than octogenarian. I am executor along with Eliza: of course I shall have practically to act alone.

„ January 16. This afternoon I handed over the will to the

solicitor who drew it up, Mr. Turner, in order that he may take
the requisite steps. The main provisions of the will are these:
House in Endsleigh Gardens to me; personal effects and £100
to Eliza; residue between Eliza, one third, and Christina, two-
thirds. I have gathered in talk with Christina that the total
value will probably exceed £5000.

1892. May 26. A dreadful complication in Christina's condition of
ill-health came to a crisis yesterday.[1] With deep thankfulness
I can say that as yet all seems to go on perfectly and even
surprisingly well. The future cannot but remain overcast; but
(a proverb which has often yielded me some consolation my life
through) "sufficient for the day is the evil thereof." Christina
has borne herself like a heroine in this matter: I first knew of
it from her on Friday last. I was in her house from 1½ p.m. on
Wednesday to 9½ a.m. on Thursday. Stewart, Lawson, Bailey.
. . . Christina had had ever since 29 December some idea of
what was in prospect for her.

„ May 28. Saw Christina for some twenty minutes in the afternoon. She is placid and comparatively comfortable—free from
any positive pain, allowing for a certain not quite easy sensation
in the left shoulder. I also saw the surgeon, Lawson, for a few
minutes: he says everything went as well as could be, and for
the present all the prospects are satisfactory.

„ June 12. Called on Christina, and for the first time found
her seated in a chair. Sat talking with her more (I suppose)
than 1½ hour, partly on religious matters. Was sorry to learn
that last night a touch of rather sharp pain woke her up. It
passed off rapidly, and she does not know what it really indicated. To-day she mentioned it to Mr. Lawson, who seemed
to pass it over as of no importance: this may perhaps be his
last visit, but Christina is not sure as to this point. His fee is
to be £52. 10s. (as settled by Stewart)—which seems very
ample. Christina does not know with any accuracy when she
can go off (as is proposed) to Brighton. I expect to accompany her. I had to write to-day to G. F. Watts, explaining
that his offer to paint Christina's portrait, to be given to the
nation among the others of his gift, cannot be further taken into
account for the present: a disappointment to me, and no
doubt, to some extent, to Christina herself.

„ September 5. Called to see Christina—still on the sofa in the
drawing-room. She feels better, and the doctor says she *is*

---

[1] The crisis (which I did not then choose to put into words) was the operation
for cancer.

better. Nevertheless, as the nurse-servant Harriett informed me on my going down-stairs, the doctor has left a special message for me, to the effect that the condition of Christina's heart is such as to give cause for grave apprehensions, and one ought to be prepared for whatever may happen. It is not for the present any recurrence of the other disease which caused so much anxiety in May. She was lately invited by the widow of Canon Burrows to write a prefatory or other memoir of him, but was reluctantly compelled to decline, owing to the state of her health.

1892. September 9. Christina seems some trifle better to-day: she was to leave her bed in the evening for the sofa in the drawing-room. Dr. James, with whom Lucy conversed, says the disease is in the nature of angina pectoris, but not that form of the malady which entails acute pain. This is an illness which afflicted Christina at a very early age—say 19 to 23: Dr. Crellin then cured it. At least he called it angina pectoris, although of late years I have been told now and again that that cannot well have been angina pectoris, as a cure could not well have been hoped for.

1893. March 3. Called on Christina. It seems to be now only too certain that the illness from which she suffered in April and May last is recurring—though as yet no definite steps to cope with it have been taken or announced. There is not any *severe* pain,—so she says. The matter of the heart-disease is kept tolerably well in check for the present. A wretchedly painful affair this.

„ June 26. Called on Christina, who looks rather well, and feels perhaps hardly worse than usual. She is executrix to my Aunt Eliza's will. My aunt left me a legacy of £650 and (after various charitable bequests, about £1,500) the residue to Christina. Christina, as she told me when last I called previously, means as executrix to assign to me shares, nominally £650, in the West Middlesex Waterworks. Each £100 share counts at present for £260: so that this amounts in fact to a gift of £1,040 from Christina, besides the legacy of £650. A very liberal sisterly act.

„ July 30. Christina suffers, but not acutely, from the illness which developed itself dangerously towards April 1892, and also from serious weakness of the heart. Her condition is certainly most precarious; yet she goes on from month to month without apparent complications of the graver kind, and her looks are mostly not amiss. She can get out of doors a very little—as for instance to sit awhile in the Square-enclosure. She can attend to her small household affairs, reading, meditating, letter-writing, &c.; and on the whole manages to get through the day with placid contentment, or resignation, and not (I think) with any extreme tedium or lowness of spirits. As residual legatee of my Aunt Eliza she will have come in for some £4,100, more or less. She has more than once told me that she regards her recent book, *The Face of the Deep*, as probably her final performance.

1893. September 29. Drew cheque to pay Christina her share for the last quarter of money coming from Gabriel's books &c. This reduces my bank-balance below £76—a lower ebb perhaps than it ever reached before. I had been expecting to have to sell-out a goodish sum from my little investments in order to meet the demands for Lucy's travelling abroad &c.: this however is staved off for the present by a gift of £100 made to Lucy the other day by Christina—who puts it on the ground that our mother had wished to leave a like sum to Lucy, but had not found it manageable. This of course is true, in its direct sense: not less true is it that Christina has acted from a spontaneous impulse of good-feeling, wishing to do what is a substantial accommodation to Lucy and me just now.

1894. February 16. Called on Christina, who continues at a low average of health. I learn that, when she was paid, some months ago, the stipulated price of her book, *The Face of the Deep*, she voluntarily returned the money. She has since then ceased to be a subscriber to the Society for Promoting Christian Knowledge, on the ground (much talked of) of their having published a book countenancing Vivisection.

„ July 24. Called on Christina, whose state is now one of considerable suffering, and I fear rapidly becoming critical. Stewart came while I was there, and I spoke to him.

„ August 15. Went to see Christina. She is now in bed, and I greatly fear will not rise again. Spoke to Stewart, who gives a very gloomy and alarming account of her condition. I don't care to enter into the details.

„ August 19. Went to see Christina. Her bed is now removed into the front drawing-room. She was not in pain to any serious extent, but drowsy—must have had a sleeping-draught. Religious bequests.[1]

---

[1] By this curt phrase I meant that Christina had asked me, as her universal legatee, to provide for certain religious bequests which she had at heart. I assented, and have made some mention of the matter in my *Reminiscences*.

1894. August 23. I called on Christina. Very low, but comparatively free from pain. Religious bequests noted, £2,000. Again spoke to Stewart. He dwelt to-day chiefly on functional irregularity (not organic disease) of the heart, and hysteria—to which he has more than once told me that Christina is extremely subject, though I can't say that I should have discerned it for myself.

„   September 3. Saw Christina. Gradual, though not very marked, worsening. A little earnest talk on matters of religion.

„   September 6. Went to see Christina. She was very low and exhausted, so that I had to cut my visit short. I am afraid to-day that she looks distinctly worse in the face than I had as yet seen her. " I should like to see you there." [1]

„   September 8. Saw Christina. She was very considerably better—*i. e.* less prostrated by weakness &c.—than when I was with her on Thursday; but of course there is not any real change of condition for the better. Form of religious bequests fully approved.

„   September 15. Saw Christina, and read the terms of my will to her. I regret to say that her pain continues on the increase, though she perseveres, as always, in making the lightest she can of it. Stewart, whom I met there, thinks the disease is now tending towards a lingering form.

„   September 18. Saw Christina. Much as usual, but I think a little weaker now in voice and aspect. Stewart said to me, however (and so far I quite agree with him), " Her face is certainly not that of a dying person."

„   September 30. Saw Christina. Suffering and weak, but perfectly conversible. She never utters a syllable of complaint, nor even, unless questioned, of information as to her troubles. A good deal of coughing of late.

„   October 3. Saw Christina. Very weak, with hysterical touches at moments. She is always, however, fully capable of a sustained talk, and to-day (with a view to the book of Gabriel's *Family-Letters*) she went over with me a list of old acquaintances of our childhood, rectifying, and reminding me of several particulars.

„   October 6. Saw Christina. She confesses now, but only if she is asked about it, to pain that must be called severe, especially in the left shoulder. She was in a bad way as I entered the house, but had revived before I saw her, and talked as usual. Stewart, who is going abroad for some months,

[1] This phrase was used by Christina in speaking to me of heaven.

informed her to-day to this effect, and that Dr. Abbot Anderson will represent him. She took the announcement placidly, though no doubt it must be unwelcome to her.

1894. October 9. Saw Christina, who is surprisingly cheerful, considering. She recited to me her old verses (say 1842) about a Chinaman's pigtail; also a stanza, which I hardly seem to have heard before (date towards 1855) about Charon &c.

„ October 22. Saw Christina. Her memory for old matters is singularly prompt and clear.

„ October 25. Saw Christina. "Thrice the tabby cat hath mewed "[1] &c. Mrs. Tooley's article on Christina in *The Young Woman* has now come out. Ridiculous blunder of printing as a portrait of Christina the portrait by Gabriel of Lucy. Must write to the editor on this and another point.

„ November 3. Saw Christina. More low and exhausted, and less capable of sustained attention, than perhaps I had yet seen her. I am afraid (if that is the right word in such a case) the end is near. She says she is not in serious pain.

„ November 15. Saw Christina. Her condition of weakness and prostration is so extreme, and her voice so near to extinction, that I hardly understand how it could be possible for her to live more than a day or two; she is not now in pain of a marked kind. Her last words to-day were "Good-bye, dear William."

„ November 17. Went to see Christina. A regular nurse now in the house.

„ November 23. Christina was sleeping when I arrived. After some while the nurse roused her to take some Brand's essence, and she and I spoke together. Her mind wanders a little now, but seems quite placid. No other marked change.

„ December 2. Christina this afternoon was a little drowsy. Said a few things in a very natural voice, better than often has been the case these three weeks or so. *Lord of the Isles.*[2]

„ December 6. Christina very quiet and composed to-day, talking with presence of mind in a deliberate though very weak voice. She got me to look into the contents of her deed-box (will, spoons, &c.) and also gave me information as to the *provenance* of the principal articles of furniture in her (front-drawing) room. . . . She has some fancy about animals, "like pussy-cats," on a piece of black satin, "looking about for sleep": but I

[1] In my *Reminiscences* I mentioned this trifling instance of a certain degree of liveliness and whim preserved by Christina up to almost the last.

[2] This means that Christina spoke about Walter Scott's poem, *The Lord of the Isles.* I don't rightly remember what she said; but it was something of a quite apposite, or even critical, kind.

think she understands that this is a mere fancy of an exhausted brain and frame.

1894. December 7. To-day again Christina was very placid, and capable of attending to whatever was said. It is remarkable how much her articulation has improved beyond what it was some fortnight or so ago.

„ December 17. Christina was not *so* bad to-day. After I had been standing a minute by her bedside she opened her eyes and addressed me in an affectionate and natural tone, and she was able to follow my reading of two longish letters. I fear her mind is always now possessed by gloomy ideas as to the world of spirits, but she has not for some weeks past said to me anything bearing in this direction. She has again taken some liquid nourishment.

„ December 25. Christina awake : taciturn, but not wholly silent. As usual now, she seems gloomy and distressed, but I find it difficult now to apprehend the precise cause. Religious ideas seem to me predominant herein.

„ December 27. Christina seemed to-day a little more self-possessed than yesterday. She did not speak. I come to the conclusion that she is constantly engaged in mental prayer, and, though not unconscious of what is going on around her, will not take any express notice of it.

„ December 29. My noble, admirable Christina passed away about 7.20 a.m. on Saturday (29). Far better so than that she should continue any longer in suffering of mind or of body. I left her on Friday about 2.45, kissing her forehead for the last time during her life. She did not seem to see me at all that day. The nurse, Harriett Read, sat holding Christina's right hand. Christina's eyes were ,mostly closed, but opened—half-opened—every few seconds, and turned on the nurse—I thought with a perceptibly affectionate look. She was still very possibly in mental prayer. That Friday morning towards 5 she "turned quite blue," as the nurse says, and the last stage of her painful passage began. Her ordinary colour however returned, and, when I saw her, there was, in this respect, nothing to be noticed different from the last few days. This morning Christina was, according to the nurse, evidently praying up to five minutes of the end. She gave one sigh, and so, in perfect peace at last, left us for ever. I went round with Olive before 11 a.m., and saw her face—peaceful, colour much sunken but aspect not distressing. I had to attend to sorrowful duties. Called in the evening on Dr. Abbot Anderson for the death-certificate. He had already posted it to Torrington Square. He considers that Christina was subject to some fanciful and varying impressions for the last 3 or 4 weeks; and this I know to be in some respects true.

1894. December 30. I went round to Torrington Square with my three younger children, who wished to take the last look at Christina. We found the coffin closed, which pained us, but I approve of its having been done. The coffin, marked with a cross, is an exact duplicate of that which was ordered for my mother, and which must have had Christina's definite approval. The medical certificate gives as causes of death — primary, scirrhus—secondary, cardiac failure.

1895. January 2. The funeral—performed with dignity, grace, and in a way quite consonant to my feelings. A considerable attendance of (uninvited) persons in church, and a certain number at the grave. Snow fell in the night of 1–2, but the day was still, fine and sunny, and not particularly cold. The only persons who accompanied us five in mourning-carriages were the clergyman (Nash), Watts, Miss Lisa Wilson, and the two servants from Torrington Square. Two hymns by Christina sung in church. Watts got from *Athenæum* office the proof of his article on Christina, and brought it round to me. A very satisfactory article. He spent the evening with us.

---

2. *Extracts from a Diary kept by Christina Rossetti on behalf of her Mother*, 1881–6.

1881. April 7. Gabriel read us his magnificent ballad, *The King's Tragedy*, founded on the history of James I of Scotland. Heard of the death of Mary Collinson, within three months after the death of her brother James.

     ,, November 26. Christina went to early dinner at the Scotts', where she met Mr. Henry Linton. Coming back she called on Gabriel, whom she found glad to see her, but weak and much depressed. A nurse had arrived the same morning to attend to him under Mr. Marshall, and to check, if possible, the excessive use of chloral &c. Mr. Watts and Mr. Caine were in the studio.

     ,, December 14. We went to see poor dear Gabriel, whom we found laid up since Sunday with loss of power on the left side

THE HOUSE IN WHICH CHRISTINA ROSSETTI DIED.
30 Torrington Square.
Photograph taken in 1908.

[*To face p.* 222.

—Mr. Marshall (thank God !) says *not* paralysis. On Sunday friends came unexpectedly to see him, and so filled up the chairs about the fire that he was restricted to the sofa; where he became so cramped and presumably so chilled as to become numbed on the left side, his hand losing power, and his foot so that he could not stand. Mrs. Abrey (nurse) with Dr. Westland Marston and Mr. Caine carried him up to bed, where he remains. Mr. Marshall was sent for, and saw him the same day. We *to-day* found him free perhaps from pain, but depressed to a pitiable degree. William knew of this terrible attack, but was charged by Gabriel not to tell me, so we arrived without knowing what had happened.

1881. December 15. Christina went to see Gabriel, and found him much the same. She saw also Mr. Watts, and understood from him that in the course of the afternoon Mr. Marshall was expected to bring with him a young medical man who would remain in the house, and watch the effect of morphia which Gabriel was to try by Mr. Marshall's orders instead of chloral.

„ December 18. To church with Christina. She in afternoon went to see Gabriel, and found him certainly not worse. The morphia is injected by puncturing the hand. The medical man in charge of the treatment is a Mr. Maudsley, aged 24, a pupil of Mr. Marshall's. Eight hours' sleep was induced by the first injection (or perhaps the *second*), but this may have been too strong a dose to repeat. Last night was restless. Mr. Caine talked kindly and feelingly to Christina. Mr. Leyland was paying Gabriel a visit.

1882. January 20. Gabriel came, looking better and talking with more animation; he mentioned having finished a little picture.

„ February 1. Mr. Cayley called. Gabriel came and invited me and Christina to accompany him down next Saturday to Birchington, where Mr. John Seddon is lending him a large and commodious "bungalow."

„ March 2. Lucy came with Olivia and Arthur. I and Christina went to West-Cliff Bungalow, Birchington-on-sea (a large one-storeyed commodious residence lent by Mr. John Seddon), to visit Gabriel; who is staying there with his trained nurse, Mrs. Abrey, and Mr. Hall Caine and his sister Lily (13 years old), endeavouring to regain health and strength, and in particular to regain the use of his left hand. But I was grieved indeed to find him much wasted away, suffering and in a measure depressed, though making us most welcome, and chatty enough on general subjects.

1882. April 6.   Christina went at 10.30 to morning service and Holy
Communion.   Gabriel so drowsy and sinking that William and
Mr. Watts were telegraphed to.   I sat up till about midnight,
when Christina took my place till 6 in the morning.

„   April 7.   The drowsiness continues.   William in great grief
and Mr. Watts arrived.   Mr. Leyland called, affectionately concerned at the unforeseen alarm.   In consequence of Gabriel's
having one night expressed to Mrs. Abrey some inclination to
see Mr. Alcock, the rector, having been informed of this, called
late in the evening and prayed with him; I and Mr. Watts
uniting.

„   April 8.   Kind Mr. Martin had an awning put up to keep the
sick-room cool.   Mr. Shields hurried down, but could not see
Gabriel at once; and slept here.   After unavoidable delays
Mr. Marshall arrived, met Dr. Harris in consultation; declared
all the present urgent symptoms to point to uræmia (blood-
poison produced by an escape of urea), and took instant vigor-
ous measures to expel if possible the poison from the system.
To produce perspiration, Gabriel was wrapped in a hot sheet
and made very hot in bed, besides medicine being adminis-
tered.   The blessed result ensued of his regaining a more natural
appearance, and rallying to a less inert general condition.
Food, heat, and medicine (though no *solid* food), were kept up
through the night, the greater part of which Christina passed
keeping nurse company at the bedside.   Mr. Marshall missed
his up-train, and so remained on the spot for the night.   Mr.
Leyland again visited Gabriel, and Mr. Martin called.

„   April 9.   *Easter Day.*   Mr. Marshall left soon after 9 o'clock,
leaving word for me (I was not yet up) that Gabriel "continued
to hold his own."   He also says that as soon as manageable
Gabriel ought to quit Birchington as being too cold for him,
and had best simply return to Chelsea.   I gather that the illness is very serious, but not hopeless.   Christina missed church
after sitting up till towards 7 in the morning.   (Forgotten from
yesterday.   Mr. Alcock called, and read and (we think) prayed
alone with Gabriel, exhorting him to simple trust in God and
our Saviour.)   Mr. Leyland came.   Mr. Alcock paid Gabriel a
short bedside visit.—[*Later on*] We had arranged to sit up, I
till 10, William till 2, Christina last; when suddenly, just after
nurse and Mr. Watts together had put a poultice on Gabriel's
back (Mr. Watts had but just left the room, nurse was attending to the fire, I was by the bed rubbing Gabriel's back),
Gabriel, who was sitting, fell back, threw his arms out, screamed

out loud two or three times close together, and then lay
breathing but insensible. Nurse raised the alarm, Mr. Watts
hurried back, and one on each side they held Gabriel down,
but there was not the slightest struggle or return of consciousness. All assembled round the bed. Mr. Shields flew for Dr.
Harris, and in the shortest time returned with him. Gabriel
still breathed, but that was all; Dr. Harris once or twice said
he still lived—then said he was dead. This took place shortly
after 9 o'clock p.m. Gabriel had scarcely breathed his last
when Lucy, having travelled all day from Manchester, arrived.
The instant cause of death assigned by Dr. Harris was that the
uræmic poison touched the brain, and he afterwards assured us
that there was no pain.

1882. April 10. *Easter Monday.* Christina went to early Holy
   Communion. A telegram sent by William brought from London
   a man from Brucciani's to take a cast of Gabriel's face and
   hand. He looked quite peaceful, with a tendency towards a
   smile. Mr. Shields made a drawing of him. Mr. Leyland came,
   and Dr. Harris. Mr. Alcock came showing sympathy with
   us : he accompanied Christina to look at dear Gabriel (whose immediate death he had not anticipated), appeared moved, and,
   kneeling down, prayed aloud with Mr. Shields and Christina.
   Afterwards Lucy went with her and William to the Rectory,
   where Mrs. Alcock was introduced to them, and expressed
   concern and good-will. This call at the Rectory was for the
   purpose of meeting Mr. Alcock, who accompanied the three to
   the churchyard, where a spot was chosen for the dear grave ;
   one or two alternative spots being fixed upon in case the first
   (on sounding) should prove to be pre-occupied. Mr. Martin
   with his usual kindness undertakes to make arrangements for
   the funeral. Mr. Shields tells us that for years past he had
   prayed for Gabriel, and on anxious inquiry he was relieved to
   learn from us that he had been visited by a clergyman.

„   April 12. Mr. Shields left us. William and Lucy returned,[1]
   and later in the day Mr. Sharp arrived, bent on having a last
   look.

„   April 13. Mr. Caine went to London. Mr. Alcock called
   to fix the exact hour for the funeral. Charlotte arrived from
   Muntham, having spent one night in London. Mr. Watts
   came back. The coffin was closed in the evening.

„   April 14. Mr. Alcock performed the funeral simply and

---

[1] Having been present at the moment of Gabriel's death, I had, with my wife,
gone up to London soon afterwards to attend to some necessary details.

solemnly. Besides myself, Christina, William, Lucy, and Charlotte, there were present Messrs. Graham, Leyland, Watts, Caine, Hueffer, John Seddon, Stephens, Boyce, Aldam Heaton, Martin, Sharp, Philip Marston, Shields, and Dr. Harris. Herbert Gilchrist and two others attended uninvited, but were not of our party. Mr. Martin having undertaken much of our trouble, all went well as to carriages (five were provided) and refreshments. Mr. Shields and Mr. Watts remained for the night, and of course Mr. Caine. In the evening Charlotte, William, Lucy, Christina, and Mr. Shields, returned to the churchyard to place on the grave (already closed and peaceful under a turfed mound) a most beautiful wreath of flowers which we believe was the one sent by Lady Mount-Temple and brought by Mr. Graham. A number of floral decorations were contributed by different friends. Philip Marston presented a wreath of bay, the Leylands wreaths and a lovely white cross, Mr. Sharp a cross of primroses. I placed in the grave a bunch of simple flowers among which were wood-spurge (or certainly *one* of the spurges) and forget-me-nots ; Christina had gathered these in the grounds and conservatory.

1882. April 15. Mr. Alcock called and said good-bye, inviting me to take a bed at his house if I liked occasionally to visit Birchington. I returned with Charlotte and Christina to Torrington Square; William, Mr. Watts, and Mr. Caine, accompanying us to the station.

„ April 18. Christina called in Cheyne Walk (92) to ask after Mr. Scott, who was gone to South Kensington and much better of his injured leg ; and she saw Mrs. Scott and Miss Boyd. Mrs. Stephens brought me a beautiful wreath of white flowers, and Mr. Cayley called.

„ May 26. I went with Charlotte, Eliza, and Christina, to dear Gabriel's house. William met us there, and we selected (I and Christina) each a drawing as a remembrance ; and all four of us chose an odd volume (at William's suggestion) from a number of imperfect books set aside as nearly valueless. The house looked desolate indeed, bereft of the dear pervading presence. Mr. Dunn showed us two water-colour drawings he has begun of the drawing-room and dining-room furnished in the old familiar manner, and he proposes to represent in the same way the studio and Gabriel's own bedroom ;[1] pretty and

---

[1] The water-colour of the studio was made. So far as I know, the bedroom was not now portrayed ; but I possess a water-colour of it made by Mr. Dunn at some preceding date.

highly interesting little pictures these promise to be. Mr. Caine, coming in before we left, greeted us very cordially.

1882. June 29. William called on his way to Chelsea, whither we followed him in the course of the afternoon; staying some time in the saddened house, and seeing a number of the familiar old objects all about the rooms ready for the sale next week. Poor William was suffering much from gout. We saw Mr. Dunn for a moment, Mr. Watts, and Mr. Caine, who fetched a cab for us.

„ July 8. William paid a long morning visit. The three days' sale, with the addition of some private sales, has produced (he estimates) about £3,000, a result far beyond anticipation. The one grievous mishap of the sale was the disappearance, how we know not, of the choice copy of *Petrarca*, given by my father to me, by me long afterwards as a keepsake to Gabriel, and containing the autograph of John Philip Kemble, by whom it was originally given to my father.

„ July 26. Mr. Sharp called, and I lent him my Main's Sonnet-book containing Gabriel's beautiful Indian-ink drawing and autograph sonnet, given me by him the day I was eighty. I am allowing both design and words to be engraved in facsimile for Mr. Sharp's forthcoming memoir of Gabriel.

„ September 21. Christina dined with William and Lucy, meeting there Mr. and Mrs. Shields, Mr. Cayley, and Mr. Dunn.

„ September 23. Charlotte returned to Muntham. Began with Christina reading through dear Gabriel's letters to me, in preparation for William's and Mr. Watts's joint volume. Mr. Cayley called with his sister Henrietta.

„ November 6. We concluded reading Gabriel's letters for William's book : Mr. Cayley called, and stayed to whist and tea.

„ December 2. Christina went to consult Sir William Jenner, who again spoke with great interest of Gabriel ; remarking on the narrow line which divides genius from mental affection, observing how it preys on its possessor, and evidently of opinion that, with his nerves and his gifts, it is no marvel that we have lost him.

„ December 19. Mr. Tebbs paid us a long sympathetic visit, selecting works by Gabriel and portraits of him for exhibition at Burlington Fine Arts Club.

„ December 30. I went with Charlotte, Eliza, and Christina, to the Royal Academy, Burlington House, to see a roomful of

15*

dear Gabriel's drawings and paintings,—strikingly beautiful. This was the private view.

1883. January 24. Olive and Arthur brought a note from Lucy saying that dear little Michael was dying. Christina went round between 10 and 11, found all in grief, and sat with poor William and Lucy till the baby died just before 1 o'clock. He was suffering from pressure on the brain, which mercifully (we are told) was unaccompanied by consciousness, although his eyes continued open. Mr. Gill, who attended him assiduously, brought a Dr. Roberts to see him in consultation last Thursday, and yesterday William called in Sir William Jenner. Christina returned to Endsleigh Gardens in the afternoon, carrying a heath in bloom to place in the room.

„ February 12. Christina called on Lucy, whom she found at home with all her children. Lucy brought in her beautiful drawing of Michael lying dead, to show Christina—at sight of which little Mary became quite excited, scuttling along towards the portrait. It seemed to attract her like a magnet, affectionately and pleasurably. Holding her mother's hand, she walked some distance round the room, accompanying the portrait held high in Lucy's other hand. Then, seated opposite it, she made kisses towards it; once broke into a laugh and uttered inarticulate baby-chatter, pointing and stretching out her little hand in her vain endeavour to touch the drawing.

„ March 9. William, Lucy, and Mr. George Hake, came to "substantial tea" with us, and we passed a very agreeable evening; in the course of which Mr. Burcham looked in by chance, in London for a short visit (from Norwich) especially to. see Gabriel's pictures now exhibiting. He brought me a small quantity of exceptionally fragrant pot-pourri, made by John[1] for a Norwich lady whose maiden name I could not learn, but who—either herself or her daughter—became a Mrs. Asker (?). This highly-valued gift I returned by presenting him with the "Home Library" (American) edition of dear Gabriel's collected poems.

„ April 7. To buy flowers (a cross of white everlastings and several small bunches, including forget-me-nots) for dear Gabriel's grave, where Mr. Caine has promised to place them next Monday, the anniversary of his death. Eliza accompanied us. We left the flowers with Mr. Caine in Clement's Inn, and

---

[1] *i. e.* Dr. John Polidori, Byron's travelling physician in 1816, Mrs. Rossetti's brother—deceased in 1821.

exchanged cordial words with him and with Mr. Watts, who happened to be there.

1883. May 12. To-day the drawings &c. left by Gabriel (on this his birthday) were sold by auction in Christie's Rooms. About £3,000 is realized for ourselves, as reported at the moment by William.

„ May 14. To church, and then to William's, where we saw himself and Helen, and for a moment Lucy. The sum realized last Saturday (not £3,000 but nearer £2,800), by sale of Gabriel's works, will probably, after all incidental expenses have been paid, rather more than suffice to clear off the remaining liabilities.

„ June 7. William came and read us a letter from Dr. Steele, containing particulars of Teodorico's seizure. He was ministering (at Florence) to a Protestant congregation, discoursing on Revelation v., when his voice failed. He sat down—for a moment his state was not perceived—then Isabella rushed forward : but he, motioning her aside, called out to his flock, "Addio, addio, addio,"—and, becoming insensible, died the same day. The funeral was to take place last Friday (5th).

„ July 12. I went with Christina to Church Hill, Birchington. Mrs. John Seddon left some roses for us, gathered (I believe) from under one of Gabriel's windows in the Bungalow.

„ July 13. I stayed at home to rest. Christina placed roses on Gabriel's grave, on which a white cross and a few withered flowers were already lying.

„ August 4. We walked and sat out. Mr. Shields called, and went with Christina to look at the church-window I wish him to fill for me. He proposes a *Publican* for one light, and a *St. Mary Magdalene* after Gabriel's own design (adapted by himself for the purpose), for the other.[1] They took a walk together along the Canterbury Road.

„ September 6. I returned to Torrington Square with Charlotte and Christina. Before we left Birchington, Christina and I paid our last visit to dear Gabriel's grave, and placed flowers upon it.

„ November 17. Mr. Burcham called, introducing to us his friend Mr. Kitton.[2]

„ December 5. To litany with Christina. Charles Bagot Cayley died in the night.[3]

[1] Neither of these proposals took effect.
[2] The late Mr. F. G. Kitton, one of the leading authorities regarding Dickens.
[3] This entry as to Cayley (who died in the night from 5 to 6 December) was evidently added after the entry for 7 December had been made.

1883. December 7. While Christina was at the litany, Profr. and Mrs. Cayley called to tell her the dreadful news that their brother Charles had been found dead in his bed the morning (Thursday) before. Coming in, Christina saw them ; then went and saw her dear friend lying just as found in the attitude of sleep ; his hand, that is, raised to his face. He is thought to have died quite painlessly, the heart stopping. Miss Cayley (Sophie) was there, and asked Christina (offering her a bed) if she would attend the funeral at Hastings, where he will be near his mother. Christina bought a beautiful wreath at Covent Garden, and herself laid it on the sheet where other flowers were already lying.

„ December 11. We walked as far as Russell Square. Christina went to Covent Garden, and bought a cross for herself and white flowers for me to send to Mr. Cayley's funeral at Hastings to-morrow.

„ December 12. To the litany. William came. Charles Bagot Cayley was buried to-day at Hastings near his mother. Lucy called with Helen.

„ December 13. Profr. Cayley brought Christina his brother's desk.

1884. January 1. Christina went a business-round for me, ending in Mr. Shields's studio, where she saw a fine cartoon for the second light of my memorial-window : our Lord leading the blind man by the hand before healing him.

„ January 15. Christina went to Hastings to visit Mr. Cayley's grave, returning in the afternoon.

„ February 29. To the litany. Mrs. Abrey called, and amongst other interesting matter assured us that, when poor Gabriel left Chelsea for Birchington, no one, so far as she knows, certainly not herself, foresaw that he would not return.

„ March 22. I and Christina went to Mr. Shields's studio to see his design for the second light of my Birchington window : our Lord leading by the hand the blind man of Bethsaida ; very fine, and, when placed opposite Gabriel's *St. Mary Magdalene*, promising a beautiful result. He showed us other fine things, and we saw Mrs. Shields.

„ May 2. Mr. Alcock came up from Birchington to talk about my memorial-window. He considers the *St. Mary Magdalene* (Gabriel's) light unsuited to the position of the particular window. So Christina went round with him to Mr. Shields's studio ; and, after thought and discussion, that kind friend promises to try to produce a "light" from Gabriel's *Passover*

in the Holy Family, of which a photograph should be submitted
to Mr. Alcock for approval before the work proceeds further.
The *Blind Man of Bethsaida* light is accepted, but must wait
till the second has got forward.

1884. June 6. The photograph of Gabriel's *Passover in the Holy
Family* arrived from Oxford, and Christina went with it to Mr.
Shields, who finds he will be able to make his second light
from it. So now we send it to Mr. Alcock, before carrying the
work any further.

„   August 26. William came to see me before I and Christina
started for Birchington, which I reached tired.

„   August 30. We revisited the grave, and I ordered a low
wooden coping to be placed round it. Mr. Bristow (carpenter,
joiner, undertaker, clerk, sexton) is to do this for me. He is
quite impressed by the number of visitors to Gabriel's grave,
and mentioned one lady in particular who fainted in her distress.

„   September 1. William in London sent us down to read the
following letter from his little Helen at Herne Bay ; believed to
be her own composition, dictated to Lucy :—

4 TELFORD TERRACE.

Thursday.

My dear Papa, I am better. I have been in great pain,
and am only allowed to eat soft things. I am not allowed
to go out or get into draughts, but the kitten is very kind and
seems to like me, and I don't know what I should do without
her. I wish you were here to take me out on the beach.
Poor Mamma has a pain in her leg, but she is always kind
to me—and Cook sat up all night helping me, and she must
have been very tired. But I love you because you do not keep
me indoors, but let me wet my feet and clothes in the water,
so do come again for I am always dry now.

Your loving child,

HELEN.

„   September 9. We changed our lodgings to next door (Mr.
Ashton, Chemist, 5 Station Road). We settled with Bristow
the sexton that he should raise a low mound over dear Gabriel,
and train ivy close over it. We visited the grave, on which
Christina placed flowers, and walked to the nearest nursery-
ground on the Margate Road.

1884. October 23.   We sat out and walked by the Bungalow.   The
memorial-window, mine to Gabriel, came down from London,
and the placing it in church was commenced.

„   October 24.   I went with Christina to look at the window,
beautiful beyond my expectation.   The bright clear morning
showed it to great advantage.   Mr. Alcock was there, and
shook hands with us.   After looking some time at the window,
and remaining somewhat longer in church, we made a pleasant
round walking home.

„   October 28.   I returned home from Birchington with Christina.

„   November 1.   Christina went for me to Lodge Place, and paid
Mr. Shields the second and final instalment for my Birchington
window, including the rejected design of *St. Mary Magdalene.*
I added £30 to what was owing, by which means Mr. Shields
received a clear £100 for himself.

1885. March 20.   We attended the litany.   A Mr. Sandeman
brought us a book of illuminations illustrative of some of
Gabriel's poems, and done by a Mrs. Traquair; who, calling in
the afternoon, fetched away her beautiful performance: they
are acquaintances of the George Hakes.

„   August 9.   In the afternoon William brought round Mr.
Brown to see what portraits of Gabriel I had, in preparation
for his commencing his memorial bronze medallion (?) to form
the chief feature of a fountain proposed to be erected near the
old house in Cheyne Walk, Mr. John Seddon furnishing the
architectural design.   Dr. Littledale called.

1886. February 25.   I fell in my room (Christina at the other end
of the room) and hurt my back.   Mr. Stewart prescribed
belladonna-poultice made with cotton-wool, and a soothing
mixture.   Considerable pain, but (thank God !) no bones broken.
Of course I keep in bed, and as quiet as possible.

„   April 7.   Christina sat up with nurse, only lying down occasionally without undressing: William and Harriett up and down
through the night.   The night over, no rally: unconsciousness
at last.   Mr. Stewart came twice.   Mr. Nash prayed by my bedside, but I knew it not (?).   Mr. Watts called much concerned.
Charlotte is better.

*   *   *   *   *   *

I, Christina G. Rossetti, happy and unhappy daughter of so
dear a saint, write the last words.   Not till nearly half-an-hour
after noon on April 8 (Thursday) did my dearest mother cease
from suffering, though for a considerable time it had (I am

assured) been unconscious suffering. William, Nurse Annie Jackson, Harriett, and I, watched by her on and off the last sad night. At the moment of death, William, Nurse, Mr. Stewart, and I, were present. Annie Jackson has been our true friend, helper, and comfort. Harriett and Alice[1] full of loving care for us. My beautiful mother looked beautiful after death, so contented as almost to have an expression of pleasure. I had her dressed in the "widow's cap" she has worn more than 30 years. Mr. Nash sent to inquire, Miss Billing came in for a last look while Mamma lay insensible. Sarah Catchpole went to look at her as she lay dead.

[1] Servants. Sarah Catchpole (named directly afterwards) had also been a servant in the family. Miss Billing I do not remember—perhaps a neighbour.

INDEX

235